Non-Western Educational Traditions:
Alternative Approaches
to Educational Thought and Practice

Sociocultural, Political, and Historical Studies in Education

Joel Spring, Editor

Non-Western Educational Traditions:
Alternative Approaches to Educational Thought and Practice

Timothy Reagan

The Cultural Transformation of a
Native American Family and Its Tribe   1763–1995
A Basket of Apples

Joel Spring

Non-Western Educational Traditions:
Alternative Approaches
to Educational Thought and Practice

Timothy Reagan
The University of Connecticut

LEA
1996

LAWRENCE ERLBAUM ASSOCIATES, PUBLISHERS
Mahwah, New Jersey

Lawrence Erlbaum Associates, Inc., Publishers
10 Industrial Avenue
Mahwah, New Jersey 07430

Cover design by Mairav Salomon-Dekel

Library of Congress Cataloging-in-Publication Data

Reagan, Timothy G.
      Non-western educational traditions : alternative
   approaches to educational thought and practice / Timothy
   Reagan.
         p. cm.
      Includes bibliographical references and index.
      ISBN 0-8058-8041-0 (alk. paper)
         1. Comparative education. 2. Education—Philosophy. 3.
   Educational anthropology. I. Title.
   LB43.R43 1996
   370.19'5—dc20   96-8690
                                                       CIP

Books published by Lawrence Erlbaum Associates are printed
on acid-free paper, and their bindings are chosen for strength
and durability.

Printed in the United States of America
10   9   8   7   6   5   4   3   2   1

Contents

Preface

In all societies, throughout human history, people have educated their children. Indeed, one of the fundamental characteristics of human civilization is a concern for the preparation of the next generation. From one generation to the next, we seek to pass on what we know and have learned, hoping to ensure not merely the survival of our offspring, but that of our culture as well.

The history of education, as it has been conceived and taught in the United States (and generally in the West), has focused almost entirely on the ways in which our own educational tradition emerged, developed, and changed over the course of the centuries. This is, of course, understandable, but it means that we have ignored the many ways that other societies have sought to meet a number of the same challenges. In this book, an effort is made to try to provide a brief overview of several other, non-Western approaches to educational thought and practice. An understanding of the ways that other peoples have tried to educate their children, as well as what counted as "education" for them, may help us both to think more clearly about some of our own assumptions and values, and to become more open to alternative viewpoints about important educational matters.

Unlike most areas traditionally included in the training of educators, very few Western individuals have had any real exposure to non-Western educational traditions, and so the audience for this book is a very broad and diverse one. The book was written to be accessible to both preservice and inservice teachers, but may also be of interest to advanced students in graduate programs as well as faculty members. Although both the book as a whole and sections in particular may be of considerable interest to educators in other societies, the book is written from the perspective of American readers, and presupposes that readers are, at the very least, familiar with the Western educational tradition.

ORGANIZATION OF THE BOOK

Non-Western Educational Traditions: Alternative Approaches to Educational Thought and Practice consists of nine chapters dealing with a wide variety of different, non-Western cultural and historical educational traditions. In chapter 1, a theoretical foundation and base for the study of non-Western educational traditions has been presented. In chapter 2, a broad overview of traditional, indigenous African educational thought and practice is offered. Chapters 3 and 4 move our focus away from Africa and onto indigenous educational thought and practice in two distinctive settings in the Americas. In chapter 3, an examination of the educational thought and practice of the Aztecs is used as a case study of indigenous education in Mesoamerica, whereas in chapter 4, the pre-Columbian North American experience is discussed. Traditional educational thought and practice in imperial China is the focus of chapter 5, with a special emphasis on the role of the imperial examination system. Chapter 6 provides an overview of the educational tradition embedded in Hinduism in India, and chapter 7 focuses on the Buddhist educational tradition. Although technically not non-Western in important ways (including its relationship to the so-called "Judeo-Christian" tradition), the Muslim educational heritage is similarly excluded in large part from Western histories of educational thought and practice, and so its inclusion in a book of this sort is certainly defensible. Therefore, chapter 8 presents a survey of traditional Islamic educational thought and practice. Finally, chapter 9, the last chapter in *Non-Western Educational Traditions: Alternative Approaches to Educational Thought and Practice*, summarizes some of the major themes and issues discussed in the book, and suggests future areas for scholarly exploration. At the end of each chapter there are a number of questions for reflection and discussion, as well as recommendations for further readings.

ACKNOWLEDGMENTS

Writing a book is an undertaking like few others, in that it is profoundly personal and individual, but at the same time it requires considerable patience and support from many others. I am deeply grateful to many colleagues for their help and assistance throughout the writing of this work. In particular, I would like to thank Naomi Tutu, Patricia Weibust, Tom Jones, Chuck Case, Eva Diaz, Frank Stone, Kay Norlander, Cheryl Spaulding, and Tom DeFranco, all at the University of Connecticut, as well as Larry Klein and Daniel Mulcahy at Central Connecticut State University, Rose Morris at the Human Sciences Research Council in Pretoria, and Claire Penn at the University of the Witwatersrand. I am also very thankful for the insights and challenges provided by many of my doctoral students, and especially those of Beatrice Ndu Okwu, Hsiung-Huei Lee, Eliana Rojas, Sharon Wilson, Gerda Walz-Michaels, Joe Veth, Adama Sow, and Kamala Willey. The librarians at the University of Connecticut, as well as those at Central Connecticut State University, the University of Hartford, the Ohio State University, the Human Sciences Research Council, and the University of the Witwatersrand, were incredibly supportive as well, tracking down difficult-to-find material and making every effort to be helpful. My friends Tammy Wood and Ann Randall provided endless cups of coffee and worthwhile discussion on many of the topics covered in this book, and I am more grateful to them than I can say. Naomi Silverman, at Lawrence Erlbaum Associates, has been a wonderful friend and supporter from the beginning of this project. The reviewers of the manuscript provided many useful and helpful ideas and questions, and I would like to thank David Conrad, W. Thomas Jamison, Paul Robinson, Joel Spring, and Olga Welch. Finally, I want to thank Jo Ann, Joshua, Bryan, and Kimberly, who with good grace put up with me, my bad temper, and my surly disposition as I worked on this book.

Timothy Reagan

It is not for him to pride himself who loveth his own country,
but rather for him who loveth the whole world.
The earth is but one country, and mankind its citizens.

— Bahá'u'lláh

This book is dedicated to my father,
Gerald Reagan.

1

The Study of Non-Western Educational Traditions

Most books and courses that deal with the history and philosophy of education include few, if any, references to indigenous educational ideas and practices in Africa and the Americas, and relatively few references to those of Asia. Although there have recently been calls for the inclusion of the perspectives of women and people of color in studies of the history and philosophy of education, such efforts, when they have taken place, have often entailed little more than the addition of vignettes indicating the contributions of women and people of color to the Western tradition. In other words, the idea that there might be valuable insights to be gained from a serious examination of non-Western educational traditions themselves—indeed, that these traditions might be fully and in all respects comparable to the Western tradition in their unique richness and diversity—is one that has been rarely voiced. Furthermore, where non-Western educational ideas and practices have been discussed, they are often subjected to a treatment roughly comparable to the "orientalism" discussed by Edward Said with regard to the Western (and specifically, Anglo-French-American) response to Islam and the Islamic world. Said argued that:

> Orientalism can be discussed and analyzed as the corporate institution for dealing with the Orient—dealing with it by making statements about it, authorizing views of it, describing it, by teaching it, settling it, ruling over it: in short, Orientalism as a Western style for dominating, restructuring, and having authority over the Orient. . . . European culture gained in strength and identity by setting itself off against the Orient as a sort of surrogate and even underground self.[1]

In other words, when scholars *do* try to examine non-Western educational thought and practice, all too often they tend to do so through a lens that not only colors what they see, but also reifies the object of study—making it, in essence, part of "the other" and hence alien. Reification results not only in the distortion of what one is trying to understand, but also in its subjugation to one's own preexisting values and norms. This problem is not, of course, unique to the study of educational thought and practice; it is a common criticism of Western scholarship about the non-Western world in general. For example, in his discussion of the study of indigenous African religions by Western scholars, the Ugandan poet Okot p'Bitek wrote of the "systematic and intensive use of dirty gossip" in place of solid and sensitive scholarship.[2] In a similar vein, the anthropologist Adam Kuper wrote of *The Invention of Primitive Society* by 19th- and 20th-century anthropologists and social theorists in the West.[3] In terms of traditional African educational practices, A. Babs Fafunwa commented that, "Because indigenous education failed to conform to the ways of the Westernised system, some less well-informed writers have considered it primitive, even savage and barbaric. But such contentions should be seen as the product of ignorance and due to a total misunderstanding of the inherent value of informal education."[4]

The same, of course, can be argued with respect to Western treatment of indigenous educational ideas and practices in Asia, the Americas, and elsewhere. In short, when we speak of the history of educational thought and practice, what we have actually meant in the past has been the history of *Western* educational thought and practice, and the effect of our meaning has been, in essence, to delegitimatize the many alternatives found elsewhere in the world. In other words, it is discourse itself—the way that one talks, thinks about, and conceptualizes educational thought and practice—that is at issue. As Stephen Ball noted in a discussion of the work of the French philosopher Michel Foucault, "Discourse is a central concept in Foucault's analytical framework. Discourses are about what can be said and thought, but also about who can speak, when, and with what authority. Discourses embody meaning and social relationships, they constitute both subjectivity and power relations."[5]

The underlying purpose of this book, then, is to begin the process by which the existing discourse in the history of educational thought and practice can be expanded in such a way as to provide a starting point for the development of a more open and diverse view of the development of various approaches to educational thought and practice. Needless to say, this work is intended to be only a beginning. If the study of the various educational traditions discussed here is to be taken seriously, these traditions (and many others as well) will require, and are certainly entitled to, the same sort of concern that has long been accorded the Western tradition. Furthermore, given their differences from the Western tradition, it is essential that we all learn to invite and to listen to the "multiple voices" and perspectives that can enlighten our understanding of these traditions, just as we must learn to recognize that different groups may, as a consequence of their sociocultural contexts and backgrounds, possess "ways of knowing" that, although different from our own, may be every bit as valuable and worthwhile as those to which we are accustomed.[6] As Carol Gilligan suggested with respect to "woman's place in man's life cycle" in *In a Different Voice: Psychological Theory and Women's Development,*

At a time when efforts are being made to eradicate discrimination between the sexes in the search for social equality and justice, the differences between the sexes are being rediscovered in the social sciences. This discovery occurs when theories formerly considered to be sexually neutral in their scientific objectivity are found instead to reflect a consistent observational and evaluative bias. Then the presumed neutrality of science, like that of language itself, gives way to the recognition that the categories of knowledge are human constructions. The fascination with point of view that has informed the fiction of the twentieth century and the corresponding recognition of the relativity of judgment infuse our scientific understanding as well when we begin to notice how accustomed we have become to seeing life through men's eyes.[7]

A very similar kind of argument can be made with respect to the differences in perspective and worldview in various non-Western cultural and historic traditions. To be sure, this argument is, at the present time, speculative in nature with respect to many of the traditions discussed in this book, whereas in the case of women, there is now a growing body of fairly compelling empirical evidence. My hope is that others, from a wide an array of different backgrounds, would challenge, modify, and add to the base that is offered here, and that someday the study of the Aztec *calmécac* and *telpochcalli*, of the imperial Chinese examination system and its content, and the role of various African initiation schools, among others, might be as commonly taught in courses in the history of educational thought as the works of Plato, Rousseau, and Dewey are today. Having said this, it is also important to stress that I am not arguing that Plato, Rousseau, and Dewey (among others) should be eliminated; they, and many others, are important figures in the development of our own historical tradition, and certainly merit serious study. My focus here is not on replacing the Western tradition, but rather on trying to expand our understanding of education, broadly conceived, through the examination and study of other approaches to educational thought and practice with which many of us tend to be less familiar. Ultimately, of course, as we better understand the educational traditions of other societies and cultures, we will also be forced to reexamine and to reflect on our own tradition in somewhat different ways—and this will be immensely beneficial to our understanding of our own traditions.

THE CHALLENGE OF ETHNOCENTRISM

As we begin the process of trying to broaden our perspectives on the history of educational thought and practice, it is important for us to understand that the activity in which we are engaged will inevitably involve challenging both our own ethnocentrism and the ethnocentrism of others. Basically, *ethnocentrism* refers to the tendency to view one's own cultural group as superior to others—a tendency common to most, if not all, human societies. In contemporary scholarly discourse, one seldom comes across such blatant ethnocentrism, however. Rather, what is far more common is simply the practice of using one's own society and sociocultural practices as the "norms" by which other societies are viewed, measured, and evaluated. Ethnocentrism of this kind takes two somewhat distinct forms: cultural ethnocentrism and epistemological ethnocentrism.[8]

Cultural ethnocentrism refers to manifestations of ethnocentrism in individual scholars and their work, as well as to the sociocultural context that has helped to form and support such individual and idiosyncratic biases. In other words, we see examples of cultural ethnocentrism when writers and scholars allow common biases, prejudices, and assumptions to color their work in various ways. Racism, sexism, and so on all contribute to cultural ethnocentrism, most often in ways that are unconscious. Thus, the topics that a scholar chooses to explore, the questions that are asked about the topic, the framework within which hypotheses are constructed, how conflicting evidence is weighed, and even what counts as evidence can all be affected by personal biases.

This brings us to the second sort of ethnocentrism, *epistemological ethnocentrism*, which deals not so much with individual assumptions and biases but, rather, with those common to an entire field of study. With epistemological ethnocentrism, we are concerned with what the philosopher of science Thomas Kuhn called the dominant "paradigm" in our own field of study.[9] A paradigm, on Kuhn's account, is far more than merely a model or a theory. As Patton explained:

> A paradigm is a world view, a general perspective, a way of breaking down the complexity of the real world. As such, paradigms are deeply embedded in the socialization of adherents and practitioners: paradigms tell them what is important, legitimate, and reasonable. Paradigms are also normative, telling the practitioner what to do without the necessity of long existential or epistemological consideration. But it is this aspect of paradigms that constitutes both their strength and their weakness—their strength in that it makes action possible, their weakness in that the very reason for action is hidden in the unquestioned assumptions of the paradigm.[10]

Thus, the dominant paradigm in a field of study at any given point in time essentially establishes the parameters within which "legitimate" discourse may take place. Kuhn explained the significance and power of the dominant paradigm in a field of study as follows:

> Scientists work from models acquired through education and through subsequent exposure to the literature often without quite knowing or needing to know what characteristics have given these models the status of community paradigms. . . . That scientists do not usually ask or debate what makes a particular problem or solution legitimate tempts us to suppose that, at least intuitively, they know the answer. But it may only indicate that neither the

question nor the answer is felt to be relevant to their research. Paradigms may be prior to, more binding, and more complete than any set of rules for research that could be unequivocally abstracted from them.[11]

In the case of the study of the history and philosophy of education, the dominant paradigm has focused almost entirely on a single educational tradition, to the exclusion of virtually all others, as mentioned earlier in this chapter. The study of traditional, indigenous educational practices has been reduced to the study of "socialization" and "acculturation," and has been left to anthropologists and others. Because scholars have tended to equate "education" with "schooling," and because they have consistently focused on the role of literacy and a literary tradition, many important and interesting—indeed, fascinating—traditions have been seen as falling outside of the parameters of "legitimate" study in the history and philosophy of education. Furthermore, even in the study of the Western educational tradition itself, scholars have been somewhat remiss in examining aspects of the traditions that seem to fall outside the bounds of their expectations. For example, even recent works concerned with educational thought and practice in classical antiquity have generally ignored the formidable work of Martin Bernal, who has, since the early 1980s, been arguing that the civilization of classical Greece has deep and important roots in Afroasiatic cultures.[12] Similarly, until fairly recently the contributions of women to the Western educational tradition were largely ignored, in part as a result of overlooking the contributions of specific individual women, but even more by defining *education* in such a way as to eliminate from discussion what might be called the "reproductive" (as opposed to the "productive") aspects of education.[13] Thus, although throughout virtually all of the Western historical tradition women have played the central role in raising and educating children, this was largely ignored in formal studies of the development of the Western educational tradition.[14]

Although dangerous and pernicious, cultural ethnocentrism is actually somewhat easier to challenge than is epistemological ethnocentrism, because individual scholars in a particular field at the same point in time may differ to a considerable degree with respect to issues related to cultural ethnocentrism. Thus, many scholars today are far more sensitive to issues of gender, race, and ethnicity than are others, while nonetheless working within the same epistemologically ethnocentric paradigm.

An example in which both cultural and epistemological ethnocentrism can be clearly seen was written in the mid-1970s by H. M. Phillips, and is presented here:

> In Africa, education was extremely limited and associated with the very small numbers who were in contact with Islam over the land routes and later with Europeans in the ports or administrative centres already starting to be set up in those parts of Africa which were colonized. But basically the continent as a whole was still completely underdeveloped and tribal. African potential, though great, was late in being mobilized.[15]

The epistemological ethnocentrism of this passage can be seen, for instance, in its conflation of "education" with "formal schooling" to the obvious detriment of traditional education in Africa, which has been informal in nature and closely tied to the social life of the community.[16] By assuming, as Phillips did, that "education" and "schooling" are synonymous constructs, one dramatically distorts the reality of the African experience. The passage also displays elements of cultural ethno-centrism, especially in its presentation of colonialism and imperialism (whether Islamic or Western) as essentially progressive in nature, whereas indigenous practices, ideals, and so on are seen as "underdeveloped" and "primitive"—spoken of only in terms of "potential," suggesting the need for "development."

In short, as one considers both cultural and epistemological ethnocentrism in the study of the history of educational thought and practice, there is good reason to believe that perhaps it is time to begin to challenge the dominant paradigm in the field, in roughly the same way that an increasing number of educational researchers have challenged the traditional, essentially positivistic, paradigm in educational research, seeking to replace it with a naturalistic, qualitative paradigm.[17] In the case of the history and philosophy of education, the paradigmatic challenge must rest in large part on the reality of diversity, and the lack of any "universal" tradition—a theme about which Paul Ricoeur, in his book *History and Truth*, wrote:

> When we discover that there are several cultures instead of just one and consequently at the time when we acknowledge the end of a sort of cultural monopoly, be it illusory or real, we are threatened with destruction by our own discovery. Suddenly it becomes possible that there are just *others*, that we ourselves are an "other" among others.[18]

The recognition that one's own tradition is simply one among many (and not necessarily even *primus inter pares*,[19] at that) will be, for many people, a difficult one to accept, and yet that is precisely what is required if the study of the history of educational thought and practice is to be more than a parochial artifact. Furthermore, in order better to understand the many educational traditions that exist and have existed in the world, it will be necessary to expand substantially the methodological tools at the disposal of scholars, using not only the standard methods of historical and philosophical scholarship but, increasingly, those of such disciplines as anthropology, cultural studies, linguistics, sociology, comparative literature, archeology, and others. Our scholarship, in short, must become far more interdisciplinary in both theory and practice than has been true in the past.

THE CONCEPT OF "TRADITION" AND ITS LIMITS

This book is about non-Western educational traditions, and throughout we talk about "tradition" in a number of very different ways. Patricia Weibust com-pellingly argued that the concept of "tradition" is a far more complex one than is generally recognized. She suggested that "tradition" can come in three very different, and in fact logically distinct, forms: the historical tradition (i.e., what really took place historically), the defined tradition (what members of the culture believe to have taken place historically), and the contemporary tradition (the way in which the tradition is manifested in people's lives today), and, furthermore, that "tradition" is best understood not in static terms, but rather as an ongoing process.[20] This distinction is a powerful and useful one as a heuristic device and analytic tool. However, in practice the three kinds of tradition are often far from distinct, and it is very difficult indeed to distinguish among them in many of the instances we examine in this text. Our task becomes even more complex in this regard when one considers that some of the traditions we study here are living ones, whereas others continue to exist in very truncated forms, if at all. Thus, although we are concerned primarily with the historical tradition in each of the cases we examine, the defined tradition may well function as a limitation to our understanding and, in some cases, confusion may arise among the historical, defined, and contemporary traditions. Finally, as we talk about different traditions, it is important that we keep in mind that traditions are in fact processes that continually change, develop, and evolve, and that at best we are looking at a snapshot of a tradition at a particular point in time.

LEARNING FROM ORAL TRADITIONS

An important element in the process of expanding our perspectives on the history of educational thought and practice is learning more about the many ways in which different societies pass on their traditions, histories, and so on. Although many of the societies that we examine in this book do have written traditions, similar to those found in the Western tradition, others have relied instead primarily or exclusively on oral traditions. Written traditions have many advantages, but so do oral ones—advantages that our own society, for the most part, lost long ago. In his landmark work *Oral Tradition as History*, Jan Vansina argued that:

> The marvel of oral tradition, some will say its curse, is this: messages from the past exist, are real, and yet are not continuously accessible to the senses. Oral traditions make an appearance only when they are told. For fleeting moments they can be heard, but most of the time they dwell only in the minds of people. The utterance is transitory, but the memories are not. No one in oral societies doubts that memories can be faithful repositories which contain the sum total of past human experience and explain the how and why of present day conditions. *Tete are ne nne*: "Ancient things are today" or "History repeats itself".
> . . . How it is possible for a mind to remember and out of nothing to spin complex ideas, messages, and instructions for living, which manifest continuity over time, is one of the greatest wonders one can study, comparable only to human

intelligence and thought itself. Because the wonder is so great, it is also very complex. Oral tradition should be central to students of culture, of ideology, of society, of psychology, of art, and, finally, of history.[21]

And, one might well add, of students of education, because education plays a key role both in the perpetuation of any oral tradition (as it does in the perpetuation of any written tradition) and in helping to determine the content of that tradition.[22]

It is important to understand that oral and written traditions are *different*, and that each is useful and valuable in its own right. Neither is intrinsically superior to the other in all ways; each has its own strengths and each has its own limitations. It is also important for us to bear in mind that much of the Western tradition has its origins in oral traditions—the epic poetry of Homer, Anglo-Saxon heroic poetry,[23] even the synoptic Gospels,[24] all have their origins in oral, rather than written, traditions.

Finally, the fact that we attempt to discuss oral traditions in a written text is itself something of a paradox. As Karl Kroeber commented about the study of American Indian tales, "One must ask if any *written* text can accurately produce an *oral* recitation."[25] The problem is that oral literature is, by its very nature, dependent on *performance*. As Ruth Finnegan explained in her discussion of oral literature in Africa:

> Oral literature is by definition dependent on a performer who formulates it in words on a specific occasion—there is no other way in which it can be realized as a literary product . . . without its oral realization and direct rendition by singer or speaker, an unwritten literary piece cannot easily be said to have any continued or independent existence at all. In this respect the parallel is less to written literature than to music and dance; for these too are art forms which in the last analysis are actualized in and through their performance and, furthermore, in a sense depend on repeated performances for their continued existence.[26]

Thus, when we discuss oral traditions in a book like this one, we are at best dealing with a mere shadow of the true reality of the oral text (somewhat similar to Plato's "allegory of the cave"). The risks of such an undertaking are made clear in the following story, an example of "dissident humor" in the former Soviet Union:

> Standing on Lenin's tomb in Red Square, Stalin was acknowledging the acclamation of the masses. Suddenly he raised his hands to silence the crowd.
>
> "Comrades," he cried. "A most historic event! A telegram of congratulations from Leon Trotsky!"
>
> The crowd could hardly believe its ears. It waited in hushed anticipation.
>
> "Joseph Stalin," read Stalin. "The Kremlin. Moscow. You were right and I was wrong. You are the true heir of Lenin. I must apologize. Trotsky."
>
> A roar erupted from the crowd.

But in the front row a little Jewish tailor gestured frantically to Stalin.

"Psst!" he cried. "Comrade Stalin."

Stalin leaned over to hear what he had to say.

"Such a message! But you read it without the right *feeling*."

Stalin once again raised his hands to the still excited crowd. "Comrades!" he announced. "Here is a simple worker, a Communist, who says I did not read Trotsky's message with the right *feeling*. I ask that worker to come up on the podium himself to read Trotsky's telegram."

The tailor jumped up on the podium and took the telegram into his hands. He read:

"Joseph Stalin. The Kremlin. Moscow."

The he cleared his throat and sang out:

"You were *right* and I was *wrong*? *You* are the true heir of Lenin? *I* must apologize?"[27]

Needless to say, the tailor's rendition of the telegram conveyed a radically different meaning to the text—a meaning disguised by the written text, and best made clear in an oral rendition. The use of italics in the text may help us to reproduce the oral event, but it requires a performance to really make sense. It is just such risks to which we must be sensitive when we examine any oral tradition or written rendering of an oral "text."

COMMONALITY AND DIVERSITY
IN NON-WESTERN TRADITIONS

The role of oral traditions is a common theme in many of the different societies that are examined in this book, and the commonality of this theme raises an important question. If different non-Western societies share many features, such as the role of an oral tradition, a communal approach to the education of children, a reliance on nonformal kinds of educational experiences, and so on, then to what extent are they really different traditions? Is it, in short, really necessary for us to study many different non-Western traditions, or would it not be sufficient for us to simply study one tradition in detail?

This is an important question; one that does not have a simple answer. The different educational traditions that we explore in this book do indeed share many common features, but they also differ in significant ways. One way to think about this that may prove useful is to draw an analogy to a concept used in contemporary linguistics. Linguists distinguish among different kinds of linguistic "universals" (i.e., properties and characteristics common to all languages). The most important distinction made in linguistics is between what are called "absolute universals," which "are properties all languages share," and "relative universals," which "are general tendencies in language." [28] In other words, there can be no exceptions whatever to absolute universals, although there may be exceptions to relative universals. Furthermore, the way in which such universals are manifested in particular languages may differ dramatically. The study of non-Western educational traditions is, in fact, fairly similar to the study of the diverse languages used by human beings around the world. Although there are likely to be certain absolute universals (such as the goal of helping the child to become a "good person," albeit perhaps defined in different ways), and although there are also likely to be relative universals (such as a concern with treating other people with respect), the ways in which such universals are in fact manifested in any particular culture—as well as the means by which the society seeks to accomplish these goals—will be very distinctive.

The purpose of studying non-Western educational traditions is both to help us understand the common principles that underlie all educational undertakings and to understand the different means that human beings have devised to accomplish these principles. Such understanding is, of course, valuable in its own right, but it may also have profound effects on the way in which we view diversity and difference writ large, and as it impacts our own personal and professional lives. An understanding of Aztec education, for instance, is unlikely to have an immediate and direct use for the classroom teacher—there is no likelihood whatsoever that a teacher will have to deal with a child whose parents wish him or her to be prepared to enter a *calmécac*. Nevertheless, an awareness of how the Aztecs educated their children, both in terms of the goals that guided their educational system and the means that they used to achieve these goals, may well help each of us as educators to develop a more critical and sensitive understanding of the educational goals and methods used in our own society.

CONCLUSION

In short, the unifying theme of this book is that it is neither idealistic nor unrealistic to suggest that we can learn much from non-Western educational traditions. As Ali Mazrui argued in the first of his BBC Reith Lectures, with respect to Africa and its relations with the west, "I cannot help feeling that it is about time Africa sent missionaries to Europe and America, as well as teachers, engineers, doctors and ordinary workers. . . . It is indeed time that Africa counter-penetrated the western world."[29] Perhaps it is time not only for Africa, but for the non-Western world in general, to begin penetrating the study of the history of educational thought and practice. It is with this goal in mind that this book was written.

QUESTIONS FOR REFLECTION AND DISCUSSION

1. What are the implications of Edward Said's notion of "orientalism" for what should be taught in the public schools in our society? For what classroom teachers should know?

2. In this chapter, it is asserted that "schooling" and "education" are by no means synonymous concepts. In our own society, how do these concepts differ? What are the implications of these differences for "public education" and "public schooling"?

3. What did Paul Ricoeur mean when he wrote that when "we acknowledge the end of a sort of cultural monopoly . . . we are threatened with destruction by our own discovery?" What are the implications of this claim for the curriculum in the public schools? For the curriculum in teacher education programs?

4. Although our own culture is predominantly a written rather than an oral culture, one could, nevertheless, make a strong case for one or more oral traditions coexisting and paralleling the written tradition. What would the elements of such oral traditions be in our own society? How are these traditions passed on from one generation to the next? Are there some oral traditions in our society that are not transgenerational? What are the implications of your answers for the classroom teacher?

5. Do you think that Ali Mazrui was speaking seriously or metaphorically when he called for Africa to send missionaries to Europe and America? If you think he was speaking seriously, what kinds of messages do you think that such missionaries might carry? If you think that he was speaking metaphorically, what are the implications of the metaphor?

RECOMMENDED FURTHER READINGS

Edward Said's book *Orientalism* (New York: Vintage, 1978) provides a powerful and challenging perspective on how cultural expectations and biases can influence and distort the way that we make sense of the "other," as does his more recent *Culture and Imperialism* (New York: Vintage, 1993). Also quite useful in helping us to understand traditions different from our own is Jan Vansina's *Oral Tradition as History* (Madison: University of Wisconsin Press, 1985).

NOTES

1. Edward Said, *Orientalism* (New York: Vintage, 1978), 3.
2. Okot p'Bitek, *African Religions in Western Scholarship* (Nairobi: East African Literature Bureau, 1971), 22.

3. Adam Kuper, *The Invention of Primitive Society: Transformations of an Illusion* (London: Routledge, 1988).

4. A. Babs Fafunwa, *A History of Education in Nigeria* (London: Allen & Unwin, 1974), 17.

5. Stephen Ball (ed.), *Foucault and Education: Disciplines and Knowledge* (London: Routledge, 1990), 2.

6. Mary Field Belenky, Blyth McVicker Clinchy, Nancy Rule Goldberger, and Jill Mattuck Tarule, *Women's Ways of Knowing: The Development of Self, Voice, and Mind* (New York: Basic Books, 1986).

7. Carol Gilligan, *In a Different Voice: Psychological Theory and Women's Development* (Cambridge, MA: Harvard University Press, 1982), 6.

8. See V. Mudimbe, *The Invention of Africa: Gnosis, Philosophy, and the Order of Knowledge* (London: Currey, 1988), 19.

9. See Thomas Kuhn, *The Structure of Scientific Revolutions*, 2nd enlarged ed. (Chicago: University of Chicago Press, 1970); Thomas Kuhn, *The Essential Tension: Selected Studies in Scientific Tradition and Change* (Chicago: University of Chicago Press, 1977).

10. Michael Patton, *Utilization-Focused Evaluations* (Beverly Hills, CA: Sage, 1978), 203.

11. Kuhn, *The Structure of Scientific Revolutions*, 46.

12. See Martin Bernal, *Black Athena: The Afroasiatic Roots of Classical Civilization, Volume 1: The Fabrication of Ancient Greece, 1785–1985* (New Brunswick, NJ: Rutgers University Press, 1987); Martin Bernal, *Black Athena: The Afroasiatic Roots of Classical Civilization, Volume 2: The Archeological and Documentary Evidence* (New Brunswick, NJ: Rutgers University Press, 1991).

13. Jane Roland Martin, "The Ideal of the Educated Person," in Daniel DeNicola (ed.), *Philosophy of Education: 1981* (Normal, IL: Philosophy of Education Society, 1982), 3–20.

14. See Jane Roland Martin, *Reclaiming a Conversation: The Ideal of the Educated Woman* (New Haven, CT: Yale University Press, 1985).

15. H. M. Phillips, quoted in Niara Sudarkasa, "Sex Roles, Education and Development in Africa," *Anthropology and Education 13*, 3 (1982): 281.

16. See chapter 2 of this book.

17. See Yvonna Lincoln and Egon Guba, *Naturalistic Inquiry* (Newbury Park, CA: Sage, 1985); Michael Patton, *Qualitative Evaluation and Research Methods*, 2nd ed. (Newbury Park, CA: Sage, 1990).

18. Paul Ricoeur, *History and Truth* (Evanston, IL: Northwestern University Press, 1965), 278.

19. "First among equals"—the way in which the role of the Pope with respect to the other Bishops of the Church is traditionally discussed.

20. See Patricia Weibust, "Tradition as Process: Creating Contemporary Tradition in a Rural Norwegian School and Community," *Qualitative Studies in Education 2*, 2 (1989): 107-122.

21. Jan Vansina, *Oral Tradition as History*, rev. ed. (Madison: University of Wisconsin Press, 1985), xi.

22. See Louis-Jean Calvert, *La Tradition Orale* (Paris: Presses Universitaires de France, 1984), 9–25. See also Russell Kaschula (ed.), *Foundations in Southern African Oral Literature* (Johannesburg: Witwatersrand University Press, 1993); Graham Furniss and Liz Gunner (eds.), *Power, Marginality and African Oral Literature* (Cambridge, England: Cambridge University Press, 1995).

23. See James Hulbert, *Bright's Anglo-Saxon Reader* (New York: Henry Holt, 1935), cvi–cxv.

24. See Vansina, *Oral Tradition as History*.

25. Karl Kroeber, "The Art of Traditional American Indian Narration," in Karl Kroeber (ed.), *Traditional Literatures of the American Indian: Texts and Interpretations* (Lincoln: University of Nebraska Press, 1981), 2.

26. Ruth Finnegan, *Oral Literature in Africa* (Nairobi: Oxford University Press, 1970), 2. See also Ruth Finnegan, "Reflecting Back on *Oral Literature in Africa*: Some Reconsiderations After 21 Years," *South African Journal of African Languages 12*, 2: 39–47.

27. Joseph Telushkin, *Jewish Humor* (New York: Morrow, 1992), 121–122.

28. David Crystal, *A Dictionary of Linguistics and Phonetics*, 3rd ed. (Oxford, England: Blackwell, 1991), 367.

29. Ali Mazrui, *The African Condition: The Reith Lectures* (London: Heinemann, 1980), 16.

2

Traditional African Educational Thought and Practice

The African continent is immense, not only in terms of its size, but more important, with respect to the cultural, linguistic, and ethnic diversity that characterize the people who live in its various parts. As Richard Olaniyan observed, "With almost a thousand separate language groups, a variety of climatic regions and greatly different levels of social and economic development . . . Africa is a continent of bewildering diversity and extraordinary dynamism."[1] This immensity and diversity might lead one to believe that it is not possible for us to discuss traditional "African" educational thought and practice in any meaningful way because there is bound to be considerable variation on such a topic from one group to another throughout the continent. This is an important issue, as Meyer Fortes made clear:

> Take, to begin with, the idea of African culture: by what criteria can we include, under this rubric, both the culture of the Kung Bushmen of the Kalahari—those gentle, peaceful, propertyless, hunting and collecting folk who have been so aptly described as "the harmless people" by Lorna Marshall—and the traditional patterns of life and thought of the sophisticated, materially wealthy, politically and socially complex, militarily organized kingdoms of West Africa—Ashanti and Benin, Yoruba and Hausa.[2]

To assume that such diversity makes impossible any discussion of "African" culture (an assumption that Fortes did not, in fact, make), however, would ignore or, at the very least distort, the many commonalities that unite the African experience. As Molefi and Kariamu Asante argued:

> Africa . . . is one cultural river with numerous tributaries characterized by their specific responses to history and the environment. In this way we have always seen Europe after the Christian manifestations. England, Norway, Ireland, France, Belgium, Germany, etc., were one culture although at the same time they were different. Asante, Yoruba, Mandinka are also one, though different in the historical sense. When we speak of unity in Africa, we are speaking of the commonalities among the people. Thus, a Yoruba who is different from an Ibo

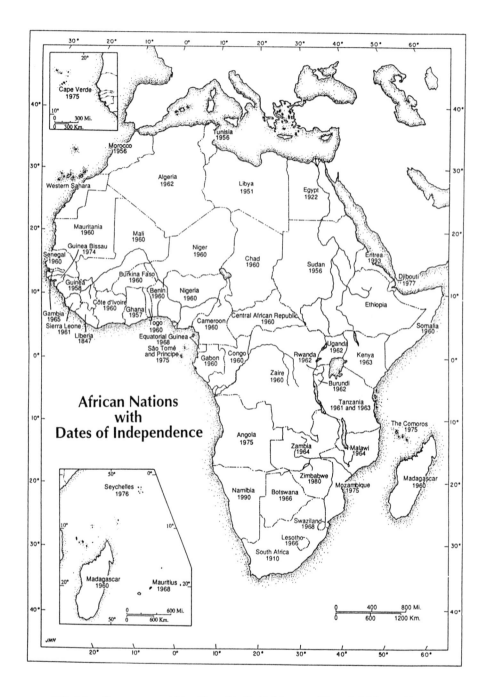

FIG. 2.1. Contemporary Africa [From Phyllis M. Martin and Patrick O'Meara, *Africa*, 3rd ed. (Bloomington: Indiana University Press, 1995), p. xv]. Reprinted with permission.

FIG. 2.2.   Location of selected ethnic groups in Africa [From Phyllis M. Martin and
Patrick O'Meara, *Africa*, 3rd ed. (Bloomington: Indiana University Press, 1995), p. xvi].
Reprinted with permission.

17

or Asante still shares more in common culture with them than with Thais or Norwegians. To the degree that the material conditions influence the choices people make, we Africans share similarities in behavior, perceptions, and technologies.[3]

In short, what we must seek in an examination of traditional African educational thought and practice[4] in what Cheikh Anta Diop, in his important book *The Cultural Unity of Negro Africa,* called the "profound cultural unity still alive beneath the deceptive appearance of cultural heterogeneity" present in Africa.[5] In this chapter, an attempt is made both to identify and discuss some of the common characteristics and assumptions shared by much traditional education in Africa and to note differences and variations that are related to sociocultural and geographic context.

THE GOALS OF TRADITIONAL AFRICAN EDUCATION

It is possible to identify a number of different goals that traditional African educational practices seek to achieve. For instance, Fafunwa, in his *History of Nigerian Education,* discussed what he termed the "seven cardinal goals of traditional African education," including:

1. to develop the child's latent physical skills;
2. to develop character;
3. to inculcate respect for elders and those in position of authority;
4. to develop intellectual skills;
5. to acquire specific vocational training and a healthy attitude toward honest labour;
6. to develop a sense of belonging and to participate actively in family and community affairs;
7. to understand, appreciate, and promote the cultural heritage of the community at large.[6]

Taken together, these educational goals constitute a descriptive inventory of the characteristics of the "good person" for traditional African societies. Such an individual, on Fafunwa's account, will be one who "is honest, respectable, skilled, cooperative and conforms to the social order of the day."[7] Although much can be said in favor of such individuals, there is also a risk involved in encouraging conformity in societies that are no longer purely traditional in nature as is, of course, the case in most of contemporary Africa. It is such people, in fact, about whom the Nigerian novelist Chinua Achebe wrote rather critically in *A Man of the People*:

Overnight everyone began to shake their heads at the excesses of the last regime, at its graft, oppression and corrupt government: newspapers, the radio, the hitherto silent intellectuals and civil servants—everybody said what a terrible lot; and it become public opinion the next morning. And these were the same people that only the other day had owned a thousand names of adulation, whom praise-singers followed with song and talking-drum wherever they went.[8]

Traditional African educational thought and practice is characterized not only by its concern with the "good person," but also by its interweaving of social, economic, political, cultural, and educational threads together into a common tapestry. In his book *Education in Africa,* Abdou Moumouni argued that traditional education in Africa is distinguished by these four features:

1. The great importance attached to it and its collective and social nature;
2. Its intimate tie with social life, in both a material and a spiritual sense;
3. Its multivalent character, in terms of both its goals and the means employed;
4. Its gradual and progressive achievements, in conformity with the successive stages of physical, emotional, and mental development of the child.[9]

Education, then, in the traditional African setting cannot (and indeed, should not) be separated from life itself. It is a natural process by which the child gradually acquires skill, knowledge, and attitudes appropriate to life in his or her community. Furthermore, in precolonial settings, such education was generally highly effective. As Moumouni argued,

> The effectiveness of this education was possible because of its very close relationship with life. It was through social acts (production) and social relationships (family life, group activities) that the education of the child or adolescent took place, so that he was instructed and educated simultaneously. To the extent that a child learned everywhere and all the time, instead of learning in circumstances determined in advance as to place and time, outside of the productive and social world, he was truly in the "school of life," in the most concrete and real sense.[10]

An important facet of education conceived of in this way is that any and every adult in the community becomes, in essence, a teacher for any child with whom he or she has contact. Thus, writing about traditional education among the Igbo, Ambrose Okeke noted that:

> education in the wider sense of the term has all along been an essential factor in the way of life of the Igbo man. Parents, guardians, relatives and a wider circle of kinsmen in Igboland consider it a sacred trust of discharging their obligations as it concerned the socialization of the Igbo child. As a matter of fact, the entire village took part in this socialization process.[11]

Children learn adult roles as well as the skills necessary for survival, in short, by imitating adults engaged in their daily activities and by assisting parents and other adults as they engage in such activities.[12] Much is learned by the child through play and imitative games, as Duminy noted:

> The work and ways of the adult provided the material for the play of the child. Often, especially among girls, the imitative games (spontaneous imitation at first) gradually passed through a phase of diverted imitation to serious work. In various South African tribes (e.g., Sotho and Venda) it was customary for young children to build small houses and play at being grown up, imitating all the actions they had seen their elders do. Young girls were grinding soft stones between harder ones and young boys went through the whole ritual of their fathers "stock-farming" with their clay oxen.[13]

In fact, in the traditional African social context it is often virtually impossible to distinguish among "play," "learning," and other kinds of social activities:

> Among all peoples children learn by imitating their elders in play so that it is often difficult to distinguish between learning and play: the San boy is given a miniature bow and arrow as soon as he is able to handle them. The arrows are not poisoned and he plays at hunting, shooting field-mice, birds and hares; but when he kills a little duiker he is deemed ready to handle poisoned arrows.[14]

Furthermore, from early childhood, the African child in a traditional society is expected to participate in the economic life and activities of the community. As de Villiers and Hartshorne commented,

> Among peoples having non-specialized cultures children begin to participate at an early age in the economic activities of the adults according to their strength and skill. The Zulu girl tends her younger siblings, fetches water and firewood, cleans the home and, as she grows older, increasingly shares in the tasks she will one day perform as an adult. What she learns thus has a direct bearing on the knowledge and skills she will require in adulthood.[15]

With this general background to traditional African educational thought and practice in mind, we can now turn to more detailed discussions of several key components of such education. Specifically, we examine the role and place of the oral tradition in education, traditional education as moral education, the process of initiation, and the vocational aspects of traditional African education.

THE ORAL TRADITION IN AFRICAN EDUCATION

Traditional African societies are, by and large, oral ones, and this is true even where an established written literary tradition exists, as in the cases of such languages as Swahili, Zulu, Xhosa, and so on.[16] Writing about traditional education in East Africa, Mazrui and Wagaw noted that:

Yet another characteristic of most indigenous systems of education in East Africa is that they are based on the oral tradition rather than the written one. This is not to suggest that the written tradition has been entirely absent. On the contrary, both the Amharic literary culture and the Kiswahili literary culture are centuries old. But most "tribal" educational systems in Eastern Africa operated on the basis of the supremacy of the oral tradition, with only a minor role for the written word. [17]

An important aspect of traditional education in the African context has, therefore, been concerned with teaching children the oral tradition as well as helping them to learn to use language creatively and effectively. In essence, such learning is a central feature of the intellectual training of the African child. With specific reference to traditional educational practice in Igboland, Okeke commented:

> The proverbs, the riddles, the ideation of "*chi*" and "*anyanwu la eseelu*," the ability to distinguish between a killing herb and a healing one—all these constitute a veritable storehouse of intellectual exercise. Proverbs and riddles are used to hide a saying from the ordinary turn of mind. They help in selecting and analysing issues and problems of the moment. Traditional education exposed the Igbo to this training. So too do tongue-twisters used to train the child's capacity to retain the sequence of events. [18]

Proverbs feature prominently in virtually all traditional African cultures and play important communicative and educational roles, as Boateng explained:

> Another means by which traditional education promoted intergenerational communication was through proverbial sayings. Proverbial sayings are widespread throughout Africa, and their themes bear strong similarity to one another. The educative and communicative power of proverbs in traditional Africa lies in their use as validators of traditional procedures and beliefs. Children are raised to believe strongly that proverbial sayings have been laid down and their validity tested by their forefathers. [19]

Furthermore, as Fajana argued,

> Proverbs which constituted an important intellectual mode of communication were used to develop the child's reasoning power and skill, and in expressing the deeper thoughts most essential in settling disputes and in decision-making processes. They had to be mastered if the child was to be fully developed and be able to cope with the various occasions when they had to be used. [20]

The basic idea underlying *proverbs* is that such sayings provide succinct, easily remembered summaries of important ideas and experiences that are part of the shared cultural knowledge of the community. Borland, writing about the oral culture of the Shona, noted that "*Tsumo* [proverbs] embody the wisdom and experience of a people lacking written records in a concise, quotable and often amusing form. The free use of *tsumo* is the accepted way of winning an argument, and *tsumo* are therefore an integral part of Shona legal procedure which is conducted by argument."[21]

Proverbs can be used to discuss virtually any aspect of social life; in his discussion of Zulu proverbs, for instance, Nyembezi classified Zulu proverbs as falling into 10 categories, which are also applicable to proverbs found in most other African languages. The categories suggested by Nyembezi, together with examples of each type of proverb, are presented in Fig. 2.3.

Examples of proverbs from traditional African contexts abound, and many of them provide us with insight into both traditional education and social and cultural values and mores.[22] Consider, for instance, the Swahili proverb *"Mgeni siki mbili, siku ya tatu mpe jembe"* [Your guest is a guest for two days; after that, give him a hoe], which conveys both practical advice and insight into interpersonal relations. A great deal can also be learned by examining proverbs that relate to the relationship between parents and children, as in these Igbo examples:

> *Akukwo nnewu talu, ka nweya nata.* [The leaf that the big goat has eaten, will be eaten by his kids.]

> *Ezinkpolo nada ezinkpolo.* [From good seed falls good seed.]

> *Ainy elur ike ili owa iru nabo.* [We can't eat the world on two sides; i.e., you can't have both many children and a lot of money.][23]

For our purposes here, it is perhaps useful to consider proverbs common in Southern Africa that relate directly to education:

> If you take a knife from a child, give him a stick.

> The teacher sometimes commits adultery himself.

> The dry stick kindles the green ones.[24]

These proverbs provide us with considerable insight into the educational philosophy that underlies traditional African education, although it is important to keep in mind that proverbs are often notoriously difficult to translate. As Taban lo Liyong noted about Acoli proverbs, "The meaning of deep Acoli proverbs are made very light by their rendition into English word for word, rather than sense for sense, or proverb for proverb."[25] Furthermore, the use of proverbs in educating children as well as in indirect social communication in general is, by its very nature, context specific. Thus, if one sees two reasonably well-matched Zulu boys fighting, one might say, *"Kubamben' ingwe nengonyama"* [the leopard and the lion are fighting]. Similarly, to describe two children who simply do not get along, one would use a proverb contrasting two animals that are natural enemies, such as:

Category of Proverb	Content of Proverbs	Examples
Ubuntu	Treatment of people, good and bad behaviour, pride, ingratitude, etc.	A kindness is reciprocated. The stomach of a traveller is small.
Ukwethembeka Nokungethembeki	Faithfulness and unfaithfulness, deception, cunning, etc.	He cries with one eye. A crime is always denied.
Ubuhlobo Nobutha	Friendship and enmity.	The harshness of young people is repaid. The one offended never forgets; it is the offender who forgets.
Impumelelo, Inhlanhla, Namashwa	Good fortune, misfortune, troubles, uncertainty, despair, futile labour, failure and encouragement.	She has married her lover. To see once is to see twice.
Ubuqhawe Nobugwala	Bravery and cowardice.	An elephant is stabbed by all before it falls.
Emakhaya	Home life, marriage, heredity, relatives, child-parent relationships, etc.	A small pot is like the big one. A minister does not beget a minister.
Ukwedlula Kwemihla	Passage of time, aging, etc.	Old age does not announce itself. Death has no modesty.
Inhlakanipho Nobuwula	Wisdom and stupidity.	He lights the fire in the wind. He who wants wisdom lives near a cunning person.
Izixwayiso	Warnings of various types, including warnings about how to raise children, avoid dangerous situations, speaking too often, etc.	The tree is bent whilst young. Solitude devoured its owner.
Ezinye	Miscellaneous.	There is no popular young man without a fault. The poor man's word is considered last. He who accuses others knows from his own acts.

FIG. 2.3.   Categories and examples of Zulu proverbs
[From C. Nyembezi, Zulu Proverbs
(Johannesburg: University of the Witwatersrand Press, 1974), pp. 46–48].

Yinkuku nempaka. [It is a fowl and a wild cat.]

Yikati negundane. [It is a cat and a mouse.]

Yinja nekati. [It is a dog and a cat.][26]

Thus, vast amounts of information can be conveyed quickly and creatively, and the use of proverbs in childrearing is widespread throughout Africa. As the Twi say, after all, "A wise child is talked to in proverbs."[27]

Finally, proverbs are sometimes used in various types of wordplay. For example, speakers of Teke in the Congo often engage in a specialized kinds of linguistic behavior called *Bisisimi*, which can be roughly translated as "the language of the wise."[28] *Bisisimi* involves the competitive chanting of proverbs, as opposed to their common use in everyday speech, and is found primarily in specialized settings such as mourning ceremonies, festive gatherings, and acts of divination.[29] Nkara described the process of *Bisisimi* as follows:

> In most contexts, participants sit in a circle, in the *mbong* (sort of communal shed in villages), in the shade of a big tree and sometimes around a fire at night. To begin with, participants converse in everyday Teke. After an hour or so, depending on the occasion, they start using *Bisisimi*. . . . The addresser or initiator stands up and starts an *Isisimi*. The other participants chant either a part of it or the whole *Isisimi* as they clap hands following the rhythm of the chant. A small drum is sometimes beaten by one of them. As soon as any other participant realizes that he is the object of the *Isisimi* he responds immediately in kind. If he fails or happens to be in no position to respond, a friend or relative of his may come to his rescue.[30]

Furthermore, it is important to understand that, in some cases, *Bisisimi* may go far beyond being merely a game: "The use of *Bisisimi* . . . may be regarded as a contest of wits or a verbal game, but this game may also turn into a kind of occult fight when the use of *mpaana* [psychic power] is involved. In such cases, it is believed that the loser may suffer physically."[31]

Another example of the way in which oral cultures are transmitted and language is used creatively in traditional African education is the use of riddles, word games, puzzles, and tongue-twisters. All of these activities, which are common throughout most of Africa, are examples of what we might call "critical thinking activities," encouraging as they do innovative, creative, and difficult uses of various symbol systems. For instance, in Shona culture *zvirahwe*, or riddles, are widely used by and with children. Examples of Shona riddles, and their correct responses, include:

1. Question: *Nzira mbiri dzinoenda mugomo?* [Two paths lead up the mountain?]

   Answer: *Mhino.* [Nostrils.]

2. Question: *Imba imiri nebango rimwe?* [The house is supported by one pole?]

   Answer: *Howa.* [Mushroom.]

3. Question: *Shumba mbiri dzakaririra gomo?* [Two lions waited on the hill?]

   Answer: *Nzeve.* [Ears.][32]

Riddles can also be used to teach a great deal of information about the natural world, as these Ndebele riddles make clear:

1. Question: *Ngabantwana bami bakha indlu banganamanzi?* [My children burning a house without water?]

   Answer: *Mmuhlwa.* [Termites.]

2. Question: *Ngesitimela sami asikhambi esiporweni?* [By my train that does not go on the railway track?]

   Answer: *Lisongololo.* [Millipede.]

3. Question: *Ngomntwa'mi unamehlo amakhulu usaba ukuqalana nomkhayo?* [By my person with big eyes who is afraid of facing the light?]

   Answer: *Sirhulurhulu.* [Owl.][33]

Finally, riddles can reinforce social and cultural knowledge, as the following Yoruba riddle demonstrates:

Question: *A be ori, a be idi re, sibe-sibe o nsowo ola?* [We cut off the top and the bottom, yet it produces wealth?]

Answer: *Ilu.* [Drum.][34]

Word games can include a wide variety of different kinds of linguistic activities, but are generally concerned with the players' speed and continuity, although such games can also depend heavily on knowledge of the social and natural worlds, as was the case with riddles. For example, a common word game is for children to quiz one another about the names for different kinds of trees, plants, animals, and so on.[35] Another common type of word game is one in which children must engage in repetition (or alteration) of words, either real or invented, in some series or sequence. Such a game strengthens the memory and helps to develop mental acuity and speed.

Similar games often serve to teach and reinforce mathematical concepts. For instance, "the Yoruba have developed a system of counting and have used a variety of human experiences to promote practice and dexterity in enumeration. The Yoruba child is introduced early in life to counting by means of concrete objects, counting rhymes, folklore, and plays and games, both at home and on the farm."[36] An example of one of the counting rhymes that Yoruba children are likely to learn, which is fairly typical of such rhymes, is:

Rhyme	Translation
Eni bi eni	One is one
Eji bi eji	Two is two
Eta metagba	Three, spin calabash
Erin woroko	Four crooked
Arun igbodo	Five, pestle pounding
Efa ti ele	Six of ele
Aro nbaro	Cymbal, which cymbal?
Aro mbata	Cymbal, bata drum
B'oo da k'esan	If one is missing [out of ten fingers]
Gbangaba l'ewa	Ten exposed.[37]

Puzzles are also used in childrearing and education, and take several different forms. Two distinct examples of puzzles are "dilemma tales" and "arithmetic puzzles."[38] Although similar to proverbs in certain ways, both dilemma tales and arithmetic puzzles are distinctive in nature. Bascom explained the difference among riddles, arithmetic puzzles, and dilemma tales: "Put concisely, riddles are to be answered; arithmetic puzzles are to be solved; dilemma tales are to be resolved."[39] Kubik, writing about both dilemma tales and arithmetic puzzles among the Valuchazi in Eastern Angola and northwestern Zambia, argued that dilemma tales are:

> a genre of oral literature; as a prose narrative that ends in an open question, a dilemma, for the audience to resolve. Thus, in contrast to ordinary folktales, a dilemma tale is not brought to a conclusion by the narrator, but it ends on a question which is followed by a lively discussion by the audience . . . in dilemma stories the aim is to stimulate discussion. A problem has to be resolved.[40]

Arithmetic puzzles, on the other hand, are stories in which a logical or mathematical challenge is presented to the listener. As with dilemma tales, both children and adults can participate in the discussion. It is important to note here, as did Kubik, that in spite of its intellectual complexity (one arithmetical puzzle discussed by Kubik involved 11 steps) and potential metaphysical implications, "This is a leisure-time activity and arithmetic puzzles serve to stimulate the intellect and test the mathematical capabilities of the participants."[41]

Thus far, we have considered the oral nature of traditional African societies primarily in terms of its role in intellectual training, but also of great significance is the content of the oral tradition. It is through fables, myths, and legends that much of the history of the community, as well as its values and beliefs, is passed on from one generation to the next. As Boateng commented, "Myths played an active part in the African's everyday life and were a vital social force . . . myths and legends not only supplied accounts of the group's origin but related precedents to present-day beliefs, actions, and codes of behavior."[42]

The African child learns fables, myths, and legends in a variety of settings and from a host of different adults, including especially the village storyteller. As N. Uka explained,

> By listening to the village story-teller [the child] acquires a knowledge of the past. Every tale is a parable; it is not just history but an educational story. The stories are manifestations of the tribal memory, the origin and history of the group, the deeds of their great men and women, their victories and defeats in war, their experiences which led to individual and group success and those which led to individual and group failure.[43]

Similarly, in describing the training of bori musicians among the Hausa, Besmer reported that:

> One common but informal institution for these lessons is the evening gossip sessions held inside or immediately in front of most Hausa compounds. A boy old enough to have "sense" (which the Hausa say should come to him by the time he is five or six years old) normally sits on the outside of the group presided over or attended by his father. Talking is the popular pastime and storytelling is an art, elderly bori musicians regularly claiming to be experts at both. The day's events are discussed and the society's problems solved during these sessions, and when spirits are the topic tale after tale is enjoyed by young and old alike. "Have I ever told you the secret of so-and-so's wealth?" or "Do you know the reason why such-and-such is a strange place?" an old man might ask. If his audience should reply "no" he would then ask them how many ears they had. Each listener would answer "two" and he would retort, "Well increase them to three and listen to this," the signal that a "true" story was about to be told.[44]

This oral tradition includes not only the history of the community, however, but also serves to "sustain morality, ritual, law, and sanctions against offenders."[45] It is manifested in everyday life in a variety of ways, none clearer than in the praise-songs or praise-poems (*izibongo*) that are sung to honor individuals, groups, and so on.[46] As Schapera noted,

> Praise-poems . . . are composed not only about chiefs, headmen, famous warriors, and other prominent tribesmen, but about ordinary commoners also, including women; there are, in addition, praise-poems of tribes and subdivisions of tribes (such as wards and lineages), of domestic animals (notably cattle), of wild animals (including birds and insects), of trees and crops, of rivers, hills, and other scenic features, and of such inanimate objects as divining-bones. In modern times some have even been composed about schools, railway trains, and bicycles.[47]

In order to understand many praise-poems, however, let alone to be able to compose one, an individual must possess a broad historical and cultural knowledge of the community, as well as a good grasp of the language of the community.[48] The recitation of such *izibongo* remains a way of maintaining and transmitting the oral tradition, and it is a feature of traditional African education to which we return later in the chapter.

TRADITIONAL EDUCATION AS MORAL EDUCATION

One of the central features of traditional education throughout Africa is its concern with the formation of the child's character. Fafunwa, discussing the education of the Yoruba, described this concern with character formation as "the corner-stone of African education."[49] Furthermore, Moumouni argued that:

> Moulding character and providing moral qualities are primary objectives in traditional African education. Almost all the different aspects of education of the child and adolescent aim towards this goal, to a greater or lesser degree. In the family, parents concern themselves with the bearing, manners, honesty and integrity of the child. Outside the house, games, the society of his friends in the same age group, and the demands they make on each other, constitute a real source of character-building. Sociability, integrity, honesty, courage, solidarity, endurance, ethics and above all the concept of honour are, among others, the moral qualities constantly demanded, examined, judged and sanctioned, in ways which depend on the intellectual level and capacities of the child and adolescent.[50]

The responsibility for teaching the child the moral and spiritual values of the community, as well as for ensuring his or her compliance with those values, as indicated in the previous passage, rests first of all with the child's mother and immediate family but, ultimately, is the concern of the entire community.[51] As Okeke noted with regard to the Igbo, "Everyone in the home, in the village and in the community wanted the Igbo child to be sociable, truthful, brave, humble, have stamina and be of unreproachable conduct at all times. For this reason, everyone joined in correcting or praising any child whenever and wherever he failed or succeeded in showing acceptable norms of behaviour."[52]

Among the more important aspects of character training common in traditional African education is its emphasis on respect for elders.[53] As Fafunwa commented in terms of the Nigerian experience:

> Age is an important element in the life of the African. Reverence for those who are older is particularly strong among the Yoruba. Seniority confers social and economic privileges, especially in the sharing of spoils, prizes, wealth, etc. The elder is assumed to be a man (or woman) of wisdom and is expected to demonstrate this in speech and action if he is to keep his position among those who look up to him for leadership. Age is such a vital factor among many. . . ethnic groups that a man (or woman) will overstate his age rather than understate it. Moreover, a young man or woman is not expected to look an elder straight in the face for this is considered a sign of disrespect.[54]

It is important to note that the concept "elders" here refers not only to those chronologically older than the individual but also to "those who are in authority, particularly the chief, the cult leaders, the diviners, relatives (especially uncles) and older neighbours,"[55] and, furthermore, that respect in this regard entails, among other things, obedience. It also involves appropriate forms of address and ritual greetings, which play an important role in many African societies,[56] and even distinct forms of language in some cases.[57]

THE PROCESS OF INITIATION

Perhaps the best known and, arguably, the most misunderstood, aspect of traditional African education is that of initiation. The process by which the adolescent is formally transformed, socially and spiritually, into an adult varies considerably from one African society to another, and a few traditional societies (i.e., the Akans[58] and the Shona[59]) do not even have a formal initiation process at all. Nonetheless, initiation remains a common, although less often observed, practice today as a result of increasing urbanization and Westernization, throughout much of Eastern, Western and Southern Africa, and traditional African initiation practices do share significant common features and characteristics. As Benjamin Ray has argued in his book *African Religions*,

> The most elaborate rites of passage usually concern the initiation of the young into adulthood. In this way a society not only socializes its young by outwardly moving them into new roles of social responsibility, but also transforms them inwardly by molding their moral and mental disposition towards the world. This is what African societies consider to be the primary purpose of initiation rituals.[60]

African initiation ceremonies and practices are different from comparable rites of passage in the West, however, in that they make public what Westerners see as intensely private, "Besides being a test of courage and the completion of education, initiation is also a collective ceremony. In European societies, reaching puberty is a private matter. Each girl and boy goes through adolescence to sexual maturity alone. In Africa the long initiation ceremonials dramatize this change and make it a social ritual."[61]

Although the process of initiation is divided into different stages by various African societies, for most groups the initiation process includes the following components:

- Separation of the initiates from the community, under the leadership of a specially selected adult,
- Both formal and informal instruction about adult duties, responsibilities, and obligations,

- Instruction in the folklore, legends, and history of the community,
- Observation of selected food, behavioral, and sexual taboos and restrictions,
- Instruction in aspects of sexuality and sexual relations in preparation for marriage,
- Physical markings, commonly permanent in nature,
- Circumcision (often for both males and females).

In addition, male initiation very often involves tests of physical and mental endurance, including various kinds of torture, which "is regarded as a test of fortitude and a conditioning to pain and discomfort which the new life in which the individual finds himself will bring in its train."[62]

Finally, a lasting feature of the initiation process in many societies is the establishment of a peer group, or "age-set."[63] Such age-sets are among the more important nonkin groupings found in traditional African societies, and are found in virtually all parts of sub-Saharan Africa. In essence, such age-sets are male association groups based on contemporaneity, and reinforced by the bonding that takes place during the initiation process. As Olaniyan explained:

> A man belongs to that set of men who are his age mates, and their set moves through the several age-grades as the men go through life, beginning with their initiation into manhood as adolescents. Membership in an age set is not voluntary, and it carries with it both obligations and privileges. Typically, age sets pass through some four grades comprising (1) newly initiated men in a training period; (2) the warrior grade responsible for defence; (3) adult men responsible for governing; and (4) the society's elders.[64]

The initiation process, which in many ways is the pinnacle of traditional African educational practice, represents a huge investment on the part of the community. As Raum noted,

> The first thing that strikes an educationist is that initiation is a tremendous pedagogic effort. There is the ritual isolation of the company of initiands in a camp set apart "in the wilderness." There is the appointment of the requisite personnel: the master of the rite, or owner of the lodge, teachers of different rank, the operator, assistants and supervisors, the carriers of food to the camp. The master of the rite has to be a man of charisma to be able to transmit special qualities to the inmates of the camp; teachers and assistants must be ritually pure. The economic preparations for initiation are often on a grand scale.[65]

Although the initiation "school" and the ceremonials related to it are, then, clearly very important and costly to the community, they are also limited in their objectives. As van der Vliet observed, "The initiation schools . . . do not mark the final stage of the development of the individual; they do, however, equip and entitle him to accept the roles which maturity will bring."[66] In short, the process by which adolescents are initiated into adulthood serves a variety of functions in traditional African societies, including religious, political, psychological, and educational ones. The initiation schools do not, however, seek to address what might be called the vocational aspects of adulthood. As Blacking argued with respect to the Venda, "Formal . . . education in traditional Venda society was never intended to give people technological training for earning a living. . . ."[67] With this point in mind, we can now turn to a discussion of how the vocational needs of both the community and the individual are met in traditional African education.

VOCATIONAL ASPECTS OF TRADITIONAL EDUCATION

The preparation of children for their future economic roles in the society is an important element in traditional African educational thought and practice. To some extent, of course, many vocational skills and a great deal of knowledge related to and necessary for such skills are acquired simply by observation, imitation, and participation as the child interacts with his or her parents on an everyday basis. Such would, for instance, be the case for many agricultural and domestic types of activity. For other occupations in traditional societies, however, various kinds of apprenticeship are employed. Generally speaking, vocational preparation in traditional African education has been divided on the basis of type of occupation into three broad categories: agriculturally related occupations, trades and crafts, and the professions.[68]

Agricultural activities have been the basis for the vast majority of traditional agricultural societies, although some groups (such as the Masai in Kenya and Tanzania) have relied on animal husbandry instead.[69] Agricultural knowledge and skills have been passed on from one generation to the next most often by involving children in all aspects of agricultural production from early on in their childhood. Gradually, the child is given increasing responsibilities as he or she becomes proficient at the tasks related to agricultural production, often being given a small farm of his or her own to tend. Here, Ishumi describes the Yoruba custom:

> At the time the young farmer was learning these techniques, he would work with his guardian all day. But by about 12–15 years when he should have mastered these techniques he would be given some evenings free to work on his own farm. At first, it might be two evenings in the week, later this would be extended to all afternoons. This in itself was a lesson in responsibility and the foundation for independent existence. From now, the boy had his own chicken, product of his own effort which he could dispose of according to his wishes. By the time he was married, between 20–25, he could stand on his own as a farmer.[70]

The experience of boys and girls in this regard differed somewhat, reflecting the later occupational division that would divide them as adults. As Sudarkasa explained, however:

Typically, in indigenous African societies, the occupational roles of women were different from but complementary to the roles of men. . . . Very often men and women worked in the same occupation (for example, in farming or trading), but the tasks undertaken tended to be sex specific (for example, preparing the land for farming versus tending the crops or trading in one line of goods as opposed to another). There does not seem to be a basis for holding that women's occupations were considered to be "inferior" to those of men, although such occupations were usually thought to be inappropriate for men, just as men's occupations were normally considered inappropriate for women. The point here is that the maintenance of separate occupational domains for the two sexes did not automatically imply a hierarchical relationship between those two domains. . . .[71]

If agricultural and domestic occupations are learned largely from parents through imitation and informal participation and, thus, as Sudarska noted, "did not usually involve formal apprenticeships," more formal apprenticeship arrangements have been common for many crafts and professions in the traditional African society.[72] Among the more common crafts learned through some type of apprenticeship system are "weaving (for instance, baskets and cloth), hunting, carving, sculpturing, painting and decorating, carpentry, building, hair-plaiting, dress-making, boat-making, mat-making, dying, isusu-collecting (cooperative banking), food-selling, wine-tapping, and a host of other trades and crafts."[73] It is important to note, however, that such craft skills and knowledge are generally passed on within specific families, as Callaway, writing about Nigeria, explained:

This vast apprenticeship training system began as a part of a wider educational process in which the indigenous societies of Nigeria passed on their cultural heritage from one generation to the next. The skills "owned" by a family were highly valued, and in some lines such as native medicine, secrets were zealously guarded. . . . Evidence of the passing on of skills within families is still strong.[74]

Ogundijo noted several important features of indigenous apprenticeship practices, not the least of which are that "children were not free to choose the trade of the their liking, for they were bound to follow the guidance of their parents. For effective training, parents always apprenticed their children to their relatives, friends or competent craftsmen. . . . "[75]

Not only are trades and crafts learned through the apprenticeship system, but so too are the professional occupations of traditional African societies. Included under the general category of "professional occupations" are such social roles as "doctors, priests, witch doctors, civil servants, village heads, chiefs and kings, tax collectors, heralds, judges, councillors, police and messengers, shrine-keepers, soldiers, etc."[76] Unlike most trade and craft occupations, at least some of these professions have traditionally been what Nadel called "free professions," which means that one could become a member of the occupation not only through birth, but also through merit. As Nadel commented about the Nupe kingdom in Nigeria, "It is not surprising that a rich and complex culture like Nupe should possess its clearly defined 'free professions'—its professional scholars, scientists and artists, or, in a terminology more akin to the native conception, its mallams, barber-doctors, and drummers and dancers."[77]

An interesting exception to the generally formal, apprenticeship-based training assumed for the professions is that of the *imbongi*, or praise-poet, among groups such as the Zulu and Xhosa in Southern Africa.[78] The *imbongi* is in many ways a unique figure in traditional society; his role is part that of historian, part that of counselor, part that of social and political critic. The *imbongi* fulfills a role similar to that played by the medieval bard, relying both on the established oral tradition and his own ability to improvise in creating the appropriate *izibongo* (praise-poem) for the occasion. The *imbongi* is granted remarkable freedom in what he can say in his *izibongo*. As Opland explained, "It is generally accepted that the *imbongi* enjoys license in his poetry to use ribald language otherwise unacceptable in public. . . . Not only can the *imbongi* use ribald language, he also enjoys the license to criticize with impunity persons in positions of power."[79]

Technically not a "professional" because he is not actually paid for his services, the *imbongi* is to a very great extent born rather than made. As Opland noted about the Xhosa *imbongi*,

> There is no formal apprenticeship or training for an *imbongi*; he needs the tacit acceptance of the people to become an *imbongi*; rarely is he officially appointed *imbongi* by the chief, merely acknowledged or recognized if he chooses to present himself; and though he may associate himself intimately with the chief and the affairs of the great place, as *imbongi* he is never paid a salary by the chief. Aspirant *iimbongi* [plural] may listen to and learn from others, but they do not attach themselves to a practicing *imbongi* in order to learn their craft. The process is strictly informal: There are no guilds of poets; *iimbongi* do not form a separate class or caste; their status is not hereditary . . . no amount of training can make an *imbongi* of a boy lacking a special talent.[80]

It must be remembered that the *imbongi*, however interesting as a social and cultural phenomenon, is atypical of the norm for vocational training in traditional African societies. Virtually all individuals in such societies learn occupational roles through either imitation of parents or apprenticeship training or, most commonly, a combination of the two.

CONCLUDING THOUGHTS

In this chapter, an overview of several key components of traditional African educational thought and practice has been presented. Although such practices are less and less commonly found in modern Africa, it is not at all clear that this is due to any intrinsic flaw in either the theory or practices that underlie such traditional conceptions of education. Rather, this is arguably the result of a rejection of all things traditional in favor of Western models, a practice whose risks are vividly evoked in p'Bitek's moving poem, "Song of Lawino":

Listen Ocol, my old friend,

The ways of your ancestors

Are good,

Their customs are solid

And not hollow

They are not thin, not easily

breakable

They cannot be blown away

By the winds

Because their roots reach deep

into the soil.

I do not understand

The ways of foreigners

But I do not despise their

customs.

Why should you despise yours?[81]

It is important that we do not overromanticize precolonial institutions and practices in Africa, as Mazrui noted in a critique of the "Négritude" movement common especially in Francophone Africa: "The mood of this branch of African romantic thought is one of nostalgia, yearning for an innocence which is eternally lost. All that can be done now is to make the best of a bad job, try to save some of the values of old Africa, and find a synthesis between these and the influences which have come with colonialism and modernity."[82]

However, although not taking such an overly romantic view of the African past, it is also important that this past not be rejected wholesale. As Okeke persuasively argued, "It is my belief that traditional education should serve as the springboard from which formal education takes off. Anything short of this shall continue to plague us and continue to make formal education non-functional and divorced from the social, political and economic realities of Igboland."[83]

In short, much can be learned from the African educational tradition that could benefit contemporary educational thought and practice throughout the continent. Indeed, there are useful and valuable lessons for non-Africans as well. The communal responsibility for the education of the young, the effective use of the oral tradition in passing on various sorts of knowledge, the centrality of concerns with moral or character training in the education of the young, the importance of a sense of belonging for the child, and the view of education as an integral component of social life (rather than as something separate from the daily lives of most adults) are all areas in which our own society might gain insight about the problems and challenges that we face today.

QUESTIONS FOR REFLECTION AND DISCUSSION

1.   How does the focus in traditional African education with respect to moral education or character training differ from various contemporary Western approaches to and concerns about moral education? In what ways is the traditional African approach similar to calls for a return to "traditional values" in our own society?

2.   Contemporary Western societies are, for the most part, literate rather than oral, and yet one could argue that the advent of much recent technology will change the way in which we view literacy. In what ways do we still possess an oral culture, and how is that culture passed on to children? To what extent is modern technology utilized in this process? Do you believe that literacy will actually be necessary in the future, or will technological innovation make possible the development of a nonliterate but nonetheless "modern" society?

3.   Does the concern in traditional African education with preparing children to accept and function in the status quo conflict with the goals of education for a democratic society? With the goal of producing "critical thinkers"?

4.   What, in your view, are the greatest strengths of traditional African education? What are its greatest weaknesses?

5.   What lessons can you draw for your own classroom practice from what you have learned about traditional African education?

RECOMMENDED FURTHER READINGS

There are a number of good general introductions to Africa and African studies broadly conceived. Especially useful are Basil Davidson's *Africa in History*, revised and exp. ed. (1991, New York: Macmillan); Davidson's edited *African Civilization Revisited: From Antiquity to Modern Times* (1991, Trenton, NJ: Africa World Press); Philip Curtin, Steven Feierman, Leonard Thompson, and Jan Vansina's *African History: From Earliest Times to Independence*, 2nd ed. (1995, London: Longman); and Sanford Ungar's *Africa: The People and Politics of an Emerging Continent*, rev. ed. (1986, New York: Simon & Schuster). Also useful for students seeking a better understanding of life in Africa are novels, and among the best for this purpose are the works of the Nigeria author Chinua

Achebe, such as *Things Fall Apart* (London: Heinemann, 1958), *No Longer at Ease* (London: Heinemann, 1960), *Arrow of God* (London: Heinemann, 1974), and *A Man of the People* (London: Heinemann, 1966), all of which are now easily obtainable in North America.

NOTES

1. Richard Olaniyan, "African History and Culture: An Overview," in Richard Olaniyan (ed.), *African History and Culture* (Lagos: Longman, 1982), 1.

2. Meyer Fortes, "Foreward," in Eric Ayisi (ed.), *An Introduction to the Study of African Culture*, 2nd ed. (London: Currey, 1979), VII. See also Jean Jolly, *Historie de continent Africain*, 2 vols. (Paris: Éditions l'Harmattan, 1989).

3. Molefi Asante and Kariamu Asante (eds.), *African Culture: Rhythms of Unity* (Trenton, NJ: Africa World Press, 1990), ix–x.

4. See the discussion of Patricia Weibust's work on the concept of "tradition" in chapter 1, this volume.

5. Cheikh Anta Diop, *The Cultural Unity of Negro Africa* (Paris: Presence Africaine, 1962), 7. See also Cheikh Anta Diop, *Civilization or Barbarism: An Authentic Anthropology* (Chicago: Hill, 1991); Kwame Appiah, *In My Father's House: Africa in the Philosophy of Culture* (New York: Oxford University Press, 1992).

6. A. Babs Fafunwa, *A History of Education in Nigeria* (London: Allen & Unwin, 1974), 20. See also S. Nwosu, "Pedagogic Problems in Africa Today," in Joseph Okpaku, Alfred Opubor, and Benjamin Oloruntimehin (eds.), *The Arts and Civilization of Black and African Peoples: Volume 6, Black Civilization and Pedagogy* (Lagos: Center for Black and African Arts and Civilization, 1986), 103–105; A. Okeke, "Traditional Education in Igboland," in F. Ogbalu and E. Emenanjo (eds.), *Igbo Language and Culture*, Vol. 2 (Ibadan: University Press, 1982), 15–26; Abiola Irele (ed.), *African Education and Identity* (Ibadan: Spectrum Books, 1992).

7. Fafunwa, *A History of Education in Nigeria*, 20.

8. Chinua Achebe, *A Man of the People* (London: Heinemann, 1966), 148.

9. Abdou Moumouni, *Education in Africa* (New York: Praeger, 1968), 15.

10. Moumouni, *Education in Africa*, 29.

11. Okeke, "Traditional Education in Igboland," 15.

12. Eric Ayisi, *An Introduction to the Study of African Culture* (London: Currey, 1979), 48–49.

13. P. Duminy, *African Pupils and Teaching Them* (Pretoria: van Schaik, 1973), 30–31.

14. Stephé de Villiers and S. Helena Hartshorne, "Education," in A. C. Myburgh (ed.), *Anthropology for Southern Africa* (Pretoria: van Schaik, 1981), 147–148.

15. de Villiers and Hartshorne, "Education," 147.

16. See, for example, M. Katengo and G. Mwale, "Can Traditional Education Be Integrated with the Modern Educational System?" in Steven Moyo, Tobias Sumaili, and James Moody (eds.), *Oral Traditions in Southern Africa*, vol. 6 (Lusaka: Division for Cultural Research, Institute for African Studies, University of Zambia, 1986), 456–481.

17. Ali Mazrui and T. Wagaw, "Towards Decolonizing Modernity: Education and Culture Conflict in Eastern Africa," in *The Educational Process and Historiography in Africa* (Paris: UNESCO, 1985), 40.

18. Okeke, "Traditional Education in Igboland," 19.

19. Felix Boateng, "African Traditional Education: A Tool for Intergenerational Communication," in Molefi Asante and Kariamu Asante (eds.), *African Culture: Rhythms of Unity* (Trenton, NJ: Africa World Press, 1990), 117.

20. A. Fajana, "Traditional Methods of Education in Africa: The Yoruba Example," in Joseph Okpaku, Alfred Opubor, and Benjamin Oloruntimehin (eds.), *The Arts and Civilization of Black and African Peoples: Volume 6, Black Civilization and Pedagogy* (Lagos: Center for Black and African Arts and Civilization, 1986), 45.

21. C. H. Borland, "The Oral and Written Culture of the Shona," *LIMI: Bulletin of the Department of Bantu Languages, University of South Africa, 8* (1969): 8.

22. C. Nyembezi, *Zulu Proverbs* (Johannesburg: University of Witwatersrand Press, 1974), 46-48; see also Northcote W. Thomas, *Proverbs, Narratives, Vocabularies and Grammar: Anthropological Report on the Ibo-Speaking Peoples of Nigeria, Part III* (New York: Negro Universities Press, 1969).

23. Thomas, *Proverbs, Narratives, Vocabularies and Grammar*, 9.

24. Cited in O. F. Raum, "An Evaluation of Indigenous Education," in P. A. Duminy (ed.), *Trends and Challenges in the Education of the South African Bantu* (Pretoria: van Schaik, 1967), 103.

25. Taban lo Liyong, *The Last Word* (Nairobi: East Africa Publishing House, 1969), 141.

26. Nyembezi, *Zulu Proverbs*, 91.

27. Boateng, "African Traditional Education," 117.

28. See J. Nkara, "*Bisisimi* or the Language of the Wise," *South African Journal of African Languages, 12*, 4 (1992): 144.

29. Nkara, "*Bisisimi* or the Language of the Wise," 144.

30. Nkara, "*Bisisimi* or the Language of the Wise," 145.

31. Nkara, "*Bisisimi* or the Language of the Wise," 144.

32. Borland, "The Oral and Written Culture of the Shona," 9.

33. D. Mahlangu, "*Imiraro*: Ndebele Riddles," *South African Journal of African Languages, 8* (Supplement 1) (1988): 154–155.

34. Fajana, "Traditional Methods of Education in Africa," 54.

35. See Borland, "The Oral and Written Culture of the Shona"; Okeke, "Traditional Education in Igboland."

36. Fafunwa, *A History of Education in Nigeria*, 28.

37. Fajana, "Traditional Methods of Education in Africa," 55.

38. See William Bascom, *African Dilemma Tales* (The Hague: Mouton, 1975); Gerhard Kubik, *"Visimu vya mukatikati:* Dilemma Tales and Arithmetical Puzzles Collected among the Valuchazi," *South African Journal of African Languages,* 10, 2 (1990): 59–68; Gerhard Kubik, "A Luchazi riddle session: Analysis of recorded texts in a South-Central African Bantu language," *South African Journal of African Languages,* 12, 2 (1992): 51–82.

39. Bascom, *African Dilemma Tales,* 12.

40. Kubik, *"Visimu vya mukatikati,"* 60–61.

41. Kubik, *"Visimu vya mukatikati,"* 67.

42. Boateng, "African Traditional Education," 113.

43. N. Uka, "Continuity and Change: A Challenge to African Educators," in Joseph Okpaku, Alfred Opubor, and Benjamin Oloruntimehin (eds.), *The Arts and Civilization of Black and African Peoples: Volume 6, Black Civilization and Pedagogy* (Lagos: Center for Black and African Arts and Civilization, 1986), 131.

44. Fremont Besmer, *Horses, Musicians, and Gods: The Hausa Cult of Possession-Trance* (Zaria, Nigeria: Ahmadu Bello University Press, 1983), 44.

45. Boateng, "African Traditional Education," 115.

46. For a distinction between *izibongo* and *izithakazelo,* or clan praises, among the Zulu, see D. Mzolo, "Social Function of Clan Praises," in A. Nkabinde (ed.), *African Linguistics and Literature* (Johannesburg: Lexicon, 1988), 132–138.

47. I. Schapera, *Praise-Poems of Tswana Chiefs* (Oxford, England: Oxford University Press, 1965), 1; see also Daniel Kunene, *Heroic Poetry of the Basotho* (Oxford, England: Oxford University Press, 1971).

48. See Schapera, *Praise-Poems of Tswana Chiefs,* 25.

49. Fafunwa, *A History of Education in Nigeria,* 21.

50. Moumouni, *Education in Africa,* 22.

51. See Nathaniel Fadipe, *The Sociology of the Yoruba* (Ibadan: Ibadan University Press, 1970).

52. Okeke, "Traditional Education in Igboland," 18.

53. See Fafunwa, *A History of Education in Nigeria,* 24–26; Nwosu, "Pedagogic Problems in Africa Today"; V. van der Vliet, "Growing Up in a Traditional Society," in W. Hammond-Tooke (ed.), *The Bantu-Speaking Peoples of Southern Africa* (London: Routledge & Kegan Paul, 1974), 224.

54. Fafunwa, *A History of Education in Nigeria,* 19.

55. Fafunwa, *A History of Education in Nigeria,* 25.

56. See Fafunwa, *A History of Education in Nigeria;* Borland, "The Oral and Written Culture of the Shona"; S. Guma, *The Form, Content and Technique of Traditional Literature in Southern Sotho,* 2nd ed. (Pretoria: van Schaik, 1977).

57. See Rosalie Finlayson, *"Hlonipha:* The Women's Language of Avoidance among the Xhosa," *South African Journal of African Languages* (Supplement 1)(1982): 35–59; Rosalie Finlayson, "Linguistic Terms of Respect among the

Xhosa," in Peter Raper (ed.), *Names 1983: Proceedings of the Second South African Names Congress* (Pretoria: Human Sciences Research Council, 1986), 128–138.

58. See Ayisi, *An Introduction to the Study of African Culture*, 47.

59. See Borland, "The Oral and Written Culture of the Shona."

60. Benjamin Ray, *African Religions: Symbol, Ritual, and Community* (Englewood Cliffs, NJ: Prentice-Hall, 1976), 91. Also of interest here are John Mbiti, *African Religions and Philosophy*, 2nd ed. (Oxford, England: Heinemann, 1989), 118–129; Geoffrey Parrinder, *Religion in Africa* (Harmondsworth: Penguin, 1969).

61. Jacques Macquet, quoted in P. Boe, "Circumcision: The Rites of Manhood in the Bille Tribe," in E. Adegbola (ed.), *Traditional Religion in West Africa* (Nairobi: Uzima Press, 1983), 88.

62. Ayisi, *An Introduction to the Study of African Culture*, 47.

63. See Ayisi, *An Introduction to the Study of African Culture*, 46; also relevant here is Olaniyan, *African History and Culture*, 30–31.

64. See Ayisi, *An Introduction to the Study of African Culture*, 46; Olaniyan, *African History and Culture*, 30–31.

65. Raum, "An Evaluation of Indigenous Education," 99–100.

66. van der Vliet, "Growing Up in a Traditional Society," 241.

67. Blacking, quoted in van der Vliet, "Growing Up in a Traditional Society," 235.

68. See Fafunwa, *A History of Education in Nigeria*, 30–31. See also Olaitan Obanewa, *Education of the Children and Youth in Ile-Ife: A Comparison of Formal and Non-Formal Systems of Education* (M.Ed. thesis, University of Ife, Nigeria, 1973), and Okeke, "Traditional Education in Igboland," 20–22.

69. See A. Ishumi, "Black Civilization and Pedagogy: A Search for Modern Methods," in Joseph Okpaku, Alfred Opubor, and Benjamin Oloruntimehin (eds.), *The Arts and Civilization of Black and African Peoples: Volume 6, Black Civilization and Pedagogy* (Lagos: Center for Black and African Arts and Civilization, 1986), 67.

70. Ishumi, "Black Civilization and Pedagogy," 51.

71. Niara Sudarkasa, "Sex Roles, Education and Development in Africa," *Anthropology and Education*, 13, 3 (1982): 280.

72. See Sudarkasa, "Sex Roles, Education and Development in Africa," 280–281.

73. Okeke, "Traditional Education in Igboland," 21.

74. Quoted in Fafunwa, *A History of Education in Nigeria*, 30.

75. M. Ogundijo, *Indigenous Education in the Ejigbo District of Oshun Division in the Pre-Colonial Days and the Coming of the Missionaries* (B.A. thesis, Faculty of Education, University of Ife, 1970), 11–12.

76. Fafunwa, *A History of Education in Nigeria*, 30; see also Okeke, "Traditional Education in Igboland," 21.

77. Quoted in Fafunwa, *A History of Education in Nigeria*, 37.

78. See Jeff Opland, *Xhosa Oral Poetry: Aspects of a Black South African Tradition* (Cambridge, England: Cambridge University Press, 1983); Jeff Opland, "Xhosa *izibongo*: Improvised Line," *South African Journal of African Languages*, *10*, 4 (1990): 239–251; Russell Kaschula, "The Role of the Xhosa Oral Poet in Contemporary South African Society," *South African Journal of African Languages*, *11*, 2 (1991): 47–54; Trevor Cope (ed.), *Izibongo: Zulu Praise Poems* (Oxford, England: Oxford University Press, 1968); D. Rycroft and A. Ngcobo, *Say It in Zulu* (Pietermaritzburg: Language and Reading Laboratories, University of Natal, 1981), Part II, Appendix I; Noleen Turner, "Comparison of the *Izibongo* of the Zulu Royal Women, Mnkabayi and Nandi," *South African Journal of African Languages*, *8*, 1 (1988): 28–33.

79. Opland, *Xhosa Oral Poetry*, 66–67.

80. Opland, *Xhosa Oral Poetry*, 64–65.

81. Okot p'Bitek, *Song of Lawino and Song of Ocol* (Ibadan: Heinemann, 1967), 41.

82. Ali Mazrui, *The African Condition: The Reith Lectures* (London: Heinemann, 1980), 11.

83. Okeke, "Traditional Education in Igboland," 25.

3

The Meso-American Educational Experience: The Case of the Aztecs[*]

When Hernán Cortés and his men first arrived in Mexico in 1519, they were astounded by the civilization that greeted them. Unlike earlier contacts between Europeans and indigenous peoples in the Western hemisphere, in their introduction to the Aztec civilization[1] Cortés and his followers faced a highly sophisticated, urban culture in full flower—a civilization, in fact, that in many ways compared favorably to that of any 16th-century European society. As Cortés himself wrote to the Spanish king, "These people live like those in Spain, and in as much harmony and order as there, and considering that they are barbarous and so far from the knowledge of God and cut off from all civilized nations, it is truly remarkable to see what they have achieved in all things."[2] This was remarkably high praise from the man who was, more than any other single individual, responsible for the destruction of the Aztec world—or, as the Aztecs themselves would have termed it, the time of the fifth sun.[3]

Education, both formal and informal, was an important and well-developed part of Aztec society.[4] As Miguel León-Portilla commented, "The written sources on the educational practices of the Nahuas are so abundant that a book could be written on that subject alone. Such a book might reconstruct—as did

---

[*]This chapter deals solely with the educational thought and practice of the Aztecs. However, the Aztec educational experience did not emerge in a vacuum, but rather was probably closely related to the experience that had characterized the earlier Mayan society. For discussions of Mayan society, see Robert Sharer, *The Ancient Maya*, 5th ed. (Stanford, CA: Stanford University Press, 1994); Michael Coe, *The Maya*, 4th ed. (London: Thames and Hudson, 1987); Michael Coe, *Breaking the Maya Code* (London: Thames and Hudson, 1992); Linda Schele and David Freidel, *A Forest of Kings: The Untold Story of the Ancient Maya* (New York: Morrow, 1990); David Freidel, Linda Schele, and Joy Parker, *Maya Cosmos: Three Thousand Years on the Shaman's Path* (New York: Morrow, 1993); Norman Hammond, *Ancient Maya Civilization* (New Brunswick, NJ: Rutgers University Press, 1988). For an analysis of Mayan education in particular, see A. Izquierdo, *La educación Maya en los tiempos prehispánicos* (México: Universidad Nacional Autónoma de México, 1983).

41

Jaeger's *Paideia* for the ancient Greeks—through the educational system all the richness and profundity of the Nahuatl concept of man."[5] And yet, despite its noteworthy successes, no mention whatever of the educational thought and practice of the Aztecs appears in the standard works in the history of education in the English-speaking world. Although a thorough analysis of education in the "time of the fifth sun" is far beyond the scope of this chapter, it is possible to present a general overview of Aztec education as it existed at the time of the arrival of the Spanish in the early 16th century.

THE AZTEC WORLD

The Aztecs were relative latecomers to the Valley of Mexico, building their society on the cultural, religious and intellectual foundations, and the architectural ruins of earlier civilizations, especially that of the Toltecs. Furthermore, their rise to prominence was, in the words of Muriel Weaver, "a dramatic rags-to-riches tale."[6] The Aztecs first arrived in the area of the Valley of Mexico in the early 13th century, by which time the more desirable areas around the lake shore were already settled by other Nahuatl- and Otomí-speaking peoples, as well as by the descendants of earlier refugees from Teotihuacan and Tula, among others.[7] Indeed, the awareness of their late arrival, as well as of their status as outsiders, remained with the Aztecs until the arrival of the Spanish. Cortés himself recorded that Monteuczoma, in their first conversation together, commented that, "From the records which we have long possessed and which are handed down from our ancestors, it is known that no one, neither I nor the others who inhabit the land of Anahuac, are native to it. We are strangers and we came from far outer parts."[8]

The new arrivals were not greeted with open arms by those already settled in the area, and in the early years after their arrival in the Valley of Mexico, the Aztecs were driven from one area to another around the western part of the lake. As Jon Manchip White wrote,

> they were looked upon as little more than squatters. . . . Nor was it simply the case that they were backward and brutish: they were downright squalid. Their little uncouth tribal war-god, Huitzilopochtli, was already notorious for the number of fresh, bleeding hearts he required, and his worshippers did not seem to be particular about where they got them. They gained a reputation for every kind of murder and brutality.[9]

Finally, the Aztecs arrived at Culhuacan, one of the established cities in the Valley. The Culhua permitted the Aztecs to settle at Tizapan, about 6 miles west of Culhuacan, in an inhospitable area where they fully expected that the Aztecs would, "perish . . . eaten by the serpents, since many dwell in that place."[10] Instead, the Aztecs prospered, ultimately acquiring not only access to the cultural heritage of the Toltecs, but also to claims of Toltec lineage as a result of intermarriage with the inhabitants of Culhuacan. The Aztecs also became mercenaries for the Culhua, and were so successful in this role that they eventually came to represent a serious threat to the Culhua. The tensions between the Culhua and the Aztecs were forced to a head when the Aztecs requested:

> the hand of one of Culhuacan's rulers, a beautiful girl whom they promptly killed and flayed. Her father arrived to attend her wedding, only to be confronted by a priest dancing in her flayed skin. Fighting broke out at once, and the [Aztecs] retreated into the swamps of the lagoon, finally reaching the safety of a reed-covered island near the center of what is now Mexico City. There they rested. Huitzilopochtli [the Aztec war god] appeared before one of the priests, ordering him to search for a cactus where a great eagle perched. This, said the god, was a place he had named Tenochtitlán, the "Place of the Fruit of the Prickly Pear Cactus."[11]

Thus was Tenochtitlán, the capital city of the Aztec Empire, established probably around 1345.[12] The Aztecs next experienced a period of growth and consolidation, culminating in the defeat of the city of Azcapotzalco in 1428, which "established the Aztecs as the dominant power in the Basin of Mexico."[13]

By the time of the arrival of Cortés and his men, the Aztec Empire was in many ways at its height,[14] consisting of some 15 million people and 489 tributary towns that were, in turn, divided into 38 provinces for administrative purposes.[15] It was, in actuality, not so much an "empire" as it was a loose collection of culturally related but distinct principalities sharing (for the most part) a common language[16] and united primarily by the paying of tribute to Tenochtitlán.[17] Local rulers continued to govern their communities, albeit under the auspices of the Aztecs. Characteristic of the Aztec approach to imperium was its emphasis on control of urban centers:

> Because of the nature of Mesoamerican warfare and the limitations on political consolidation, conquest did not mean complete territorial control. Rather, conquest was of political centers. Control of territory per se was not a major consideration. Once a political center was dominated, so too were its dependencies, and tribute, flowing from dependency to cabecera to provincial capital, could be drained from an entire region simply by dominating the center.[18]

The empire was held together, in short, not by the establishment of military garrisons throughout its territories, nor by overt control from Tenochtitlán but, rather, by tribute to be paid to Tenochtitlán and well-developed commercial ties.[19] The paying of tribute as well as the commercial ties were both, in turn, strengthened by what might be termed *ideological hegemony*, as Hassig noted:

> The Aztecs' reliance on hegemonic rather than territorial control produced an empire of distinctive character and vast expanse but loose control. Mesoameri-

can technological constraints limited the size, strength and duration of forays outside the empire, and such engagements took on strategic characteristics that varied with the political nature of the target. Furthermore, the Aztec Empire was essentially an alliance, and was expectedly fraught with rebellion. Nevertheless, the system functioned admirably within its cultural context, and through it the Aztecs expanded their domain to a size unprecedented in Mesoamerica.[20]

By 1519, Tenochtitlán was a large, thriving urban metropolis of some 200,000 people, with at least as many living in the satellite cities that surrounded it, making it far larger than any European city of the time.[21] The city was connected to the mainland by three elevated causeways, and was provided fresh water by a serious of carefully engineered aqueducts.[22] Food came to the capital not only as tribute from the provinces, but also, and more importantly, from the *chinampas*, the island gardens that made possible the intensive agricultural cultivation that supported the urban civilizations of the Valley of Mexico.[23]

The spiritual heart of the Aztec Empire was the Templo Mayor, the largest structure in the central plaza of Tenochtitlán,[24] which represented not only the ritualistic center of the empire but, even more, embodied in its architecture itself of the Aztec view of the universe, as Eduardo Matos Moctezuma noted: "The Templo Mayor thus becomes the fundamental center where all sacred power is concentrated and where all the levels intersect. I propose that it not only occupies a privileged location but that in its architecture, form, and particular characteristics it also represents the entire Mexica conception of the cosmos."[25]

Aztec society was hierarchical in nature, characterized by rank and kinship.[26] The population was broadly divided into those of noble birth and those of common birth, although some degree of social mobility did exist primarily as a result of success in commerce, military success, or entrance into the priesthood.[27] Gender also played a key role in individual identity in Aztec society,[28] as did ethnicity for those of non-Aztec ancestry. Central to social status in Aztec society, however, was military rank. As Hassig explained, "Military ranking was intimately tied to the overall social structure of Aztec society, and social ranking was intimately tied to political offices, the latter defining rights and requiring the holder to have a specified status."[29]

It is interesting to note that although, as Nicholson has noted, "The sharply aristocratic bias of the society as a whole, naturally correlated with a high degree of social stratification,"[30] this social stratification was manifested in practice by far greater expectations of those at higher social levels. For example, as Muriel Weaver argued:

> An interesting concept of Aztec law was that the severity of punishment was measured in accordance with the offender's station in life. A high priest would be put to death for a crime that might be tolerated if committed by a bondsman. That is, a man of high office assumed greater moral responsibilities and his conduct was expected to be beyond reproach.[31]

Also important in terms of the organization of Aztec society was the role played by the *calpulli*, the ancient territorial kinship groups to which every member of the society belonged. The *calpulli* "served as the interface between the citizens and the government,"[32] as well as maintaining religious and educational institutions and communally holding a certain amount of land.[33] As Fagan commented:

> The *calpulli* was probably the most important social institution in Aztec society. It provided a mechanism by which people cooperated with one another and gave a large measure of security to everyone. The state used it not only to govern a teeming and diverse urban and rural population, but to recruit large numbers of people at short notice for public works or armies of conquest.[34]

Underlying virtually all aspects of Aztec society were the two closely interrelated pillars of Aztec society—militarism and religion.[35] For the Aztecs, warfare was a means not only of gaining personal glory, social status, and, ultimately, tribute and expanding territorial control, but even more was a kind of sacrificial activity. In fact, warfare involved two kinds of sacrifice, as one of the terms used by the Aztecs to refer to war makes clear: *teoatl tlachinolli*, which translates literally as "divine liquid and ashes."[36] The term itself incorporates a vast wealth of meaning:

> The first element signifies "blood," and the second is a shorthand statement for the practice of cremating dead warriors on the battlefield, a Toltec custom that released the fortunate soul like a sunburst to ascend into the heavens. War meant the spilling of human blood, which was by definition a liquor destined for the support of the gods; war, in other words, was an act of sacrifice carried out voluntarily by those who killed as well as by those who were killed.[37]

Indeed, the need for such sacrifice was so great that when real warfare was not possible or advisable, the Aztecs engaged in what was called a *xochiyaoyotl*, or "war of flowers."[38] The *xochiyaoyotl* was a ritual military contest, "in which the two sides set out to capture the maximum number of sacrificial victims from the other while inflicting a minimum of damage in other respects."[39]

Sacrifice was essential in the Aztec religious system, because it was the shedding of human blood that ensured "the continued existence of the cosmos."[40] The sun itself, as well as the other deities of the Aztec pantheon, were nourished by human blood.[41] As Davies suggested, "In general terms, the religion of the Aztecs was an elaborate defence mechanism, born not out of hope but of anxiety. Every aspect, and in particular human offering, implies a struggle to ward off disaster, whether immediate catastrophes such as crop failure or the ultimate doom of the Fifth, and last, Sun."[42] Such an understanding is also consistent with the Aztec view of history, as the noted scholar Miguel León-Portilla maintained:

> It was believed that the present sun, moon, stars and earth integrate the fifth universe within a series of ages, known to the Nahua people as "Suns." Four

other Suns had emerged and come to an end through the machinations of the gods: the ages of Earth, Air, Water, and Fire. The present is that of *Olintonatiuh*, "The Sun of Movement," which began to exist and to move thanks to a primeval sacrifice of the gods, who, with their own blood, brought it into being and thus also gave life to a new generation of humans. This fifth age not only may perish but actually carries within itself the very principle of death and destruction.[43]

Another view of the role of sacrifice in Aztec religious thought is that offered by López Austin, who:

> claimed that the relationship between god and man was mercantilistic: man gave blood, hearts, and fire to the gods, and was given in return crops, water, and freedom from disease and plagues. This claim is supported etymologically. The word for sacrifice to the gods is *nextlahualiztli* ("the act of payment"), and the offering of fire to the gods, *tlenamaca*, means "to sell fire."[44]

Such sacrifice occurred, of course, not only on the battlefield, but in the temples and in everyday life as well. The role of human sacrifice and the related practice of ritual cannibalism in Aztec society has been well documented,[45] and it is clear that such sacrifice involved males and females, adults and children,[46] and as many as 20,000 human sacrifices a year may have taken place by the time of the arrival of Cortés.[47] Also important in Aztec life, however, was the practice of autosacrifice, which involved personal bloodletting. As Cecelia Klein argued, "In Aztec society, from all reports, virtually everyone, regardless of age, sex, or social class, was expected to bleed himself."[48] The practice of such autosacrifice, which the Aztecs believed to have originated with the god Quetzalcoatl, was in fact closely related to human sacrifice, and it appears to have served as a symbolic substitute for human sacrifice in some instances.[49]

Aztec religious thought entailed far more than just sacrifice, of course. Religion played a central role in social life in general, touching every aspect of the society.[50] In addition to the rituals performed in the temples, their religion provided the Aztecs with a well-developed creation mythology, a powerful moral code, the basis for their political and economic social order, a complex view of life after death, a priesthood responsible for the maintenance of both the oral and written traditions of their society, the calendrical system used not only to maintain records but to make predictions, a highly developed astrological system, and the foundations for a metaphysical and ultimately philosophical world view.[51] Thus, it is hardly surprising that religious concerns are in many ways at the heart of the Aztec notion of the educated person, the concept to which we now turn.

THE AZTEC CONCEPTION OF THE "EDUCATED PERSON"

The development of the individual's personality, which the Aztecs called "face and heart," played an important role in their conception of *education* and the *educated person*, although the primary focus of education was "the assimilation of individuals into the life and highest ideals of the community."[52] As one ancient text described what we would today call the "educated person":

In omacic oquichtli,

Yollotetl, yollotlaquavac,

ixlamati,

ixehyollo,

mozcalia.

The mature man

is a heart solid as a rock,

is a wise face.

Possessor of a face, possessor of a heart,

he is able and understanding.[53]

The core values that were expected to guide the behavior of all individuals in Aztec society, regardless of social station, and that provide a clear indication of the Aztec view of what the "educated person" might look like include:

1. maintenance of control and discipline;
2. fluency of speech and good manners;
3. a composed and reserved attitude;
4. a sense of responsibility for the common people;
5. respect for one's elders;
6. interest in and knowledge of the gods; and
7. courage, submission to one's fate, a desire to die a heroic death rather than to die without having made a serious effort to expand and strengthen the Aztec's supremacy.[54]

These core values are clearly intended to promote the general good of society, and have a social rather than individual focus, as one would expect. This focus can be seen vividly in the following model homily delivered by an Aztec father to his son:

Revere and greet your elders; console the poor and the afflicted with good works and words. . . . Follow not the madmen who honour neither father nor mother; for they are like animals, for they neither take nor hear advice. . . . Do not mock the old, the sick, the maimed, or one who has sinned. Do not insult or abhor them, but abase yourself before God and fear lest the same befall you. . . . Do not set a bad example, or speak indiscreetly, or interrupt the speech of another. If someone does not speak well or coherently, see that you do not the same; if it is not your business to speak, be silent. If you are asked something, reply soberly and without affectation or flattery or prejudice to others, and your speech will be well regarded. . . . Wherever you go, walk with a peaceful air, and do not make wry faces or improper gestures.[55]

Similar messages were conveyed less directly, but perhaps more effectively, to children in Aztec society through the use of proverbs, conundrums, and metaphors.[56] For example, typical proverbs that children might hear include the following, reported in the *Florentine Codex:*

1. *Nonouian.* Here, there and everywhere. (This is said about a person who enters where he or she should not enter, sticks his or her hand where he should not stick his hand, and quickly takes part in whatever others are doing.)[57]
2. *Ayac xictili in tlalticpac.* No one on earth is an umbilical cord (i.e., to be thrown away). (We should not sneer at anyone; meaning, we should not disdain anyone even though he appears to warrant disdain, as he might be a wise man, or learned, or able.)[58]
3. *Tlacoqualli in monequi.* Moderation is proper. (We should not dress in rags, nor should we overdress. In the matter of clothing, we should dress with moderation.)[59]

The conundrums that characterized much of the verbal play of Aztec children, as Sullivan noted, "are like conundrums everywhere—charming, simple, and concerned with everyday things."[60] Some interesting examples of common conundrums, again drawn from the *Florentine Codex,* include:

1. *Zazan tleino, icuitlaxcol quiuilana, tepetozcatl quitoca. Aca quittaz tozazaniltzin, tla ca nenca uitzmallotl.* (What is it that drags its intestines as it ambles along the foothills of the mountain? Someone is sure to guess our riddle; it is a sewing needle.)[61]
2. *Zazan tleino, tezcatzintli acxoyacaletica. Tixtelolo.* (What is a little mirror in the middle of fir trees? Our eyes.)[62]
3. *Zazan tleino, tepetlamimilolli yitic ameia. Toyac.* (What is a mountain-side that has a spring of water in it? Our nose.)[63]
4. *Zazan tleino, quauhtla calaqui nenepilotiuh. Tepuztli.* (What is it that goes into a tree and its tongue is hanging out? An ax.)[64]

The purpose of Aztec education, in short, was largely to promote socially appropriate and basically conformist behavior and, in this objective, it is clear that Aztec education was remarkably successful.[65] As the Jesuit José de Acosta noted in the latter part of the 16th century, "Nothing caused me so much admiration and seems to me more worthy of praise and remembering than the care and discipline with which the Mexicans raised their children. In effect, it would be quite difficult to find a nation which in its times of paganism gave more attention to this element of highest importance to the state."[66]

We turn now to an examination of how the Aztecs accomplished the making of such "educated persons," first looking at the child's earliest years at home, and then at the formal educational institutions of Aztec society.

THE EDUCATIONAL FUNCTIONS OF THE FAMILY
IN AZTEC SOCIETY

As Fagan commented, "From the moment of birth, an Aztec child became aware that the world was a place of hard work and suffering."[67] Early childhood education for the Aztecs was guided by the twin concerns of teaching self-control and accommodation to adversity on the one hand and self-knowledge and introspection on the other.[68] By the age of 4, both boys and girls were performing chores around the home—boys began by carrying water and accompanying their fathers to work and the market; girls by helping their mothers in various household activities.[69] The nature of the activities in which children were engaged became increasingly sophisticated as they grew older and were given more responsibility—for girls, such training was intended to prepare them for their futures as wives and mothers, whereas for boys the focus was increasingly on learning their father's craft.[70] Children also learned the importance of learning to control their appetites during this early period—a lesson reinforced by the relatively small food ration they were allowed.[71] Boys learned to tolerate not only hunger, but also extremes of heat and cold, as preparation for their later lives as warriors.[72]

Much of the concern of parents for their children during this early period in their children's upbringing concerned what might be called "character education," with punishments for inappropriate behavior ranging from mere scolding to beatings, being pricked with maguey spines and, perhaps as a last result, being forced to inhale the fumes of burning chilis—punishments vividly portrayed in the Aztec manuscript the *Codex Mendoza*.[73]

FORMAL SCHOOLING IN AZTEC SOCIETY

The first taste of formal schooling outside of the home that Aztec children took place between the ages of twelve and fifteen, when both boys and girls attended the *cuicacalli* ("the House of Song").[74] Each *calpulli* maintained its own *cuicacalli*, in which the elderly members of the community taught the songs, dances, and music with which everyone in Aztec society needed to be familiar.[75] The *cuicacalli* took place toward the end of the day, about 1 hour before sunset, and children learned:

> the correct songs and orations for every major religious ceremony on the Aztec calendar. These incantations spoke of the Aztec cosmos, the creation, and the great migrations of the ancestors. They dealt with the roles of mortals on earth,

and of the relationships between gods and humans. At the *cuicacalli* everyone learned about their cultural heritage and about the mystical and highly symbolic world that surrounded them.[76]

For the sons of the common people, additional schooling normally took place in the *telpochcalli* (the "House of Youth"), in which the curriculum included the study of history, religion, ritual, proper behavior, and music, singing, and dancing.[77] The *telpochcalli*, however, was primarily concerned with preparing its charges for war, and the students in the *telpochcalli* engaged in extensive military training and even participation in real battles on occasion.[78] As Hassig explained:

> Beyond greater numbers, the Aztecs also had a fully professional corps of soldiers, the result of a formal educational system. Initially, the Aztecs offered formal military training only to the elite, but within two decades of their emergence as an independent power, King Monteuczomah Ilhuicamina instituted training for all males. . . . The commoners' schools [the *telpochcalli*], located in each of the city's wards, were responsible for educating all the youths therein between the ages of fifteen and twenty years . . . each commoners' school had a staff of accomplished verteran soldiers who trained the youths in military skills. Youths . . . accompanied the army on its campaigns to teach them about battle, usually as burden bearers.[79]

Boys slept at the *telpochcalli* at night, and were required to perform a variety of different kinds of physical work necessary to the maintenance of the *telpochcalli*, but they ate their meals at home with their families, and spent part of their day with the fathers, continuing to learn the vocational skills they would someday need to support themselves.[80]

The sons of the nobility, on the other hand, generally attended the *calmécac*, which were attached to the temples and were under the direct control of the religious authorities.[81] The *calmécac* provided an academically superior education, focusing not only on the military skills needed by all Aztec males, but also on religious instruction, history, painting, music, law, astrology, mathematics, government, and architecture.[82] Also important in a *calmécac* education was learning to speak well; the Aztecs valued the ability to use what they called *qualli tlatolli* ("good language"), by which they meant noble (as opposed to common) speech, and even distinguished between *macehuallatolli* ("the language of the common people") and *tecpillatolli* ("lordly language").[83]

Because the Aztec writing system was "not a transliteration of spoken words but an elaborate code that was reserved to those who had learned its intricacies and the orations behind it,"[84] students at the *calmécac* spent much of their time memorizing vast quantities of historical and religious material.[85] This limitation of the Aztec literary tradition has turned out to have significant benefits for us today as we try to more fully understand the Aztecs, as John Cornyn noted:

> The great body of the national literature was memorized in the Aztec schools over a period of scholastic life that was almost as long as our own. To this fact

we owe the preservation of the very considerable body of Aztec metric compositions which have come down to us, for, had the Aztecs been able to write their literature, it would all have disappeared in the ruthless destruction of Indian libraries wrought by the Spanish conquerors and their native allies in the first few years after the conquest.[86]

Unlike in the *telpochcalli*, students in the *calmécac* lived at the school, in what has been suggested to have been an environment "more like that of a monastery than an ordinary school."[87] It was from the *calmécac* that the priests of Aztec society were drawn, as well as the senior government officials, military leaders, judges, and so on, and thus the *calmécac* served an important role in "the spread of elite dogma and the consolidation of belief" in Aztec society.[88] Interestingly, whereas the patron god of the *telpochcalli* was Tezcatlipoca, the war god, the patron god of the *calmécac* was Quetzalcoatl, the Creator god who was also "the god of learning and culture, of ancient lore, the god of civilization itself."[89]

Although attendance at the *telpochcalli* and the *calmécac* was largely determined by social class background, there was, nevertheless, a certain degree of choice involved in the selection of the school one's son would attend.[90] It is well established that children of non-noble backgrounds attended the *calmécac*, primarily to become priests, just as it is documented that some children of the nobility attended the *telpochcalli*.[91] In any event, all young men in Aztec society, regardless of their social background, attended one or the other of these institutions.[92]

Although all boys went on for further schooling, the *cuicacalli* was the end of formal schooling for many, and perhaps most, girls. There were, however, equivalent institutions to both the *telpochcalli* and the *calmécac* available for girls,[93] as discussed in the "Bancroft Dialogues":

> Likewise within the houses, where the ladies were in their quarters, the girls were taught all the different things women do: sweeping, sprinkling, preparing food, making beverages, grinding (maize), preparing tortillas, making tamales, all the different things customarily done among women; also (the art of) the spindle and the weaver's reed and various kinds of embroidery; also dyeing, how rabbit down or rabbit fur was dyed different colors. And in the same way (as with the boys) those who did something wrong or did not take care were severely punished. And they were all well cared for: no men, no matter who, entered there; taking care of them was the exclusive domain of the elderly noblewomen. . . . And the commoners were raised in the same way; the youths were raised in the school at the youths' house, and the girls at the women's temple, where the female penitents were enclosed and fasted.[94]

CONCLUSION

In short, formal schooling in Aztec society was well-developed and effective. Perhaps most impressive was the fact that at a time when in virtually every European society, schooling of any sort was limited to a small elite in the Aztec world there was mandatory, universal schooling for both boys and girls regardless of social class.[95] Furthermore, for the Aztecs "education" entailed a variety of different attributes; in fact, the Aztecs had two very distinct words for "education": *neixtlamachiliztli* ("the act of giving wisdom to the face") and *tlacahuapahualiztli* ("the art of strengthening or bringing up men").[96] Given this model of *education* and the *educated person*, it could certainly be argued that the Aztecs were far more successful in achieving their educational aims than are many contemporary societies.

QUESTIONS FOR REFLECTION AND DISCUSSION

1.   Social class clearly played an important role in both informal and formal education in Aztec society. To what extent, and in what ways, was the educational system open to social class mobility, and how might this have strengthened Aztec society?

2.   The Aztec conception of the *educated man* is discussed in detail in this chapter. What, given your knowledge of Aztec society, would have been the Aztec conception of the *educated woman*? How does this conception fit with the passage from the "Bancroft Dialogues" presented in the chapter?

3.   In many ways, Aztec educational goals and practices are similar to the those of a number of other societies throughout history. For example, what are the similarities to and differences from Spartan education? What about the educational ideals and institutions of Nazi Germany? How might the similarities that you have identified be explained?

4.   Aztec schooling sought to promote the social status quo and reproduce Aztec society. To what extent and in what ways is this true for contemporary schooling as well? Is this, in your view, a reasonable goal for schooling?

5.   This chapter concludes by noting that Aztec education may have been more effective than are many contemporary systems of education. If this is true, is it in fact desirable? With what issues other than effectiveness might one be concerned when evaluating educational thought and practice?

RECOMMENDED FURTHER READINGS

An excellent overview of Aztec society for the beginner is Richard Townsend's *The Aztecs* (London: Thames and Hudson, 1992), whereas a somewhat more sophisticated account is provided in Inga Clendinnen's *Aztecs: An Interpretation* (Cambridge, England: Cambridge University Press, 1991). Among the best works describing the intellectual and cultural world of the Aztecs are Miguel León-Portilla's *Aztec Thought and Culture* (Norman: University of Oklahoma Press, 1963) and his *The Aztec Image of Self and Society: An Introduction to Nahua Culture* (Salt Lake City: University of Utah Press,

1992). Finally, although somewhat dated, Jacques Soustelle's *Daily Life of the Aztecs on the Eve of the Spanish Conquest* (Stanford, CA: Stanford University Press, 1961) provides a classic summary of many educationally relevant aspects of Aztec life.

NOTES

1. There is something of a terminological problem involved in discussing the Aztecs. First, as Fagan quite correctly noted, "At the time of the Spanish Conquest, the Aztecs called themselves either Tenocha Mexica or Tlatelolca Mexica, depending on which part of the capital they lived in. 'Mexica' could also be used alone, depending on the context" [Brian Fagan, *The Aztecs* (New York: Freeman, 1984), x]. Furthermore, the Aztecs were but one group among the closely related Nahuatl groups in Mesoamerica, and so one might also quite properly use the term "Nahuatl" to refer to them—as, indeed, Miguel León-Portilla did. However, "Aztec" is the most commonly and easily understood term used today for the people about whom I am writing, and so I have chosen to take the easiest way out for the benefit of the reader, as have many other writers on the Aztecs.

2. Quoted in Ross Hassig, *Trade, Tribute, and Transportation: The 16th Century Political Economy of the Valley of Mexico* (Norman: University of Oklahoma Press, 1985), 4.

3. From the Aztec perspective, of course, the "time of the fifth sun" did not actually end with the Spanish Conquest—technically speaking, only the end of the world as we know it, on a predetermined date, would constitute the end of the "time of the fifth sun." However, in a very real social and political sense, the world of the Aztecs did indeed end in the early 16th century, as Brundage and others seem to implicitly recognize in utilizing the phrase "the fifth sun" to refer solely to the world of the Aztecs. See Burr Brundage, *The Fifth Sun: Aztec Gods, Aztec World* (Austin: University of Texas Press, 1979).

4. See Ruben Campos, *La producción literaria de los Aztecas* (México: Talleres Gráficos del Museo Nacional de Arqueología, Historia y Ethnografía, 1936), 65–72; F. Infante, *La educación de los Aztecas* (México: Panorama Editorial, 1983); Mina Markus, "Estudio comparativo entre la educación nahuatl y la griega," *Estudios de Cultura Náhuatl*, 4 (1963): 281–292; P. Aizpuro, *Historia de la educación en la época colonial: El mundo indígena* (México: El Colegio de México, 1990); Jacqueline Sáenz, "Reto y educación en el México prehispánico," in J. Kathryn Josserand and Karen Dakin (eds.), *Smoke and Mist: Mesoamerican Studies in Memory of Thelma D. Sullivan, Part II* (Oxford, England: B.A.R., 1988), 681–695.

5. Miguel León-Portilla, *Aztec Thought and Culture* (Norman: University of Oklahoma Press, 1963), 135.

6. Muriel Weaver, *The Aztecs, Maya, and Their Predecessors: Archeology of Mesoamerica*, 2nd ed. (New York: Academic, 1981), 420.

7. See Nigel Davies, *The Ancient Kingdoms of Mexico* (New York: Penguin, 1982), 167–171; John Thompson, *Mexico Before Cortez: An Account of the Daily Life, Religion, and Ritual of the Aztecs and Kindred Peoples* (New York: Scribner's, 1933), 23–27; Weaver, *The Aztecs, Maya, and Their Predecessors,* 420; Jacques Soustelle, *Les Aztèques,* 6th ed. (Paris: Presses Universitaires de France, 1991).

8. Quoted in Burr Brundage, *A Rain of Darts: The Mexica Aztecs* (Austin: University of Texas Press, 1972), 22.

9. Jon White, *Cortés and the Downfall of the Aztec Empire: A Study in a Conflict of Cultures* (New York: St. Martin's Press, 1971), 93.

10. Quoted in Fagan, *The Aztecs,* 57–58.

11. Fagan, *The Aztecs,* 58.

12. See Davies, *The Ancient Kingdoms of Mexico,* 171; Weaver, *The Aztecs, Maya, and Their Predecessors,* 421.

13. Weaver, *The Aztecs, Maya, and Their Predecessors,* 422.

14. Although in many ways the Aztec Empire was indeed at its height in 1519, in other ways it was profoundly troubled. As Benjamin Keen noted:

> Was Aztec society going through a moral crisis, a *crise de conscience,* on the eve of the Conquest? Certainly the native chronicles reveal a state of jangled nerves, of profound insecurity on the part of the Aztec leadership. Economic and social factors undoubtedly contributed to this state of affairs: chronic discontent of conquered peoples under the mounting burden of tribute demands, perhaps population pressure on exhausted soils, dissension between warrior nobles and increasingly powerful merchants, a decline of tribal solidarity as a result of growing inequalities of wealth and status. Yet ideological factors also played their part. . . . Aztec civilization has reached an impasse that perhaps could have been overcome only by a decisive advance in technology, of the kind that attended the invention of ironworking in the Old World.

[see Benjamin Keen, *The Aztec Image in Western Thought* (New Brunswick, NJ: Rutgers University Press, 1971), 47–48].

15. Warwick Bray, *The Everyday Life of the Aztecs* (New York: Dorset, 1968), 25.

16. Throughout Mesoamerica, Nahuatl, the language of the Aztecs and related peoples, functioned as a *lingua franca.* See James Andrews, *An Introduction to Classical Nahuatl* (Austin: University of Texas Press, 1975); Jorge Suárez, *The Mesoamerican Indian Languages* (Cambridge, England: Cambridge University Press, 1983); Gunter Lanczkowski, *Aztekische Sprach und Überlieferung* (Berlin: Springer-Verlag, 1970).

17. See Frances Berdan, "La organización del tributo en el imperio azteca," *Estudios de Cultura Náhuatl, 12* (1976): 185–195; Hassig, *Trade, Tribute and Transportation,* 276–280.

18. Hassig, *Trade, Tribute and Transportation,* 104.

19. See Weaver, *The Aztecs, Maya, and Their Predecessors,* 451–455; see also Hassig, *Trade, Tribute and Transportation.*

20. Ross Hassig, *Aztec Warfare: Imperial Expansion and Political Control* (Norman: University of Oklahoma Press, 1988), 26; see also Ross Hassig, *Trade, Tribute and Transportation*, 92–103.

21. Fagan, *The Aztecs*, 109; Bray, *The Everyday Life of the Aztecs*, 98.

22. See Bray, *The Everyday Life of the Aztecs*, 98.

23. Fagan, *The Aztecs*, 84–89.

24. Fagan, *The Aztecs*, 99–103; Elizabeth Boone (ed.), *The Aztec Templo Mayor: A Symposium at Dumbarton Oaks, 8th and 9th October 1983* (Washington, DC: Dumbarton Oaks Research Library and Collection, 1987).

25. Eduardo Moctezuma, "Symbolism of the Templo Mayor," in Elizabeth Boone (ed.), *The Aztec Templo Mayor: A Symposium at Dumbarton Oaks, 8th and 9th October 1983* (Washington, DC: Dumbarton Oaks Research Library and Collection, 1987), 191.

26. Diane Chase and Arlen Chase (eds.), *Mesoamerican Elites: An Archeological Assessment* (Norman: University of Oklahoma Press, 1992); Nigel Davies, *The Aztec Empire: The Toltec Resurgence* (Norman: University of Oklahoma Press, 1987), 106–116; Fagan, *The Aztecs*, 137–138; Friedrich Katz, *Situación social y económica de los Aztecas durante los siglos XV y XVI* (México: Universidad Nacional Autónoma de México, Instituto de Investigaciones Históricas, 1966), 123–149; H. Nicholson, "The Efflorescence of Mesoamerican Civilization: A Resume," in Betty Bell (ed.), *Indian Mexico: Past and Present* (Los Angeles: University of California at Los Angeles, Latin American Center, 1967), 46–71.

27. Hassig, *Aztec Warfare*, 28.

28. See A. Hellbrom, *La participación cultural de las mujeres: Indias y mestizas en el México precortesiano y postrevolucionario* (Stockholm: The Ethnographic Museum, Monograph Series, Publication 10, 1967); Susan Kellogg, "Cognatic Kinship and Religion: Women in Aztec Society," in J. Kathryn Josserand and Karen Dakin (eds.), *Smoke and Mist: Mesoamerican Studies in Memory of Thelma D. Sullivan, Part II* (Oxford: B.A.R., 1988), 665–681.

29. Hassig, *Aztec Warfare*, 28.

30. Nicholson, "The Efflorescence of Mesoamerican Civilization," 64.

31. Weaver, *The Aztecs, Maya, and Their Predecessors*, 446.

32. Fagan, *The Aztecs*, 146; see also C. Davies, *Los mexicas: Primeros pasos hacia el imperio* (México: Universidad Nacional Autónoma de México, Instituto de Investigaciones Históricas, 1973), 81–83; Jane Day, *Aztec: The World of Moctezuma* (Niwot, CO: Denver Museum of Natural History and Roberts Rinehart Publishers, 1992), 8–9.

33. See Katz, *Situación social y económica de los Aztecas durante los siglos XV y XVI*, 117–121; Day, *Aztec*, 8.

34. Fagan, *The Aztecs*, 148.

35. See Cecilia Klein, "The Ideology of Autosacrifice at the Templo Mayor," in Elizabeth Boone (ed.), *The Aztec Templo Mayor: A Symposium at Dumbarton Oaks, 8th and 9th October 1983* (Washington, DC: Dumbarton Oaks Re-

search Library and Collection, 1987), 293–370; Brundage, *A Rain of Darts*, 96–102; White, *Cortés and the Downfall of the Aztec Empire*, 113–115.

36. Brundage, *A Rain of Darts*, 97.
37. Brundage, *A Rain of Darts*, 97.
38. Brundage, *A Rain of Darts*, 99–101.
39. Davies, *The Aztec Empire*, 93; see also R. Hassig, *War and Society in Ancient Mesoamerica* (Berkeley: University of California Press, 1992), 147–148.
40. Fagan, *The Aztecs*, 228.
41. Bray, *The Everyday Life of the Aztecs*, 171–175.
42. Davies, *The Ancient Kingdoms of Mexico*, 229–230.
43. Miguel León-Portilla, *Fifteen Poets of the Aztec World* (Norman: University of Oklahoma Press, 1992), 46; Miguel León-Portilla, *Trece poetas del mundo azteca* (México: Universidad Nacional Autónoma de México, 1967).
44. Bernard Ortiz de Montellano, *Aztec Medicine, Health, and Nutrition* (New Brunswick, NJ: Rutgers University Press, 1990), 41.
45. See Brundage, *A Rain of Darts*, 101–107; Davies, *The Ancient Kingdoms of Mexico*, 228–231; Fagan, *The Aztecs*, 228–237; M. Othón de Mendizábal, "La cultura azteca y los sacrificios humanos," in Miguel León-Portilla (ed.), *De Teotihuacán a los Aztecas: Antología de fuentes e interpretaciones históricas* (México: Universidad Nacional Autónoma de México, Instituto de Investigaciones Históricas, 1971), 208–214; White, *Cortés and the Downfall of the Aztec Empire*, 119–121.
46. See Juan Berrelleza, "Offering 48 of the Templo Mayor: A Case of Child Sacrifice," in Elizabeth Boone (ed.), *The Aztec Templo Mayor: A Symposium at Dumbarton Oaks, 8th and 9th October 1983* (Washington, DC: Dumbarton Oaks Research Library and Collection, 1987), 131–143; Brundage, *The Fifth Sun*, 212–214; Davies, *The Aztec Empire*; Fagan, *The Aztecs*, 232; Miguel León-Portilla, ed., *Ritos, sacerdotes y atavíos de los dioses: Textos de los informantes de Sahagun*, 1 (México: Universidad Nacional Autónoma de México, Instituto de Historia, 1958).
47. Brundage, *The Fifth Sun*, 215; Fagan, *The Aztecs*, 230; see also Davies, *The Aztec Empire*, 218–221, for a description of the inflationary nature of human sacrifice in Aztec society.
48. Klein, "The Ideology of Autosacrifice at the Templo Mayor," 350.
49. Klein, "The Ideology of Autosacrifice at the Templo Mayor," 297.
50. See Bray, *The Everyday Life of the Aztecs*, 152–185; Weaver, *The Aztecs, Maya, and Their Predecessors*, 446–451.
51. See Munro Edmonson, *The Book of the Year: Middle American Calendrical Systems* (Salt Lake City: University of Utah Press, 1988); Wayne Elzey, "Some Remarks on the Space and Time of the 'Center' in Aztec Religion," *Estudios de Cultura Náhuatl*, 12 (1976): 315–334; Keen, *The Aztec Image in Western Thought*, 30–48; León-Portilla, *Ritos, sacerdotes y atavíos de los dioses*; León-Portilla, *Aztec Thought and Culture*; Alberto Lhuillier, "El pensamiento náhuatl respecto de la muerte," *Estudios de Cultura Náhuatl*, 4 (1963): 251–261.

52. León-Portilla, *Aztec Thought and Culture*, 135.

53. Quoted in Markus, "Estudio comparativo entre la educación nahuatl y la griega," 292.

54. Rudolf van Zantwijk, *The Aztec Arrangement: The Social History of Pre-Spanish Mexico* (Norman: University of Oklahoma Press, 1985), 170–171.

55. Quoted in Davies, *The Ancient Kingdoms of Mexico*, 240.

56. See Thelma Sullivan, "Nahuatl Proverbs, Conundrums and Metaphors Collected by Sahagun," *Estudios de Cultura Náhuatl*, 4 (1963): 93–178.

57. Sullivan, "Nahuatl Proverbs, Conundrums and Metaphors Collected by Sahagun," 97.

58. Sullivan, "Nahuatl Proverbs, Conundrums and Metaphors Collected by Sahagun," 99.

59. Sullivan, "Nahuatl Proverbs, Conundrums and Metaphors Collected by Sahagun," 121.

60. Sullivan, "Nahuatl Proverbs, Conundrums and Metaphors Collected by Sahagun," 95.

61. Sullivan, "Nahuatl Proverbs, Conundrums and Metaphors Collected by Sahagun," 131.

62. Sullivan, "Nahuatl Proverbs, Conundrums and Metaphors Collected by Sahagun," 133.

63. Sullivan, "Nahuatl Proverbs, Conundrums and Metaphors Collected by Sahagun," 133.

64. Sullivan, "Nahuatl Proverbs, Conundrums and Metaphors Collected by Sahagun," 135.

65. See Infante, *La educación de los Aztecas*.

66. Quoted in León-Portilla, *Aztec Thought and Culture*, 135.

67. Fagan, *The Aztecs*, 149–150.

68. See León-Portilla, *Aztec Thought and Culture*, 136.

69. Bray, *The Everyday Life of the Aztecs*, 58–59.

70. Fagan, *The Aztecs*, 151.

71. León-Portilla, *Aztec Thought and Culture*, 136.

72. See Campos, *La producción literaria de los Aztecas*, 65-66.

73. See Kurt Ross (ed.), *Codex Mendoza* (Fribourg, Switzerland: Miller Graphics, 1978).

74. Day, *Aztec*, 23; Fagan, *The Aztecs*, 151–153; Joyce Marcus, *Mesoamerican Writing Systems: Propaganda, Myth, and History in Four Ancient Civilizations* (Princeton, NJ: Princeton University Press, 1992), 50; Elizabeth Boone and Walter Mignolo (eds.), *Writing Without Words: Alternative Literacies in Mesoamerica and the Andes* (Durham, NC: Duke University Press, 1994); Bernardino Sahagun, *El Mexico antiguo: Selección y reordenación de la historia general de las cosas de Nueva España* (Caracas: Biblioteca Ayachucho, 1981), 165–166; Remi Siméon, *Dictionnaire de la langue Nahuatl ou Mexicaine* (Graz: Akademische Druck U. Verlagsanstalt, 1963), 120; Richard Townsend, *The Aztecs* (London: Thames and Hudson, 1992), 158.

75. Townsend, *The Aztecs*, 158.

76. Fagan, *The Aztecs*, 153.

77. Bray, *The Everyday Life of the Aztecs*, 63; Day, *Aztec*, 23; Infante, *La educación de los Aztecas*, 57-63; Marcus, *Mesoamerican Writing Systems*, 51; Townsend, *The Aztecs*, 158–159.

78. See Hassig, *Aztec Warfare*, 30–37.

79. Hassig, *War and Society in Ancient Mesoamerica*, 142.

80. Bray, *The Everyday Life of the Aztecs*, 62–63; Fagan, *The Aztecs*, 154; Sahagun, *El Mexico antiguo*, 163–166; van Zantwijk, *The Aztec Arrangement*, 144.

81. Bray, *The Everyday Life of the Aztecs*, 63; E. Calnek, "The *Calmécac* and *Telpochcalli* in Pre-Conquest Tenochtitlán," in J. Jorge Klor de Alva, H. Nicholson, and Eloise Keber (eds.), *The Work of Bernardino de Sahagun: Pioneer Ethnographer of Sixteenth-Century Aztec Mexico* (Albany: Institute for Mesoamerican Studies, State University of New York, 1988), 169–177.

82. See Bray, *The Everyday Life of the Aztecs*, 64; Infante, *La educación de los Aztecas*, 63–71; Marcus, *Mesoamerican Writing Systems*, 50–51; Townsend, *The Aztecs*.

83. León-Portilla, *Aztec Thought and Culture*, 140.

84. Fagan, *The Aztecs*, 198; see also León-Portilla, *Fifteen Poets of the Aztec World*, 5–15.

85. See Marcus, *Mesoamerican Writing Systems*, 50–51.

86. John Cornyn, *The Song of Quetzalcoatl* (Yellow Springs, OH: Antioch Press, 1930), 9–10.

87. Bray, *The Everyday Life of the Aztecs*, 64.

88. Geoffrey Conrad and Arthur Demarest, *Religion and Empire: The Dynamics of Aztec and Inca Expansionism* (Cambridge, England: Cambridge University Press, 1984), 43.

89. Fagan, *The Aztecs*, 244.

90. Calnek, "The *Calmécac* and *Telpochcalli* in Pre-Conquest Tenochtitlán."

91. See Calnek, "The *Calmécac* and *Telpochcalli* in Pre-Conquest Tenochtitlán;" Hassig, *Aztec Warfare*, 34; León-Portilla, *Aztec Thought and Culture*, 137–138.

92. León-Portilla, *Aztec Thought and Culture*, 138.

93. See Bray, *The Everyday Life of the Aztecs*, 64; Day, *Aztec*, 33; Infante, *La educación de los Aztecas*, 71–74; Marcus, *Mesoamerican Writing Systems*, 51–52.

94. Frances Karttunen and James Lockhard (eds.), *The Art of Nahuatl Speech: The Bancroft Dialogues* (Los Angeles: UCLA Latin American Center Publications, 1987), 153-155.

95. See José Luis de Rojas, *México Tenochtitlan: Economía y sociedad en el siglo XVI* (México: El Colegio de Michoacán, Fondo de Cultura Econónica, 1988), 22, 24.

96. León-Portilla, *Aztec Thought and Culture*, 134–135.

4

Education in Pre-Columbian
North America

There is an extensive literature concerned with the education of Native American children,[1] and it includes a significant body of excellent historical works.[2] With very few exceptions, however, this historical literature deals with the education of Indian children after the arrival of European settlers. In other words, the focus of scholarship has been not so much on Native American education as it has been on the formal, Western schooling processes to which Indian children have been exposed (or, some would say, subjected). The history of the treatment of the indigenous peoples of North America is an important, and largely shameful, part of our history, and the historical studies of Indian education constitute a significant and potent piece of the broader history of American education. Our concern in this chapter, however, is not with the history of the interaction of Indians and others in North America but, rather, with the educational ideas and practices that existed before that interaction began, many of which continue to play roles in Native American cultural and childrearing practices even today.

In discussing Native American educational ideas and practices, we are faced with a problem very similar to that discussed in chapter 2 with respect to traditional African education. North America is geographically large, and the indigenous peoples of North America were and are very diverse culturally and linguistically (see Fig. 4.1). Some 250 distinct languages were spoken in North America when Europeans first arrived and, although many of these languages are now extinct, a significant number still survive.[3] American Indians, both in the past and the present, live in a wide variety of very different physical settings and, as a consequence, have developed very different cultural patterns, norms, social structures, and behaviors. As Joseph Oxendine commented, "The great diversity among traditional Indian cultures makes it impossible to discuss Indian customs . . . as a cohesive entity. Differences in languages, means of livelihood, social structures, and traditions inhibit attempts to generalize absolutely about . . . cultural phenomena."[4] In fact, Carol Locust argued that it is the diversity of both beliefs and practices among different Indian peoples

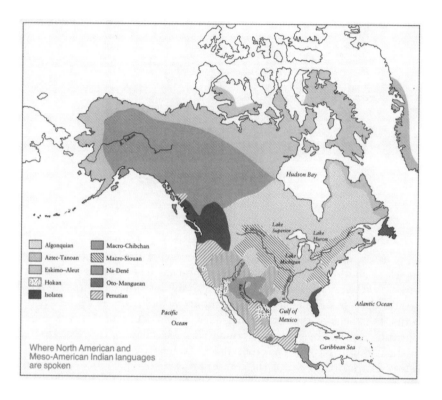

FIG. 4.1. The diversity of Native America: where North American and Mesoamerican
languages are spoken [From David Crystal, *The Cambridge Encyclopedia of Language*
(Cambridge, England: Cambridge University Press, 1987), p. 321].
Reprinted with permission.

that contributes to a general lack of understanding of Indians in our society.
As she explained:

> One of the reasons many non-Indian people do not understand much about
> Indian belief systems is that they vary from tribe to tribe and from clan to clan.
> For example, Apaches believe that supernatural spirits seek out an individual to
> become a medicine person. The Tohono O'odham, on the other hand, believe
> that one must be born into a lineage of medicine persons or must be a twin in
> order to become a medicine person.[5]

Nevertheless, just as in the case of sub-Saharan Africa, it is possible to
discuss a common, core unity in the midst of diversity; this is also possible in
the case of Native Americans. There are, in fact, a common core of beliefs and
remarkably similar practices that are common to most (although by no means,
all) American Indians. This is true not only with respect to their belief systems,
as Locust argued, but also with respect to traditional ideas about education

and childrearing. Having said this, it is important to keep in mind that variation and diversity will, nonetheless, characterize the reality of American Indian thought and practice, and that the general claims offered here are just that—generalizations rather than absolutes. Furthermore, it is important to remember that even within a particular tribe, there may well be differences of opinion and practice related to clan distinctions, as well as differences related to the degree and amount of contact with other groups.[6]

Added to this complexity has been the tendency of historians to view American Indian history as synonymous with the history of contact with Europeans. As Calvin Martin noted:

> "There are two Indians of history," recently mused an eminent anthropologist: "one is the Indian of ethnology; the other, the Indian of recent history. The first is the Indian of cultural elements: the snowshoe, puberty ceremonies, kinship organization, and the potlatch. The second is the Indian of the mines, the *encomiendas*, the missions, and the fur trade."[7]

In order to understand traditional educational thought and practice, it is with the former, more anthropologically based view of the Native American that we are concerned here. We turn now to a brief discussion of the underlying, core belief system of Native Americans.

THE CORE BELIEF SYSTEM OF AMERICAN INDIANS

Carol Locust identified 10 core beliefs that she believes are common to most Indian tribes in the U.S. and that are probably valid for North American Indians in general. These ten core beliefs, which are basically an attempt to summarize the key elements of what many Indians would call the "Old Teachings," include:

1. American Indians believe in a Supreme Creator. In this belief system, there are lesser beings also.
2. Humans are threefold beings made up of a spirit, mind, and body.
3. Plants and animals, like humans, are part of the spirit world. The spirit world exists side by side with, and intermingles with, the physical world.
4. The spirit existed before it came into a physical body, and will exist after the body dies.
5. Illness affects the mind and spirit as well as the body.
6. Wellness is harmony in spirit, mind, and body.
7. Unwellness is disharmony in spirit, mind, and body.
8. Natural unwellness is caused by the violation of a sacred or tribal taboo.
9. Unnatural unwellness is caused by witchcraft.
10. Each of us is responsible for his or her own wellness.[8]

The overall focus of this set of core beliefs is on health, which may initially seem to be related to educational beliefs at best only tangentially. And yet this is, in fact, far from the case, because for Native Americans one's health is not only a physical condition but a spiritual one as well. Furthermore, the separation of the spiritual from other aspects of culture not only does not exist in traditional Indian thought, it does not make sense conceptually. In other words, if we want to understand traditional Native American ideas about education and childrearing, we must begin with traditional Native Americans' ideas of good health and illness.

Central to Native American educational thought and practice is the view of the human being as a threefold being, consisting of a spirit, a mind, and a physical body. Each of these parts has a role to play, but the roles are distinctive and by no means of the same relative importance. As Locust explained:

> Of the three elements—spirit, mind, and body—the spirit is the most important, for it is the essence of the being. The instrument by which the spirit may express itself is the body. It can learn spiritual lessons and may progress toward the ultimate goal of being united with the Supreme Creator. The mind is the link between the spirit and the body and functions as an interpreter between the two.[9]

Education, understood in this context, should involve all three of the elements of which we are all composed and, furthermore, should aid in helping the individual to achieve the goal of *harmony*. Harmony had a somewhat distinctive meaning here, referring to: "the peaceful, tranquil state of knowing all is well with one's spirit, mind, and body. To be in harmony is to be at oneness with life, eternity, the Supreme Creator, and oneself. . . . But harmony is not found within the environment, nor does it come from others; it comes from within and from the Supreme Creator."[10]

Although harmony is indeed associated with wellness, it is wellness of a spiritual sort.[11] Thus, learning to cope with various physical ailments may well be part of achieving harmony.[12] Just as harmony is the proper goal for education, the alternative—disharmony—is precisely what education ought to be concerned with preventing. Disharmony is the root cause for physical and psychological unwellness:

> One cannot be in a state of disharmony caused by suppressed anger, frustration, heartache, or fear without sooner or later developing unwellness in the physical body from that disharmony. Disharmony may be a vague feeling of things "not being right" in one's life, and a time of meditation may be needed in which to discover what is not right.[13]

The responsibility of each individual for his or her own wellness extends back beyond birth, because it is believed that each spirit chooses the body that it will inhabit. Thus, as Locust explained:

In the case of a handicapped body, the spirit chooses the body knowing its limitations but choosing to use it for some purpose determined by that spirit and the Supreme Creator. Furthermore, tribal members envision the spirit inside a handicapped body as being whole and perfect and capable of understanding everything that goes on in the environment, even when it appears that the physical body cannot comprehend anything.[14]

Typical of this approach to education, and to individual differences, is the following quote from the Crow leader Plenty Coups:

> My people were wise. . . . They never neglected the young. Our teachers were willing and thorough. They were our grandfathers, our fathers, or uncles. All were quick to praise excellence without speaking a word that might break the spirit of a boy who might be less capable than others. The boy who failed at any lesson got only more lessons, more care, until he was as far as he could go.[15]

Such a view also has important implications for differences among learners, because such differences are not viewed normatively. Rather, they are simply taken to be part of nature and are dealt with accordingly. No sanction applies to the child who is less bright, nor does any particular reward accrue to those who are exceptionally bright. With this point in mind, we turn now to a discussion of the traditional educational beliefs and practices of the American Indians.

TRADITIONAL EDUCATIONAL BELIEFS AND PRACTICES

Traditional education among Native Americans was, for the most part, informal in nature, taking place as an undemarcated part of social life in general.[16] Children learned the skills and knowledge necessary for successful survival as adults through observation and imitation as well as from direct instruction from parents and other adults.[17] Included among the skills and knowledge that children learned were gender-specific skills, attitudes, values, beliefs, and content knowledge that encompassed vocational skills (hunting, fishing, trapping, agricultural skills, etc., as appropriate to the tribe), social skills and behaviors, and religious knowledge (including rituals, ceremonies, etc.).[18] All of this took place in a broadly spiritual context, which emphasized the need to live in balance with nature. As Jean Barman, Yvonne Hébert, and Don McCaskill noted, "An emphasis was placed on maintaining reciprocal relationships between the individual and the natural environment in order to ensure the provision of the subsistence required to live."[19]

The ultimate purpose of traditional Indian education, however, was spiritual in nature, as our earlier discussion of the place of harmony and wellness would lead one to expect. Indeed, among the Nisga'a, for instance, there is a saying, "Ts'im gan wilaak'il's wil luu sisgihl gandidils," which translates as "within the pursuit of knowledge, therein one will find the true meaning of life." In other words, education comes to be seen as a "total way of life."[20] As Jack Forbes commented in his discussion of traditional Native American philosophy:

> What is the purpose of education? . . . [I]t is not primarily the acquisition of specific skills or factual knowledge. Rather it is learning how to be a human being. That is, how to live a life of the utmost spiritual quality. A person who has developed his character to its highest degree, and who is on that path, will also be able to master specific skills. But if they don't have that spiritual core, they will use those skills to hurt other people. . . . So knowledge without the spiritual core is a very dangerous thing.[21]

A central feature of traditional Indian education is its communal nature. Traditional educational practices were not separate from daily life, and teaching was an activity engaged in by all adults, and even by older children, in the community. As one Canadian elder noted, "In the old days not only your own elders would discipline you, but also an outsider would come in and lecture the young. This could happen anytime, just happen naturally."[22]

The responsibility for the education of the young, although a community one in the broadest sense, rested primarily on parents, relatives (in particular on maternal uncles in many tribes),[23] and on tribal elders. The role played by tribal elders is especially important in this regard because it is the elders who function as both the repositories and transmitters of the cultural traditions of the community.[24] Elders are elders by virtue not only of age, but also as recognition by other members of the community; their role in the community has been a significant one:

> The elders, comprising the accumulation of tribal wisdom and experience, have always been a vital group in opinion-making, if not in actual decision-making. Many, if not all, of the political leaders depend on "their elders" for advice in decision-making. Some . . . perform the role of adding the cultural perceptions to the decision-making process.[25]

Although the "entire question of the status, configuration, and function of elders in educational contexts is extremely nebulous and imprecise,"[26] it is nevertheless clear that their role historically was an incredibly important one with respect to the proper upbringing of children. As one contemporary Elder recalled:

> As children we learned from the very beginning, by teaching and discipline, and later on through lecturing, and also by example. You saw how your elders lived, how respectful they were of one another, and how they loved each other. . . . The training went on as a child grew older, became more severe, harder, tougher. . . . It became a habit to live in a sane, sensible way, and intelligent way.[27]

One facet of the educational role of the elder in traditional Native American education was in the passing on of ritual and ceremonial knowledge. Rituals and ceremonies of various sorts played and continue to play a very important role in most Native American cultures. As Gary Witherspoon noted with respect to the Navajo:

> The Navajo term *nahaghá* ("ritual") labels a large and significant category of Navajo behavior which non-Navajos least understand, and thus constitutes a major dimension of the estrangement that divides Navajos and non-Navajos. Navajos possess and perform over sixty major rites and numerous minor ones. They perform rituals for blessing, for curing, and for purification. They bless (make immune to illness and tragedy) their land, their livestock, their crops, their homes, their property, their relatives, and themselves.[28]

Oratory often played an important role in ritual and ceremony, and was integrated, in speeches, myths, legends, folktales, chants, and so on, in virtually all aspects of traditional Indian social life.[29] As Joel Sherzer pointed out with respect to the Iroquois:

> there was an ancient oratorical tradition which entered into all facets of traditional religious and political life, including death, curing, and agricultural ceremonies. Most Iroquois ceremonies involved many speakers, representing families, clans, or whole nations, making formal speeches. . . . This oratory was a central feature of ritual and kept the Iroquois world spiritually alive and well.[30]

Indeed, the ability to use language creatively and effectively was among the key characteristics sought by many tribes in their leaders, and often such ability was at least as important as one's skills as a warrior or hunter.[31] A related point here is that traditionally Native American societies were oral ones and thus, as was the case with Africa, in North America was there an emphasis on the oral transmission and maintenance of knowledge. As Rik Yellow Bird explained, "Our system of learning was based on oral tradition although syllabics were used later. The nomadic lifestyle determined and strengthened the use of orally transmitted information. . . ."[32]

Although by no means a universal phenomenon, various initiation processes and ceremonies were quite common in traditional Indian societies, and such initiation ceremonies are often maintained today, although not uncommonly in modified ways. As Donald Miller wrote, with respect to the Hopi:

> At about the age eight or nine, when children become involved in mischief, they are initiated into one of the ritual societies. This occasion arrives annually, usually during February, at the time of the Powamu ceremony. . . . Initiation marks the beginning of attaining adult social status. A child is sponsored by a set of ceremonial parents who guide him through the ritual and perform various functions at appropriate times as described below. This new relationship sets up future "ceremonial kinship ties" with subsequent rights, duties, and reciprocal obligations attached to them, thus adding an additional significant dimension to social cohesion. . . . During the initiation a child has his head washed in yucca suds by his ceremonial mother, after which he is given a new name. It is at this

time that formal instruction is given about the gods. . . . During the day, those to be initiated are taken by their ceremonial fathers into one of the village kivas where instruction begins. Each child is brought forth before the whipper Kachinas [gods] who ritually purify by literally whipping the child's backside. . . . The ceremonial father may take some or all of the lashes for him, but if the child has been particularly naughty, the father will not interfere. The whipper Kachinas are believed to have ritual power to cleanse and to heal. Later, after an evening of ritual dancing, all non-initiates and women are dismissed from the kiva, after which the Kachinas remove their large masks to reveal themselves as fathers and "uncles" of the village. Initiation marks a turning point in Hopi life. It is not unlike a graduation ceremony—a rite of passage which ritually removes childhood and admits one to the greater responsibilities of an adult world.[33]

An important aspect of traditional Indian educational practice is that of children's play and games played by both children and adults.[34] Joseph Oxendine argued that the traditional play of Indian children can be organized into three broad, if overlapping, categories: games that functioned as preparation for adult activity, games in which toys were the focus of attention, and more formal games that were played by older children and adults.[35] We explore each of these types of play briefly here.

American Indian children, like children in all societies, often engaged in play that was imitative of adult activities. Such play was largely gender-specific in nature, with boys engaging in role playing related to such traditionally male roles as hunter, warrior, and athlete, whereas girls "played games that closely paralleled childrearing, household chores, farming, or pastimes of their mothers."[36] As Ohiyesa commented with respect to play activities found among the Sioux, such play was:

molded by the life and customs of our people; indeed, we practiced only what we expected to do when grown. Our games were feats with the bow and arrow, and foot and pony races, wrestling, swimming, and imitation of the customs and habits of our fathers. We had sham fights with mud balls and willow wands; we played lacrosse, made war upon bees, and coasted upon the ribs of animals and buffalo robes.[37]

Although imitation and role playing certainly come naturally to children, this is not to say that it occurred independent of either adult supervision or input. Indeed, as George Pettitt observed nearly 50 years ago:

That these activities were recreational is beyond question, but that they were carried on as spontaneous uncontrolled imitations, either of adults or of slightly older juveniles, is hardly supported by the facts . . . it is clear that desired imitative activities are effectively fostered and undesired imitative activities neglected or discouraged.[38]

The second broad category of traditional play identified by Oxendine is play that involved the use of toys. Toys were made both by adults for children and by the children themselves. A wide variety of toys were made by adults for infants, including mobiles to be suspended over beds, colorful and noisy toys, feathers and, at least in some tribes, rattles.[39] Typical toys for older children included bows and arrows, tops, noisemakers, and dolls. Very often, such toys played roles in imitative activities; of course, and adults would engage in direct instruction (as in the case of archery) to help children learn how to use their toys properly.[40]

Finally, there were games played by both children and adults, generally of a self-testing nature. Among the more common games of this sort were tobogganing, playing string games (including "Cat's Cradle"), stilt walking, "battledoor" (also called "shuttlecock"), skin or blanket tossing, ring and pin, ball juggling, and hot ball.[41] These kinds of games involved challenging oneself, often both physically and intellectually, and so played an important educational as well as social role in traditional society.

CONCLUSION

The spiritual nature of traditional Indian educational thought and practice permeates virtually all aspects of its educational practice. This can be seen most clearly, perhaps, in the way that the child is viewed and treated, and the respect that is to be accorded to each individual.[42] Beyond this, though, is the sense of kinship with not only other members of one's own community, but with the larger human community and, indeed, with everything around us. As Jack Forbes wrote:

> So everything is like a big family. We are children of the Great Spirit, children of Mother Earth, children of the sky, and so on. We have that relationship, that kinship that is part of our identity. That is knowing who we are . . . we live in a world of many circles and these circles constitute our identity and they go out to encompass every thing that there is in this Universe. That is our kinship. Those are our relatives. The Universe is a family and we have to deal with other things in that Universe with that in mind.[43]

Although the context in which traditional Native American educational thought and practice emerged and prospered for centuries has undergone dramatic change in the last few centuries, there is, nevertheless, much to be learned and even emulated, not only in educational activities and programs for Indians themselves, but for all of us, as the previously quoted Forbes passage makes clear.

QUESTIONS FOR REFLECTION AND DISCUSSION

1. Based on your reading, how do you believe that Native Americans would traditionally have defined an *educated person* in their societies? How does this view of an *educated person* differ from our contemporary view?

2. The American Indian view of the role of *elders* in both social life in general and in education in particular is arguably very different from that found in contemporary American society. What are the advantages of the Native American view of the role of the elder? What are its disadvantages?

3. Using this chapter's discussion of play activities as a component of traditional Native American education as a guide, try to develop a similar classification system for play in contemporary American society. What differences do you find? How might these differences be explained?

4. The Indian concept of kinship, as expounded in the conclusion of this chapter, is potentially a very powerful one. What are its educational implications, both in terms of the aims of education and the content of education?

5. Reflect on the Native American concept of *disharmony*. What are the implications of this concept for society, in general, and for the education of children, in particular? Is the concept a pedagogically useful one in your view?

RECOMMENDED FURTHER READINGS

There are a number of excellent works that present a Native American view on both American history and contemporary American society. Especially valuable are Ronald Wright, *Stolen Continents: The "New World" Through Indian Eyes* (Boston: Houghton Mifflin, 1992), Alvin Josephy Jr.'s, *500 Nations: An Illustrated History of North American Indians* (New York: Knopf, 1994), as well as the recent revision of his 1968 *The Indian Heritage of America* (Boston: Houghton Mifflin, 1991), Alvin Josephy, Jr., ed., *America in 1492: The World of the Indian Peoples Before the Arrival of Columbus* (New York: Vintage, 1991), and Dee Brown, *Bury My Heart At Wounded Knee: An Indian History of the American West* (New York: Bantam, 1971).

NOTES

1. There is a terminological problem with respect to the proper term for the indigenous peoples of North America. In this chapter, I have chosen to use both *Indian* and *Native American* interchangeably, as is a fairly common practice by such people themselves. It should also be noted that the term *North America* is being used here in a common, but nonetheless inaccurate, way to refer to what is today the United States and Canada. Thus, the civilizations of Mesoamerica (which were geographically in North America) are excluded from the focus here.

2. See, for example, Margaret Szasz, *Education and the American Indian: The Road to Self-Determination, 1928–1973* (Albuquerque: University of New Mexico Press, 1974); Guy Senese, *Self-Determination and the Social Education of Native Americans* (New York: Praeger, 1991); K. Tsianina Lomawaima, *They Called It Prairie Light: The Story of Chilocco Indian School* (Lincoln: University of Nebraska Press, 1994); Ruth McDonald Boyer and Narcissus Gayton, *Apache Mothers and Daughters: Four Generations of a Family* (Norman: University of Oklahoma Press, 1992); Michael Coleman, *American Indian Children at School, 1850-1930* (Jackson: University Press of Mississippi, 1993).

3. See Joel Sherzer, "A Richness of Voices," in Alvin Josephy, Jr. (ed.), *America in 1492: The World of the Indian Peoples Before the Arrival of Columbus* (New York: Vintage, 1991), 251–275.

4. Joseph Oxendine, *American Indian Sports Heritage* (Champaign, IL: Human Kinetics Books, 1988), xiii.

5. Carol Locust, "Wounding the Spirit: Discrimination and Traditional American Indian Belief Systems," *Harvard Educational Review, 58*, 3 (1988): 317.

6. Locust, "Wounding the Spirit," 317.

7. Calvin Martin, "Ethnohistory: A Better Way to Write Indian History," in Albert Hurtado and Peter Iverson (eds.), *Major Problems in American Indian History: Documents and Essays* (Lexington, MA: Heath, 1994), 23.

8. Locust, "Wounding the Spirit," 317–318.

9. Locust, "Wounding the Spirit," 318.

10. Locust, "Wounding the Spirit," 321–322.

11. Native American approaches to education are, in fact, profoundly spiritual in nature. See Gloria Snively, "Traditional Native Indian Beliefs, Cultural Values, and Science Instruction," *Canadian Journal of Native Education, 17*, 1 (1990): 44–59. Also of interest here are Mary Atwood, *Spirit Healing: North American Magic and Medicine* (New York: Sterling, 1991) and Steve Wall, *Shadowcatchers: A Journey in Search of the Teachings of Native American Healers* (New York: HarperCollins, 1994).

12. See John Coulehan, "Navajo Indian Medicine: Implications for Healing," *Journal of Family Practice, 10* (1980): 55–61.

13. Locust, "Wounding the Spirit," 322.

14. Locust, "Wounding the Spirit," 325.

15. Quoted in Jack Forbes, "Traditional Native American Philosophy and Multicultural Education," in *Multicultural Education and the American Indian* (Los Angeles: American Indian Studies Center, University of California, 1979), 10.

16. Jean Barman, Yvonne Hébert, and Don McCaskill, "The Challenge of Indian Education: An Overview," in Jean Barman, Yvonne Hébert, and Don McCaskill (eds.), *Indian Education in Canada, Volume 2: The Challenge* (Vancouver: University of British Columbia Press, 1987), 3.

17. See Donald Miller, "Hopi Education: Before Schools and Teachers," *Tennessee Education, 18,* 2 (1988), 28–32.

18. Barman, Hébert, and McCaskill, "The Challenge of Indian Education: An Overview," 3.

19. Barman, Hébert, and McCaskill, "The Challenge of Indian Education," 3.

20. Alvin McKay and Bert McKay, "Education as a Total Way of Life: The Nisga'a Experience," in Jean Barman, Yvonne Hébert, and Don McCaskill (eds.), *Indian Education in Canada, Vol. 2: The Challenge* (Vancouver: University of British Columbia Press, 1987), 64.

21. Forbes, "Traditional Native American Philosophy and Multicultural Education," 11.

22. Quoted in Beatrice Medicine, "My Elders Tell Me," in Jean Barman, Yvonne Hébert, and Don McCaskill (eds.), *Indian Education in Canada, Vol. 2: The Challenge* (Vancouver: University of British Columbia Press, 1987), 146.

23. For an extensive discussion of the role of relatives in traditional American Indian education, see George Pettitt, *Primitive Education in North America* (Berkeley: University of California Press, 1946), 15–24. Published as part of the University of California "Publications in American Archaeology and Ethnology" series, this monograph is valuable despite its dated and highly ethnocentric bias.

24. Medicine, "My Elders Tell Me," 142–152; see also Rik Yellow Bird, "Position Paper on Native Education," *Humanity & Society, 14,* 3 (1990), 298–299; Teresa Scott Kincheloe, "The Wisdom of the Elders: Cross-Cultural Perspectives," *Journal of Thought, 19,* 3 (1984), 121–127.

25. Quoted in Medicine, "My Elders Tell Me," 147.

26. Medicine, "My Elders Tell Me," 143; see also Miller, "Hopi Education: Before Schools and Teachers," 28–32.

27. Quoted in Medicine, "My Elders Tell Me," 145–146.

28. Gary Witherspoon, *Language and Art in the Navajo Universe* (Ann Arbor: Univeristy of Michigan Press, 1977), 13.

29. Sherzer, "A Richness of Voices," 271. See also Karl Kroeber, "The Art of Traditional American Indian Narration," in Karl Kroeber (ed.), *Traditional Literatures of the American Indian: Texts and Interpretations* (Lincoln: University of Nebraska Press, 1981), 1–24.

30. Sherzer, "A Richness of Voices," 265.

31. Sherzer, "A Richness of Voices," 265.

32. Yellow Bird, "Position Paper on Native Education," 297.

33. Miller, "Hopi Education," 30–31.

34. See Steward Culin, *Games of the North American Indians* (New York: Dover, 1975).

35. Oxendine, *American Indian Sports Heritage,* 121.

36. Oxendine, *American Indian Sports Heritage,* 122.

37. Quoted in Oxendine, *American Indian Sports Heritage,* 123.

38. Pettitt, *Primitive Education in North America,* 41, 58.

39. Oxendine, *American Indian Sports Heritage*, 124. In some Native American cultures, rattles are viewed as sacred objects, and are used only in specific religious ceremonies. Thus, in these groups they would be seen as inappropriate as children's toys.

40. See Pettitt, *Primitive Education in North America*, 41–44.

41. For detailed discussions of these games, see Oxendine, *American Indian Sports Heritage*, 131–137. An even more extensive examination of such games is provided in Culin, *Games of North American Indians*.

42. See Forbes, "Traditional Native American Philosophy and Multicultural Education."

43. Forbes, "Traditional Native American Philosophy and Multicultural Education," 5–6.

5

The Chinese
Educational Heritage

Elements of Chinese civilization can be traced back at least as far as six thousand years, and perhaps considerably further.[1] By the time of the Shang dynasty (roughly 1700 B.C. to 1100 B.C.; see Fig. 5.1), schools and other social institutions of a complex culture had developed, as had the foundations for the examination system that would serve throughout the history of imperial China to select government officials.[2] Although Chinese civilization evolved, developed, and changed throughout its history, it nevertheless retained a core set of features that characterize it as a single cultural tradition. Although much of the Chinese cultural heritage has been rejected in contemporary China, much remains as well. In other words, much of the culture of China that still thrives has a direct link to the civilization that emerged nearly as long ago as those of ancient Egypt and Mesopotamia.[3] The difference, of course, is that although the civilizations of Egypt and Mesopotamia may be fascinating for us to study, the ties that bind modern people to them are, at best, very distant indeed, whereas the ties that bind modern Chinese people to their past remain powerful. Further, as Michael Loewe wrote in his book *The Pride That Was China*, the impact of traditional Chinese civilization went far beyond the borders of China itself:

> China's achievements have been unique. Just as the glory that was Greece and the grandeur that was Rome have left their indelible mark on Europe, so have the features of China's traditional way of life nurtured the cultural growth of East Asia; for it was largely the ideas, beliefs and ideals of China that shaped the humanities of the east, with their counterparts to the spirit and grace of Greece and the dignity and organization of Rome.[4]

If traditional Chinese culture had such a significant impact on the historical development of Asia, it was able to do so in large part because of the values and institutions that underlie its educational system. This system had to address problems related to the size of the country (China has been, and remains, one of the largest countries in the world), its geographical diversity, the ethnic and linguistic diversity of its population (see Fig. 5.2),[5] and the

Xia Dynasty	21st to 16th centuries B.C.
Shang Dynasty	16th to 11th centuries B.C.
Western Zhou Dynasty	11th century to 771 B.C.
Spring and Autumn Period	770 to 476 B.C.
Warring States Period	475 to 221 B.C.
Qin Dynasty	221 to 207 B.C.
Western Han Dynasty	206 B.C. to 24 A.D.
Eastern Han Dynasty	25 A.D. to 220 A.D.
Three Kingdoms Period	220 A.D. to 265 A.D.
Western Jin Dynasty	265 A.D. to 316 A.D.
Eastern Jin Dynasty	317 A.D. to 420 A.D.
Northern and Southern Dynasties	420 A.D. to 589 A.D.
Sui Dynasty	581 A.D. to 618 A.D.
Tang Dynasty	618 A.D. to 907 A.D.
Five Dynasties Period	907 A.D. to 960 A.D.
Northern Song Dynasty	960 A.D. to 1127 A.D.
Southern Song Dynasty	1127 A.D. to 1279 A.D.
Liao Dynasty	916 A.D. to 1125 A.D.
Jin Dynasty	1115 A.D. to 1234 A.D.
Yuan Dynasty	1271 A.D. to 1368 A.D.
Ming Dynasty	1368 A.D. to 1644 A.D.
Qing Dynasty	1644 A.D. to 1911 A.D.

FIG. 5.1. Chinese dynasties.

tensions in an overwhelmingly agrarian society with large urban centers competing for resources. The traditional Chinese educational system was able to meet these challenges remarkably effectively for millennia. The endurance of Chinese civilization, as well as its intellectual, cultural, and artistic contributions to world civilization, make it well worth an examination of the educational thought and practice that played a key role in its maintenance, transmission, and development.

The study of the history of Chinese educational thought and practice is, in many ways, somewhat easier to understand than that of many other non-Western societies. Not only are many facets of traditional Chinese education still maintained in Chinese communities around the world but, even more, there is a wealth of material related to the history of the Chinese educational tradition available. As Will Durant noted in *The Story of Civilization*, "China has been called 'the paradise of historians.' For centuries and millenniums, it has had official historiographers who recorded everything that happened, and much besides. We cannot trust them further back than 776 B.C.; but if we lend them a ready ear they will explain in detail the history of China from 3000 B.C. . . ."[6]

This abundance of sources means that the challenge in discussing traditional Chinese educational thought and practice is not one of trying to reconstruct

Northern Mandarin
Northwest Mandarin
Southern Mandarin
Southwest Mandarin
Wú
Mǐn
Kèjiā
Yuè
Huīzhŏu
Xiāng
Gàn

500 km
300 miles

FIG. 5.2. Ethnic and linguistic diversity in China [From Jerry Norman, *Chinese* (Cambridge, England: Cambridge University Press, 1988), p. 184].
Reprinted with permission.

the past from limited information but, rather, trying to sort through an incredibly complex and monumental historical record to identify the key issues that we need to address. In this chapter, we begin with a discussion of traditional Chinese educational thought, focusing on the special role of Confucian thought in that tradition. We then turn to the ways in which Confucian thought was manifested in practice in educational institutions and, even more, in the imperial examination system.

THE ROLE OF CONFUCIAN THOUGHT
IN TRADITIONAL CHINESE EDUCATION

It would be impossible to discuss traditional Chinese educational thought without repeated reference to Confucian thought; indeed, to a considerable extent one could argue that traditional Chinese educational thought in large part *is* Confucian educational thought.[7] Tu Wei-ming argued that "Confucianism is still an integral part of the 'psycho-cultural construct' of the contemporary Chinese intellectual as well as the Chinese peasant; it remains a defining characteristic of the Chinese mentality,"[8] and, in a similar vein, Cheng Tien-Hsi commented, "The whole Chinese social system, or rather what may be called Chinese civilization and culture . . . is saturated with the teachings of Confucius and those of Mencius, the sage next to him and the most brilliant exponent of his doctrines."[9] As Cheng Tien-Hsi implied, however, it is important that we distinguish between the body of teaching that can be reliably ascribed to Confucius himself, and the far broader body of theories and doctrines that developed after his death and are today identified as *Confucian.*[10]

Confucius (whose real name was K'ung Ch'iu) was, according to tradition, born in the town of Ch'ü-fu, in the state of Lu, in the year 551 B.C., and died in the year 479 B.C.[11] Of relatively humble background , Confucius seems to have been largely self-educated, as well as both ambitious and relatively successful in his own time.[12] Living in a time of considerable social, political, and economic unrest and uncertainty, Confucius advocated a conception of the *good man* (*chün-tzu*)[13] that emphasized the twin qualities of benevolence (*ren*) and propriety (*li*). There is, in Confucian texts, an emphasis on the writings of Chinese antiquity, and his philosophy is often identified as a conservative one seeking a return to a more moral and just past.[14] This is especially interesting because, as Jacques Gernet observed about Confucius' work, "A body of teaching which aimed primarily at being faithful to tradition in fact threw up ideas that were new."[15]

The core of Confucian thought is found in a short text produced by Confucius' disciples after his death, called the *Lun-yü* or, more commonly in English, the *Analects.*[16] It would be difficult to underestimate the significance of the *Analects* in the history of Chinese thought. As Patricia Ebrey wrote:

Confucius' ideas are known to us primarily through the sayings recorded by his disciples in the *Analects*. This book does not provide carefully organized or argued philosophical discourses, and the sayings seem to have been haphazardly arranged. Yet this short text became a sacred book, memorized by beginning students and known to all educated people. As such it influenced the values and habits of thought of Chinese for centuries. Many of its passages became proverbial sayings, unknowingly cited by illiterate peasants.[17]

The closest analogy that one could draw to the role of the *Analects* in the western tradition would probably be the role of the Bible. For us, regardless of our personal religious beliefs, the Bible provides a virtually limitless source of proverbs, folk wisdom, and references to people and events that color our language and fill our speech, as well as offering a framework within which much of our everyday experience is, both knowingly and unknowingly, organized. It would be inconceivable to be a member of Western civilization and not recognize reference to the burning bush, to Noah and the ark, to Lot's wife, or to the miracle of the loaves and fishes. The *Analects*, in short, have played a comparable role in traditional Chinese culture.

The notion of *li*, mentioned previously, is a very important one in understanding Confucian thought.[18] Originally, the term referred merely to proper conduct in general, and in religious and ritualistic settings in particular, but for Confucius it came to encompass far more than simply ceremonial correctness. Although ritual and its proper performance was an important aspect of Confucian thought,[19] *li* entailed both a knowledge of traditional practice and behavior, and a sensitivity that would allow their modification as required by contemporary circumstances.[20] In short:

> *Li* was in fact a kind of balance wheel of conduct, tending to prevent either deficiency or excess, guiding toward the middle path of socially beneficial conduct. Confucius stated it thus: "Courtesy, if not regulated by *li*, becomes labored effort; caution, if not regulated by *li*, becomes mere timidity; courage, if not regulated by *li*, becomes mere unruliness; frankness, if not regulated by *li*, becomes mere effrontery."[21]

It is important to keep in mind, however, that *li* is not just a Chinese version of the ancient Greek dictum, "Moderation in all things." Moderation, to be sure, is an important part of *li*, but the concept goes well beyond this. The goal of *li* is both a social and individual one, grounded in the proper expression of social and cultural tradition. Education is the means by which the individual learns what *li* will require in a particular situation; *li* is not so much character as the means by which character is manifested.

If *li* is the way in which character is manifested, the cultivation of character itself—defined in terms of virtues—is a significant component of education.[22] For Confucius, the *chün-tzu* will seek to develop what are called the "Five Constant Virtues": right attitude, right procedure, right knowledge, right moral courage, and right persistence.[23] Taken together, the practice of these virtues would lead to a new society based on justice and wisdom.[24] The nature of the *chün-tzu*, as described in the *Analects,* included the following characteristics:

> The Master said, (the good man) does not grieve that other people do not recognize his merits. His only anxiety is lest he should fail to recognize theirs. (Book I: 16)
>
> The Master said, In the presence of a good man, think all the time how you may learn to equal him. In the presence of a bad man, turn your gaze within! (Book IV: 17)
>
> The Master said, A gentleman is ashamed to let his words outrun his deeds. (Book XIV: 29)

Furthermore, Confucian moral thought is grounded in the concept of the five basic human relationships: ruler and subject, father and son, husband and wife, older brother and younger brother, and between friends.[25] Each of these relationships is hierarchical, with each individual tied and obligated to the other in keeping with his or her station. Thus, children are bound to their parents by filial piety, wives to husbands, subjects to rulers, and so on. However, it is important to understand that each of these relationships, as envisaged by Confucius, was to be one of mutual responsibility. As Ron-Guey Chu explained, "Filiality originates from one's sense of obligation or gratitude. It is a natural response to the parents' love and care for one—a consequence of their initial parental solicitude. Indeed, this kind of reciprocity underlies all human relationships."[26]

This reciprocity, however, although very much affecting both parties in the relationship, was nonetheless in no way intended to be one of equality. Wang Gungwu, for instance, commented that:

> In talking about reciprocity and reciprocal rights, I am talking about unequal reciprocity in a hierarchical structure. In short, duties and implicit rights were between unequals not between equals, and therefore the shares of both duties and rights were also necessarily unequal and this was implicit in the very concept of reciprocity.[27]

The analogy drawn by Confucius of the family to the state was built on precisely this same notion of the reciprocity of the ruled and the ruler. In essence:

> Confucianism thus built a new moral interpretation of the world upon the oldest and soundest foundation, the family system. It could be fitted to the political system, thus ensuring that monarchy, as an apotheosis of paternalism, would be the only conceivable form of government. The government must, however, be restrained and guided by ethical teaching and exercised in conformity with high moral principles.[28]

In summary, Confucian theory, especially as it was articulated and expanded by latter Chinese philosophers (most notably Mencius[29] and Chu Hsi[30]), provided what was taken by its proponents to be a powerful and compelling justification for a highly stratified social order that proved to be remarkably conservative and resistant to change. Confucius himself often distinguished between the *chün-tzu* (here best translated as *gentleman*) and the common people, always to the detriment of the latter, and there can be little doubt that Confucian thought did indeed have a profoundly conservative effect on Chinese society—precisely, of course, as Confucius would have wished.

And yet, there is another side to Confucian theory and practice as it relates to the role of education in the social order. Education was the key to Confucius' view of how the ideal social order could be achieved, and he was far from naive about the intellectual and moral qualities of many of those born into positions of power and influence. In essence, Confucius believed that: "a good education would change men for the better, and that this should be available to those capable of benefitting from it. His remark that by nature men are nearly alike; but through experience they grow wide apart supported the efficacy of schooling, and he was famed for his meritocratic outlook. . . ."[31]

Among Confucius' own pupils were individuals from virtually all social and class backgrounds, and he emphasized that wealth and honor were just "fleeting clouds."[32] Education should identify those of talent, and help them to become men fit to rule over others.[33] In other words, education for Confucius served a very pragmatic purpose—the creation of individuals who would be able to ensure better government. Indeed, Confucian philosophy in general has often been described by Western scholars as "this-worldly," in contrast to the "other-worldly" focus of much Western philosophical thought.[34] However, at the same time the purpose of education:

> was by no means narrowly practical. Although the end of education was to bring about good government, this did not mean that the end product of education should be an efficient administrator and nothing more. Far from it, he should, in fact, be as nearly as possible the ideal man, from every point of view. He definitely should not be a mere specialist in some particular technique. . . . Confucius' object was not successful careers but good government, and this he believed to be possible only when government was administered by men who, in addition to being educated in the ordinary sense, were also endowed with integrity and poise.[35]

This brings us to one of the more criticized aspects of Confucian educational thought, which is its negative view of manual labor in general and agricultural pursuits in particular. Confucius himself once rebuked a student who had asked him about growing crops as a "little-minded man."[36] Thus, although education for Confucius had a practical focus, there were limits on how this practicality was to be manifested.

Although it is true that to a considerable extent that the Confucian system in practice "reinforced the rigidly hierarchical social class structure" of imperial

China,[37] it nevertheless did permit limited social class mobility based on talent, and was not incompatible with certain characteristics of a democratic social order. As H. G. Creel argued, Confucius appears to have believed, among other things, that:

- The proper aim of government is the welfare and happiness of the whole people.
- This aim can be achieved only when the state is administered by those most capable of government.
- Capacity to govern has no necessary connection with birth, wealth, or position; it depends solely on character and knowledge.
- Character and education are produced by proper education.
- In order that the best talents may become available, education should be widely diffused.
- It follows that the government should be administered by those persons, chosen from the whole population, who prove themselves to have profited most by the proper kind of education.[38]

Such a perspective is not only reminiscent of the view of the role of education in Plato's *Republic,* but is also very close to the view of education found in Thomas Jefferson's "Bill for the More General Diffusion of Knowledge."[39]

Finally, it should be noted that although Confucianism has indeed played a central role in the development and evolution of Chinese culture, it has not been alone in providing a conceptual and philosophical context for Chinese educational thought and practice. Challenges to Confucianism, especially those of the "Legalists" in the years preceding the rise of the Han dynasty,[40] as well as the impact of Taoism (most clearly identified with Lao-tzu's *Tao Te Ching*),[41] also impacted Chinese educational thought in important ways. Nor, as suggested earlier, was Confucian thought static; rather, it evolved and changed over time, and the articulation of Confucian thought that we know today undoubtedly has at least as much to do with the later formulations of Mencius and Chu Hsi as with Confucius himself.[42] With this in mind, we turn now to a discussion of traditional Chinese educational practice.

TRADITIONAL CHINESE EDUCATIONAL PRACTICE

Schooling in imperial China reflected social class background to a very great extent. Although private schools and private tutors existed for the children of merchants and artisans, the focus of most schooling in China was on the preparation of the sons of the elite for the imperial civil service examinations.[43] It was this latter type of school that was actively supported by the government, largely out of self-interest, because it was from the ranks of successful examinees that government officials would come. Thus, it is not surprising to find that during the early years of the Ming dynasty, as China was recovering from a century of Mongol rule and civil strife, the government invested heavily in schooling: "To provide for the nation's needs, radical steps were taken to improve the means of training; no less than 1,200 local schools were established in the prefectures and counties, at the expense of the central government and with officially appointed teachers."[44]

Indeed, as Raymond Dawson argued in *The Chinese Experience*, "Throughout imperial Chinese history emperors were regarded as the grand patrons of education, frequently paying formal visits to the national university, issuing edicts for the establishment of schools, and paying honour to Confucius as the 'first teacher.'[45]

Nonetheless, it is important not to overemphasize the role of the government in supporting education; elementary schooling remained primarily the province and responsibility of parents,[46] which inevitably meant that such institutions were generally neighborhood based and somewhat informal in terms of their status. As the Reverend Justus Doolittle described the system in 1865, "There is no village tax nor any aid from government received for the support of schools. Each parent must pay the teacher for the instruction of his children."[47] Schooling, in short, was available to those most able to pay for it, and the quality of basic education was to a significant degree reflected in one's social class background.

Preparation for the civil service examinations actually began well before the birth of a boy. Detailed advice was given to pregnant women to help them ensure the birth of a gifted son; the advice included sitting erect, avoiding strange food, and having poetry and classical literature read to her.[48]

The more formal education of the male child began a bit later, around the age of three, when the boy began learning to read his first characters.[49] Because of the complexity of written Chinese, the acquisition of literacy played an important and time-consuming role in the educational process. From the time he was able to hold a brush, the boy would copy characters from various books intended for use with children, among which were the *Three Character Classic* and the *Thousand Character Essay*. The former "is the world's longest surviving and best selling textbook and is still in print in China."[50] These books served two distinct kinds of educational purposes: first, they provided the child with the basic lexicon he would need to become literate and, second, they provided extensive moral education in keeping with the Confucian ethic.

Schooling, as such, began for the boy around the age of seven or eight, after he had mastered the basic elements of literacy. Working with a tutor or teacher in a small group, he began an educational process that relied extensively on the memorization of the Four Books (which included both the *Analects* and the *Mencius*, as well as two shorter works, the *Great Learning* and the *Just Mean*) and the Five Classics (which included the *Book of Changes*, *Book of Records*, *Book of Odes*, *Book of Rites*, and the *Spring and Autumn Record*).[51]

By the time he was 12, a boy would have memorized texts consisting of more than 400,000 characters[52]—and these texts were the same ones learned by every student preparing for the civil service examinations, ensuring a broad and deep common intellectual base for each generation of Chinese officials. Once he had mastered the basic texts, the student would progress to the commentaries written about the texts and finally, to learning the proper form for writing essays for the civil service examinations. This latter point is an important one; essay themes were set in the examinations, and examinees were required to produce what was called the "eight-legged essay"—a highly formal and rule-governed kind of writing that has been criticized for stressing technique over creativity. As Dawson commented, "This type of essay . . . required technical expertise rather than intellectual distinction for its composition, so it has been a byword in modern times for the sterility and formalism of the classical tradition."[53]

While some boys were engaged in this intensive educational undertaking, their sisters were educationally (and in a variety of other ways) less fortunate in traditional Chinese society. As John Cleverley wrote, "The world for many women was one of segregation and seclusion, often crippled by bound feet, and subject to child marriages arranged by parents."[54] Although there are a number of well-educated and politically powerful women in the long history of China, such women were clearly the exception rather than the rule.[55] For the most part, the role of the woman in traditional China was limited to the duties and obligations of being a wife and a mother, and her education was oriented toward these goals.

We turn now to an exploration of the nature and purposes of the imperial civil service examination, the focal point of traditional Chinese education and the feature of that education for which it is best known today.

THE IMPERIAL EXAMINATION SYSTEM

Written examinations to aid in the selection of government officials were used as early as the Han period (206 B.C. through 220 A.D.),[56] although it was only the Tang dynasty (618 A.D. to 907 A.D.) that they came to play a key role in the selection of such officials.[57] The purpose of the examination system was to ensure the quality of the civil service by making it more meritocratic, as well as to provide civil servants (as well as all educated people) with a common body of knowledge and experience on which they could draw.[58] Initially, the system co-existed with one of aristocratic privilege, in which recruitment to the civil service was based largely on heredity and recommendation. Under the usurper Empress Wu, however, this changed as the examination system was utilized as a political tool to challenge the power of the aristocracy, and by the eighth century the system operated as a highly effective, meritocratic means of providing a reasonably fair and objective means by which officials could be chosen.[59] As John Cleverley argued,

Stage I: Preliminary Examinations

District-level (*hsien-k'ao*)
Prefectural-level (*fu-k'ao*)
Examination for *sheng-yüan* degree

↓

Stage II: Provincial Examinations

Examination for *chü-jen* degree

↓

Stage III: Metropolitan Examinations

Major examination (known as *Hui-Shih*) for *chin-shih* degree
Palace examination (*tien-shih*)

FIG. 5.3.   An overview of the Chinese Imperial Examination System.

The imperial civil service examination made it possible for a man from humble origin to move into a position of political power, and it also enabled districts to gain national prominence through their native sons. Because it served the cause of social mobility, it had an integrating and stabilising effect on Chinese life generally. Further, the infusion of new blood, which the examining process permitted, reduced the political power of the hereditary aristocracy and clans, and strengthened the throne.[60]

Although the examination system was not static over the long course of its existence, of course, it is nevertheless possible to present a general overview of how it operated, especially under the Ming and Ch'ing periods of Chinese history. Basically, the examination system consisted of tests at three distinct levels: the district examinations, the provincial examinations, and the metropolitan examinations.[61] The examinations were of increasing difficulty, and each required the candidate to have passed the preceding level (see Fig. 5.3). The first examination level, which was conducted in local cities by provincial education officials, granted successful examinees the title *hsiu-ts'ai* ("Flowering Talent"). Passing this first examination allowed one to wear special, distinctive clothing, as well as granted one's family a tax exemption but, more important, allowed one to progress to the next level of the examination system.[62]

Lines of Cells

Inside of the Cells

FIG. 5.4.   The Chinese Imperial Examination System: examination cells.

The second level of the examination system consisted of a test given every 3 years in the various provincial capitals of the empire. The examination took place in a special complex, consisting of individual cells in which the candidates spent 9 days writing their answers to the set questions.[63] The cells, which contained only three boards to function as a shelf, desk and chair, were too small to allow the individual to comfortably sleep at night (see Fig. 5.4). Successful candidates, who were generally a tiny fraction of those taking the examination, gained the title *chü-jen* ("Recommended Man"), and were now eligible for lower-level government appointments.

Next, metropolitan examinations were held in order to identify those scholars who would be suitable for higher posts in the government. Only 1 of 20 or 30 candidates at this level could hope to become a *chin-shih* ("Presented Scholar").[64] Finally, also at the metropolitan level, came the pinnacle of the examination system, the palace examination, which was (in theory if not in practice) presided over by the Emperor himself. At this final level, candidates did not fail but, rather, were ranked in order of merit.[65] Success at this level, although not ensuring career advancement was, nonetheless, a necessary condition for it, as Dawson explained:

Success in this rigorous competition did not, however, bring automatic appointment. It merely made one a member of a social and intellectual elite from among whom appointments were made. The top palace graduates would . . . expect high office after a period in the imperial secretariat; but there were not enough jobs to go round for those who were qualified. . . . [66]

The examinations were open to most men in Chinese society; excluded were members of certain occupations and, hardly surprising given the patriarchal nature of traditional Chinese society, women. Furthermore, there was no restriction on the number of times an individual might try to pass an examination, and so some men spent their entire lives attempting to pass the difficult examinations. Although the rewards for success in the examination system were great, so too were the challenges and expenses and, in practice, few individuals from poor backgrounds could hope to succeed. [67]

If originally a creative and thoughtful solution to the complex and difficult challenge of providing the empire with the best possible civil servants and officials, over the course of the centuries the imperial examination system gradually declined as it "failed to preserve the freshness and ingenuity of earlier days." [68] To some extent, such an outcome was understandable. As Jacques Gernet explained, "As the sole means of access to political honours and responsibilities, the examinations served to inculcate in those who sat for them the virtues of devotion and submission indispensable to the autocratic empire. At the same time they also drained the energies of generations of the literati." [69]

Furthermore, the system was increasingly plagued by problems with cheating, [70] as well as by the narrowness of view encouraged by both the content of the examination (which excluded virtually all knowledge not related to the classics) and its form (especially the "eight-legged essay" discussed earlier). [71] In any event, by the end of the 19th century the examination system had come into widespread disrepute, and its abolition in 1905 came as a surprise to few.

CONCLUSION

Traditional Chinese educational thought and practice both reflected and helped to reproduce traditional Chinese society, as do all educational systems to some extent, and this was both its strength and weakness. Because traditional Chinese society was highly patriarchal and involved the oppression of girls and women in a number of ways, educational thought tended to pay little attention to the education of girls, and this meant that, in practice, girls were likely to receive little education beyond those things deemed necessary for wives and mothers to know. The social class organization of Chinese society was both hierarchical and fairly rigid and, again, both educational thought and practice reflected the social class structure of the society. If imperial China invested huge resources in education—and it did so throughout its history—these resources were far from equitably distributed. For some, educational endeavors would dominate their lives, whereas for the vast majority of the population illiteracy was the norm.

At the same time, the system did, in fact, work well for most of its history to produce what was, in essence, as aristocracy of intellect. The system, although by no means truly meritocratic, did have features of meritocracy, and there were noteworthy instances of social class mobility based on intellectual skill and talent. China was well ahead of its time in terms of the development of a professional civil service based on talent rather than on birth. Finally, if traditional educational thought and practice in China was, as Gerald Gutek noted somewhat critically, "used for highly conservative maintenance purposes [and] not intended to promote social change,"[72] this was precisely what it was designed to do. The idea that the schools can, and should, contribute to social change flies in the face of Confucian teaching about the nature and purposes of the "good society." The point of traditional Chinese educational thought and practice was to ensure stability, and it did so effectively for most of its history.

QUESTIONS FOR REFLECTION AND DISCUSSION

1. An important theme in American education, since the time of the Common School Movement, has been on the role of the school in promoting social change. Traditional Chinese education, as we have seen, placed its emphasis instead on social stability. To what extent is contemporary schooling in our society concerned with social maintenance, and to what extent is it concerned with promoting social change? How are each of these concerns manifested in practice?

2. The imperial civil service examination system ensured that all educated people in China would share a common educational background based on knowing the same body of literature and having the same types of skills. What are the advantages of such a common educational background? What are the disadvantages?

3. "Imperial China addressed the challenges posed by the presence of ethnic and linguistic diversity in a way that seems to share characteristics with both assimilationism and cultural pluralism." Respond to this claim, paying special attention to the role of social class and education.

4. The eight-legged essay consisted of a set format for responding to an examination question, and has been widely criticized for promoting an emphasis on form over content. To what extent do you believe that teaching students a particular form or format for the presentation of their ideas is a legitimate goal for education? Does the requirement of a particular form necessarily conflict with the educational goal of creativity?

5. Do you believe that a formal, institutionalized examination system such as that found in imperial China can be successfully utilized to promote meritocracy in a society? What are the constraints on such a system? In your view, is the goal of a meritocratic social order worth pursuing?

RECOMMENDED FURTHER READINGS

There are several good general introductory works on Chinese history, including W. Scott Morton, *China: Its History and Culture* (New York: McGraw-Hill, 1995), John K. Fairbank, *China: A New History* (Cambridge, MA: Harvard University Press, 1992), Jacques Gernet, *A History of Chinese Civilization* (Cambridge, England: Cambridge University Press, 1982), and Immanuel C. Y. Hsü, *The Rise of Modern China* (New York: Oxford University Press, 1990). The best general introduction to Chinese education, both traditional and modern, is John Cleverley, *The Schooling of China: Tradition and Modernity in Chinese Education* (Sydney: Allen & Unwin, 1985). Among primary sources, D. C. Lau's excellent translations of *The Analects* (Harmondsworth: Penguin, 1979) and *Mencius* (Harmondsworth: Penguin, 1970) are very much worth reading. Finally, for an interesting treatment of Taoism, see Eva Wong (trans.), *Seven Taoist Masters: A Folk Novel of China* (Boston: Shambhala, 1990).

NOTES

1. Jacques Gernet, *A History of Chinese Civilization* (Cambridge, England: Cambridge University Press, 1982), 37–38; Marcel Granet, *La Civilisation Chinoise: La Vie Publique et la Vie Privée* (Paris: Éditions Albin Michel, 1968); John Cleverley, *The Schooling of China: Tradition and Modernity in Chinese Education* (Sydney: Allen & Unwin, 1985), 1; W. Bauer, *China and the Search for Happiness: Recurring Themes in Four Thousand Years of Chinese History* (New York: Seabury, 1976); H. Cordier, *Histoire Général de la Chine*, 4 vols. (Paris: Geuthner, 1921).

2. Cleverley, *The Schooling of China*.

3. Gerald Gutek, *American Education in a Global Society: Internationalizing Teacher Education* (New York: Longman, 1993), 178.

4. Michael Loewe, *The Pride That Was China* (New York: St. Martin's Press, 1990), xix.

5. See Gernet, *A History of Chinese Civilization*, 3–13; Jerry Norman, *Chinese* (Cambridge, England: Cambridge University Press, 1988).

6. Will Durant, *The Story of Civilization: Our Oriental Heritage* (New York: Simon and Schuster, 1963), 642.

7. See David McMullen, *State and Scholars in T'ang China* (Cambridge, England: Cambridge University Press, 1988); Tadao Sakai, "Confucianism and Popular Educational Works," in William de Bary (ed.), *Self and Society in Ming Thought* (New York: Columbia University Press, 1970), 331–366; Don Wyatt, "A Language of Continuity in Confucian Thought," in Paul Cohen and Merle Goldman (eds.), *Ideas Across Cultures: Essays on Chinese Thought in Honor*

of Benjamin I. Schwartz (Cambridge, MA: Harvard University Press, 1990), 33–34.

8. Tu Wei-Ming, "The Confucian Tradition in Chinese History," in Paul Ropp (ed.), *Heritage of China: Contemporary Perspectives on Chinese Civilization* (Berkeley: University of California Press, 1990), 136. See also Michael Bond and Kwang-kuo Hwang, "The Social Psychology of the Chinese People," in Michael Bond (ed.), *The Psychology of the Chinese People* (Hong Kong: Oxford University Press, 1986), 213–266.

9. Cheng Tien-Hsi, *China Moulded By Confucius: The Chinese Way in Western Light* (London: Stevens & Sons, 1947), 23.

10. Gernet, *A History of Chinese Civilization*, 88. See also Patricia Ebrey, *Confucianism and Family Rituals in Imperial China: A Social History of Writing About Rites* (Princeton, NJ: Princeton University Press, 1991).

11. H. Creel, Confucius and the Chinese Way (New York: Harper & Row, 1949), 25–26; Tu Wei-Ming, "The Confucian Tradition in Chinese History," 113–114.

12. Creel, *Confucius and the Chinese Way*, 25–26; Tu Wei-Ming, "The Confucian Tradition in Chinese History," 113–114.

13. The term *chün-tzu* literally means "son of a ruler," but is used in the more general sense of "gentleman." Even this translation is somewhat problematic, however, because it refers not so much to an assumed superiority of birth as to a superiority of character and behavior. See Arthur Waley (trans.), *The Analects of Confucius* (New York: Vintage, 1938), 34–38.

It should be noted that the use of male pronouns here is deliberate and meaningful; the role of women in Confucian thought is restricted, in large part, to their roles as wives and mothers. Traditional Chinese society was very much patriarchal, and this was reflected in the place of women in the social order. See Patricia Ebrey, "Women, Marriage, and the Family in Chinese History," in Paul Ropp (ed.), *Heritage of China: Contemporary Perspectives on Chinese Civilization* (Berkeley: University of California Press, 1990), 197–223; Patricia Ebrey, *Confucianism and Family Rituals in Imperial China*.

14. See Creel, *Confucius and the Chinese Way*, 142–144; Ebrey, *Confucianism and Family Rituals in Imperial China*.

15. Gernet, *A History of Chinese Civilization*, 88.

16. D. C. Lau (trans.), *The Analects* (Harmondsworth: Penguin, 1979).

17. Patricia Ebrey (ed.), *Chinese Civilization: A Sourcebook*, 2nd ed. (New York: Free Press, 1993), 17.

18. See Cheng Tien-Hsi, *China Moulded By Confucius*, 30–36.

19. See Ebrey, *Confucianism and Family Rituals in Imperial China*, 3–13.

20. Creel, *Confucius and the Chinese Way*, 85.

21. Creel, *Confucius and the Chinese Way*, 86.

22. Creel, *Confucius and the Chinese Way*, 129.

23. Howard Ozmon and Samuel Craver, *Philosophical Foundations of Education*, 5th ed. (Englewood Cliffs, NJ: Prentice-Hall, 1995), 93.

24. Ozmon and Craver, *Philosophical Foundations of Education*, 93.

25. Charles Commeaux, *La Vie Quotidienne en Chine Sous les Mandchous* (Paris: Librairie Hachette, 1970), 162–194.

26. Ron-Guey Chu, "Chu Hsi and Public Instruction," in William de Bary and John Chaffee (eds.), *Neo-Confucian Education: The Formative Stage* (Berkeley: University of California Press, 1989), 272.

27. Wang Gungwu, *The Chineseness of China* (Hong Kong: Oxford University Press, 1991), 171.

28. Louis Heren, C. P. Fitzgerald, Michael Freeberne, Brian Hook, and David Bonavia, *China's Three Thousand Years: The Story of a Great Civilisation* (New York: Collier Books, 1973), 23–24.

29. See D. C. Lau (trans.), *Mencius* (Harmondsworth: Penguin, 1970); also useful is Tu Wei-Ming, "The Confucian Tradition in Chinese History."

30. See Peter Bol, "Chu Hsi's Redefinition of Literati Learning," in William de Bary and John Chaffee (eds.), *Neo-Confucian Education: The Formative Stage* (Berkeley: University of California Press, 1989), 151–185; William de Bary, "Chu Hsi's Aims as an Educator," in William de Bary and John Chaffee (eds.), *Neo-Confucian Education: The Formative Stage* (Berkeley: University of California Press, 1989), 186–218; M. Theresa Kelleher, "Back to Basics: Chu Hsi's *Elementary Learning (Hsiao-hsüeh)*," in William de Bary and John Chaffee (eds.), *Neo-Confucian Education: The Formative Stage* (Berkeley: University of California Press, 1989), 219–251; Ron-Guey Chu, "Chu Hsi and Public Instruction."

31. Cleverley, *The Schooling of China*, 4.

32. Cleverley, *The Schooling of China*, 4.

33. Creel, *Confucius and the Chinese Way*, 77.

34. See Wyatt, "A Language of Continuity in Confucian Thought," 33–34.

35. Creel, *Confucius and the Chinese Way*, 76.

36. Cleverley, *The Schooling of China*, 7.

37. Gutek, *American Education in a Global Society*, 179.

38. Creel, *Confucius and the Chinese Way*, 165–166.

39. See Steven Tozer, Paul Violas, and Guy Senese, *School and Society: Educational Practice as Social Expression* (New York: McGraw-Hill, 1993), 29–31; Gordon Lee, *Crusade Against Ignorance: Thomas Jefferson on Education* (New York: Teachers College Press, 1967).

40. Raymond Dawson, *The Chinese Experience* (London: Weidenfeld and Nicolson, 1978), 108–115; Gernet, *A History of Chinese Civilization*, 90–93.

41. See T. H. Barrett, "Religious Traditions in Chinese Civilization: Buddhism and Taoism," in Paul Ropp (ed.), *Heritage of China: Contemporary Perspectives on Chinese Civilization* (Berkeley: University of California Press, 1990), 138–163; Phyllis Ghim Lian Chew, "The Great Tao," *The Journal of Bahá'í Studies*, 4, 2 (1991): 11–39; Liu Ts'un-Yan, "Taoist Self-Cultivation in Ming Thought," in William de Bary (ed.), *Self and Society in Ming Thought* (New York: Columbia University Press, 1970), 291–330; C. Hansen, *A Daoist Theory of Chinese Thought: A Philosophical Interpretation* (New York: Oxford University Press, 1992); Gernet, *A History of Chinese Civilization*, 93–95.

42. See de Bary and Chaffee, *Neo-Confucian Education*.

43. See Édouard Biot, *Essai sur l'histoire de l'instruction publique en chine et de la corporation des lettrés* (Paris: Benjamin Duprat, 1847); H. Galt, *A History of Chinese Educational Institutions*, Vol. 1 (London: Arthur Probsthain, 1951); McMullen, *State and Scholars in T'ang China*; Cleverley, *The Schooling of China*, 15.

44. Loewe, *The Pride That Was China*, 145.

45. Dawson, *The Chinese Experience*, 20.

46. See Richard Smith, *China's Cultural Heritage: The Ch'ing Dynasty, 1644–1912* (Boulder, CO: Westview, 1983), 250.

47. Justus Doolittle, *Social Life of the Chinese*, Vol. 1 (orig. published 1865; Taipei: Ch'eng-Wen, 1966), 376–377.

48. Cleverley, *The Schooling of China*, 16.

49. As few words about the nature of written Chinese are in order here. The Chinese writing system is not phonetic in the way that Western, alphabetically based systems are. Rather, each Chinese character represents a single morpheme, and contains two elements, one of which carries semantic information and the other phonological information, which is used for sound value alone. Thus, the character for the word *liáng* (*wolf*) contains the graph for *dog* on the left and a graph for the word *liáng* (literally meaning *good*) on the right. Thus, the combination gives the reader an idea of the semantic content, coupled with the appropriate sound. Although far more complicated to learn than an alphabetically based system, the Chinese system has the advantage that it can be used to represent different spoken languages, which is, in essence, what has taken place historically, because China is in fact very diverse linguistically. An orthographic system such as that used by Chinese basically functions as a sort of written *lingua franca*, serving as an additional unifying force where spoken language would tend to work against unity. See Norman, *Chinese*, 58–63.

50. Cleverley, *The Schooling of China*, 17.

51. See Kiang Kang-Hu, *On Chinese Studies* (Shanghai: Commercial, 1934); S. Wells Williams, *The Middle Kingdom: A Survey of the Geography, Government, Literature, Social Life, Arts, and History of the Chinese Empire and its Inhabitants*, Vol. 1 (New York: Scribner's, 1907), 627–673.

52. Smith, *China's Cultural Heritage*, 47.

53. Dawson, *The Chinese Experience*, 34.

54. Cleverley, *The Schooling of China*, 27.

55. See Bettine Birge, "Chu Hsi and Women's Education," in William de Bary and John Chaffee (eds.), *Neo-Confucian Education: The Formative Stage* (Berkeley: University of California Press, 1989), 325–367; Ebrey, "Women, Marriage, and the Family in Chinese History."

56. Dawson, *The Chinese Experience*, 33.

57. Ebrey, *Chinese Civilization*, 128.

58. See Thomas H. C. Lee, *Government Education and Examinations in Sung China* (Hong Kong: Chinese University Press, 1985); Ping-Ti Ho, *The*

Ladder of Success in Imperial China (New York: Columbia University Press, 1962); John Chaffee, *Education and Examinations in Sung Society* (PhD dissertation, University of Chicago, 1979).

59. Dawson, *The Chinese Experience*, 33-34; see also Hsiung-Huei Lee, *Education in Taiwan During the Ch'ing Dynasty, 1683-1895* (PhD dissertation, University of Connecticut, 1995), 193-272.

60. Cleverley, *The Schooling of China*, 19.

61. See Immanuel C. Y. Hsü, *The Rise of Modern China* (New York: Oxford University Press, 1990), 75. For a detailed discussion of the examination system, see Smith, *China's Cultural Heritage*, 47–51; also interesting is Doolittle, *Social Life of the Chinese*, chaps. 15, 16, and 17.

62. Dawson, *The Chinese Experience*, 34.

63. Hsiung-Huei Lee, *Education in Taiwan During the Ch'ing Dynasty*, 217–222.

64. Dawson, *The Chinese Experience*, 36.

65. Dawson, *The Chinese Experience*, 36.

66. Dawson, *The Chinese Experience*, 36.

67. See Hsiung-Huei Lee, *Education in Taiwan During the Ch'ing Dynasty*, chap. 5.

68. Dawson, *The Chinese Experience*, 34.

69. Gernet, *A History of Chinese Civilization*, 505.

70. Cleverley, *The Schooling of China*, 20; Hsiung-huei Lee, *Education in Taiwan During the Ch'ing Dynasty*, 212–216.

71. Cleverley, *The Schooling of China*, 20–21.

72. Gutek, *American Education in a Global Society*, 179.

6

Hinduism and Education
in Classical India

The Indian subcontinent is the home of three important related, cultural, and religious traditions: Hinduism, Buddhism, and Jainism, each of which has educational traditions meriting a book of its own.[1] In this book, the traditional educational thought and practices associated with two of these three religious is examined. Specifically, in this chapter we explore selected aspects of the Hindu educational tradition and, in the following chapter, the educational tradition associated with Buddhism is examined (see Fig. 6.1).

It is difficult to both identify the origins of Hinduism and provide a succinct, clear summation of what the essence of Hinduism actually is. To some extent these problems are related, because Hinduism is incredibly ancient and has been open to diversity and the assimilation of new ideas and practices throughout its long history.[2] According to Hindu tradition, the *Vedas* (or "body of knowledge") that constitute the sacred literature of Hinduism date back as far as 6000 B.C. in their oral form, whereas most historians would argue that the written literature, although not nearly as old as the tradition would suggest, nonetheless dates to around 1500 to 1000 B.C.[3] In fact, we know relatively little about the early history of Hinduism and what today is called *Hinduism*[4] is actually the product of the blending of four distinct religious traditions. These four traditions, in chronological order of their impact of the development of Hinduism, are:

1. The religious and spiritual traditions of the original, indigenous people of the subcontinent, whose stone age culture dates back some half million years,
2. The religious and spiritual traditions of the Indus civilization, which encompassed much of Northern and Northwestern India,
3. The religious and spiritual traditions of the Dravidian culture, and
4. The Vedic religion, which was brought to the subcontinent by Aryan invaders roughly between 200 B.C. and 900 B.C.[5]

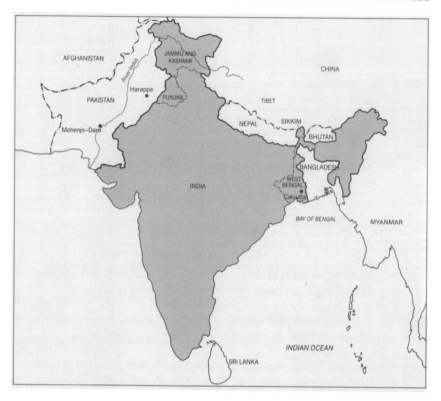

FIG. 6.1. The Indian subcontinent [From Mary Pat Fisher, *Living Religions*, 2nd ed. (Englewood Cliffs, NJ: Prentice Hall, 1994), p. 63]. Reprinted with permission.

Later contacts with Jews, Christians, and Muslims, as well as with Buddhists whose religious tradition is related to and in part derived from that of Hinduism, also impacted Hinduism in various ways, as have both Jainism and Sikhism. This openness to other religious traditions has not, however, meant that the fundamental essence of Hinduism has differed significantly through its long history. As Klaus Klostermaier noted in *A Survey of Hinduism*, "Despite its openness to many influences and the considerable changes that it has undergone throughout the ages, there is a distinct character, an unbroken tradition, and a unifying principle that allows Hinduism to be faithful to itself while inviting others to share whatever treasures they may possess."[6]

Hindus themselves call their religion *sanatana dharma*, which is generally translated as "eternal religion," although it might just as well be translated as "eternal truth." However, the term implies far more than the English translation.[7] *Sanatana* means "eternal" or "ageless" in the sense that the religion is believed by its practitioners to have always existed and to be *the* religion.[8] *Dharma*, often translated simply as "religion," actually encompasses such concepts as *duty*, *righteousness*, and *natural law*, thus suggesting a much broader understanding than that generally accorded the term *religion* in the west.[9] In fact, as Troy Organ argued in *The Hindu Quest for the Perfection of Man,* underlying the notion of *dharma* is a far more encompassing conception of the duties of the individual, involving "the total disciplinary methods of training the will, rather than to the moral rightness or wrongness of single acts as measured by a fixed law."[10]

Not only is the translation of *sanatana dharma* problematic, but the actual nature of the religion itself is somewhat difficult to define. Indeed, as Stephen Cross commented, "One of the ways in which Hinduism differs strikingly from those religions which we in the West are most used to is that it has no fixed minimum doctrine. There is no Hindu creed and no central authority. . . . Hinduism is not a tightly defined religion but rather the way of thought of an entire ancient and populous civilization."[11]

Further complicating this situation have been the close ties between Hinduism as a religious tradition and Indian nationalism in recent times.[12] Although certainly not all Indians are Hindu, and although there are, of course, non-Indian Hindus, for the most part there is a commonly assumed connection between Hinduism and Indian cultural identity. To assume such a connection is hardly unreasonable because, as Arvind Sharma explained, "95 percent of the Hindus in the world live in India, over 80 percent of whose population is Hindu."[13] The contemporary reality of the situation is that Hinduism actually exists (or, perhaps more accurately, coexists) both as an ethnic religion and as a universal religion.[14] This has led to a degree of conceptual tension within Hinduism, as Sharma noted: "The ethnic and universal aspects of Hinduism thus together constitute the paradoxical axes of Hindu pluralism, keeping the map of Hinduism, as it were, forever on the drawing board of history."[15]

Identification of oneself as Hindu, then, inevitably depends less on doctrinal agreement than on self-definition and acceptance by the Hindu community, to a far greater extent than would be the case with most other religious traditions, especially those with which we in the West tend to be most familiar. Having said this, however, one common way of distinguishing Hindus from non-Hindus is that the former accept the authority of the *Vedas* in spiritual matters.[16] The centrality of the *Vedas* to Hinduism provides a valuable entry point for us as we try to understand Hinduism and the traditional educational thought and practice associated with Hinduism.

THE VEDIC TRADITION

The body of sacred writings in Hinduism is extensive and includes a number of different kinds of literature. As Klostermaier pointed out, "No other living tradition can claim scriptures as numerous or as ancient as Hinduism; none can boast an unbroken tradition preserved as faithfully as the Hindu tradition. The sources of Hinduism are not only historical materials to be studied by the scholar of antiquity, they have been recited and studied by the faithful throughout the ages."[17] The two most significant of the elements in the sacred literature of Hinduism's "living tradition" are *shruti* and *smrti*,[18] each of which is now briefly discussed. We also talk about the unique the role of Sanskrit in the Hindu literary tradition.

Shruti

Shruti means "that which is heard," and is commonly associated primarily with the *Vedas*. The *Vedas* are believed to constitute divine revelation. As Fisher explained, "According to orthodox Hindus, the *Vedas* are not the work of any humans. They are believed to be the breath of the eternal, as heard by the ancient sages, or *rishis*. The scriptures are thought to transcend human time and are thus as relevant today as they were thousands of years ago."[19]

Although the *Vedas* have been written down, they are, first and foremost, oral texts, and there is a strong view in the Hindu tradition that they are best transmitted orally.[20] There are actually four distinct bodies of work that together make up the *Vedas*; specifically, there are the *Rig Veda*, the *Yajur Veda*, the *Sama Veda*, and the *Atharva Veda*.[21] Each of these *Vedas* is, in turn, divided into four parts, including devotional hymns (*Samhita* or *Mantra*), priestly texts (*Brahmanas*), forest treatises (*Aranyakas*), and philosophic texts (the *Upanishads*), which were actually produced later and are more correctly called *Vendantic* texts.[22]

The *Vedas* play a role in Hinduism that is in some ways similar to that of texts believed to be divinely inspired in other religions, but that is also different in important ways. As Sharma noted,

> The *Vedas*, by virtue of their historical priority and canonical primacy, play a very significant role in Hinduism but in unsuspecting ways. . . . The *Vedas*, for the tradition as a whole then, functioned as a symbol of the tradition and as the ultimate rather than the proximate basis of its beliefs and practices, for anything not inconsistent with the *Vedas* was considered admissible as Hindu. This negative criterion for orthodox inclusion once again attests to Hinduism's reluctance to limit itself.[23]

Smrti

Smrti is the body of religious literature in Hinduism that seeks to explain how the timeless spiritual truths of the *Vedas* are to be understood and applied in one's daily life.[24] In practice, the term *smrti*, which means "that which has been remembered," can be used either to refer to works that are basically codes of conduct, or "extended to embrace virtually all forms of sacred writings of human origin."[25] *Smrti*, at least in the former sense, consists of a variety of different books that seek to provide guidance for virtually all aspects of human life, the most widely accepted of which is the *Manusmrti* (the "Laws of Manu"). They tend to be highly prescriptive, complex, and analytic in nature but, as Sharma explained, there is an underlying reason for this: "Their passion for classification baffles modern readers. A "method" may, however, underlie the "madness." Marriage is classified as being of eight kinds. A deep compassion perhaps underlies this classification, which is so exhaustive that it is virtually impossible for anyone to be born out of wedlock!"[26]

Although recognized by Hindus as being of human origin, *smrti* is arguably of considerably greater immediate importance than are the *Vedas* themselves for most Hindus, because it regulates daily life in a way that *shruti* does not.[27] Finally, it is worth noting that although Hindus accept *shruti* as divine scripture, Hinduism as it is generally recognized has, since the Classical Hindu Period (roughly 300 A.D. to 1200 A.DE.) been characterized to a far greater extent by compliance with *smrti* than *shruti*.[28]

The Role of Sanskrit in the Vedic Tradition

Sanskrit, a language brought to India by the Aryan invaders of the subcontinent between 1500 B.C. and 1200 B.C., has played and continues to play an important role in Hinduism. The *Vedas* are written in Sanskrit, as are many other important religious writings. Although there is also an extensive religious literature in the various vernacular languages of India, Sanskrit remains very much the "sacred tongue *par excellence*" of Hinduism.[29] Furthermore, having ceased to function as a spoken language in daily life more than 2,000 years ago, Sanskrit was maintained for much of its history not merely as a sacred language, but as a sacred language of which knowledge was reserved for a small elite in Indian society who maintained both their religious and social status in part through their knowledge of it.[30]

Sanskrit, incidentally, is also important in another, far different, context. European scholars gained access to both the language and the texts written in Sanskrit only in the 18th century—an undertaking that had been quite difficult, because the Brahmins were hesitant to let foreigners (*mlecchas*) learn the sacred language. In 1786, a British scholar, Sir William Jones, delivered a paper on Sanskrit, in which he argued that the language bore striking similarities to Latin and Greek.[31] These similarities were later explored in considerable detail, and led to the discovery that Sanskrit, and many other languages as well, were indeed related. In fact, it proved to be the beginning of the discovery of the Indo-European language family, to which not only Sanskrit, but also English and the other Germanic languages, the Celtic languages, the Romance languages, the Slavic languages, the Hellenic languages, the Baltic languages, and the Indo-Iranian languages all belong.

HINDU BELIEFS AND PRACTICES

As we have already seen, it is very difficult indeed to identify the core beliefs of Hinduism. However, keeping in mind that there is, and probably could be, no "creed" to which all Hindus subscribe, it is nevertheless possible to summarize some of the key beliefs that are most prevalent and common among Hindus. A good start in this effort has been made by the Himalayan Academy, an American Hindu organization, which has identified the following "Nine Beliefs of Hinduism":

1. That there is "one, all-pervasive Supreme Being";
2. That there are "endless cycles of creation, preservation and dissolution" (that is, a cyclical view of time and history);
3. That "all souls are evolving" toward or seeking "*Moksha*" or "liberation";
4. That there is a "law of cause and effect" known as Karma;
5. That there is "reincarnation";
6. That there are "divine beings and forces" that require "temple worship" and "personal worship," or Puja, in the home;
7. That there is a need for "an awakened Master of Sat Guru" (that is, a reliable, personal teacher) for one's personal and ethical life;
8. that "all life is sacred" and that one should pursue "*ahimsa* or non-violence"; and
9. That "no particular religion teaches the only way to salvation about all others, but that all genuine religious paths are . . . deserving (of) tolerance and understanding."[32]

Although this list is useful, it has also been carefully and understandably constructed to avoid, for the most part, issues that Americans might find problematic. It is not, however, universally accepted by Hindus—the need for a *guru* for instance, is by no means generally accepted as a core belief of Hinduism. One additional feature of Classical Hinduism that must be explicitly addressed here in order to help make sense of traditional Hindu educational thought and practice is that of the caste system that is so closely associated with Hinduism.

The Hindu caste system had its origins in the culture brought to India by the Aryan invaders who, like other Indo-European peoples, divided their society into three classes of people: a priesthood, a class of warriors and rulers, and a class concerned with meeting the economic needs of the society (farmers, merchants, craftsmen, etc.). In addition, the Aryans developed a fourth class, who functioned as servants for the members of the other three classes. These four classes of people, called *varnas*, were called *Brahmins*, *Kshatriyas*, *Vaishyas*, and *Shudras*, respectively.[33] To this division of society, the Aryans added a fifth group, consisting of the indigenous people of India whom they had conquered, to whom were delegated various socially necessary but "impure" activities. This group were the untouchables because it came to be believed that even contact with them could pollute others. The social divisions among these five classes of people, which were established in the *Vedas*, were in practice replaced with an hereditary system based on *jati* (birth) in traditional Hindu society.[34] Thus, the divisions, which had always been hierarchical, came to be religiously sanctioned and, for the most part, permanent and binding in nature. Thus, what had begun as social classes gradually became castes. Over time, the caste system further developed so that today there are actually more than 3,000 different castes, reflecting different trades, professions, backgrounds, and so on.[35] Although an understanding of traditional Hinduism certainly requires a familiarity with the caste system, especially in terms of traditional Hindu educational thought and practice, it is important to note that the caste system is not, in fact, part of the religion itself. As Cross noted, "The whole system has thus become attached in the popular mind, and in that of many foreign observers, to Hinduism, but in reality it has little to do with it. The caste system is a social phenomenon masquerading as religion."[36]

It is also possible for us to talk about Hinduism in terms of the legitimate goals for human life. Specifically, an important component of Hinduism has been what is termed the *doctrine of the four goals of life* or *purusharthas*.[37] These four goals include:

1. *Dharma* (the leading of a moral life),
2. *Artha* (the earning of wealth),
3. *Kama* (the enjoyment of the pleasures of the senses),
4. *Moksha* (the seeking of liberation).[38]

Ideally, these four goals are to be reflected chronologically in one's life as distinct "stages of life," with *dharma* as the goal for one's first 25 years, followed by each of the other goals in turn, although in practice most Hindus only progress through the first two.[39] The ultimate goal for the individual that underlies all of these four goals is, of course, the quest for perfection,[40] but the focus of this goal in Hinduism is on the process rather than on the product. As Organ argued in *The Hindu Quest for the Perfection of Man*, "Hinduism is a pursuit, an endeavor, a striving. According to the *Mahabharata* it is the pursuit of Brahman or self-knowledge that is immortality. This continuous endeavor toward fulfillment is a promise, and, like all ideals, a forever falling short of the goal.[41]

We now turn to an examination of how individuals were educated for this pursuit in traditional Hindu society.

TRADITIONAL HINDU EDUCATIONAL THOUGHT

At the base of traditional Hindu educational thought is a deep concern with epistemology, or the theory of knowledge. Human beings are believed to be held captive by our ignorance and, thus, ways of knowing (*pramana*) become very important in Hinduism.[42] Hindu theologians and philosophers have identified six different methods of knowing: sense perception (*pratyaksha*), inference (*anumana*), authority (*shabda*), analogy (*upamana*), hypothetical

supposition (*arthapatti*), and negation (*anupalabdhi*).[43] Although the ultimate purpose of epistemology in Hinduism is spiritual in nature, it is important
to keep in mind that none of these six methods of knowing is intended to
provide direct knowledge of the Absolute; rather, each is useful in assisting us
to "discern the realities which are assumed to be manifestations of the Reality
and, hence, are instrumental in the quest for Absolute Reality."[44] Each of
these methods of knowing are briefly discussed in the following list:

1. *Pratyaksha*, or sense perception, is arguably the most important source
of knowledge. It refers to those things that we learn by means of our senses
(which, in Hinduism, are taken to include the five external senses—touch,
taste, sight, sound, and smell—as well as an internal sense, mind [*manas*]).[45]

2. *Anumana*, or inference, refers to what might be called logical argument,
and includes both inductive and deductive reasoning. Typical of *anumana* is
the five-part syllogism characteristic of Hindu philosophy, which precedes the
development of syllogistic reasoning in the west. The five-part syllogism
includes the following steps:

a. The thesis that is to be established.
b. The reason for maintaining the thesis.
c. The example of the reason.
d. The application of the reason and example.
e. The conclusion (that is, the thesis established).[46]

3. *Shabda*, or authority, is concerned primarily with scriptural authority,
whether *shruti* or *smrti*. The study and analysis of the scripture plays an
important role in Hinduism, and the concern with *shabda* led early on to
extensive Hindu scholarship on the nature and structure of language. Religious
knowledge is derived primarily from *shabda*.[47]

4. Analogical reasoning, or *upamana*, has a higher status in Hindu philosophical thought than it does in the west. Analogies are, in essence, compari-
sons of two things that share certain common characteristics, and suggest that
because they share those characteristics, they are likely to share other characteristics as well. Basically, in the West analogy is used as a possible source for
hypotheses, whereas in Hindu thought it is considered a possible source of
knowledge.[48]

5. *Arthapatti*, or hypothetical supposition, is also sometimes called the
"method of implication." It involves identifying a missing premise in a
dilemma or argument. Thus, if a person is fasting during the day, but
nonetheless is gaining weight, one would be led to suspect that the person
is eating at night.[49]

6. The last of the six methods of knowing is called *abhava*, or negation,
and is, in a way, a sort of extension of *pratyaksha*, or sense perception. The
idea here is that "non-existence . . . can be known by non-cognition."[50] In other
words, the fact that I do not sense x around me can be taken to be evidence
for the nonexistence of x in my immediate vicinity.

Beyond its epistemological concerns, traditional Hindu educational thought emphasizes the need to think of the individual apart from his or her social context. As Radha Mookerji explained in his monumental work *Ancient Indian Education*:

> Hindu thought takes up the position that the individual as conceived in the context of social life, and the laws of the State, is essentially a psychological and biological fact. But the individual, in order that his ultimate datum of personality may be understood, must be viewed from other perspectives, those of his elemental nature, his potentiality for growth and transformation, his self-suffi-ciency, his capacity for effecting harmony between conflicting trends of im-pulses. Such a view of the self will necessarily take it out of its usual habitat. It means that the normal functions in terms of which the biological self ties itself to its material home must be checked so as to lay bare the core and kernel of one's being, the true self, the naked personality, stripped of the envelope with which it is shrouded by the accretions of passing impulses and emotions.[51]

In other words, the focus and purpose of education is on the spiritual growth and development of the individual rather than on any particular instrumental goal or objective. However, the purpose of emphasizing the individual is, in fact, to move the learner beyond individuation and toward emancipation. This involves moving away from the physical, material world around us, as well as beyond the limits of our own individual minds:

> When the mind is withdrawn from the world of matter, and does not engage in individuation, Omniscience, the Knowledge of the Whole, dawns on it. Indi-viduation shuts out omniscience. Individuation is concretion of the Mind. The Mind takes the form of the object in knowing it. It limits itself to the object, like the water rained down from the clouds limiting itself in a tank. Thus Individuation is Bondage. It limits vision, knowledge, omniscience.[52]

The goal of the traditional Hindu educational endeavor, then, will not be on the acquisition of bits of knowledge or on "objective knowledge," but rather on the knowledge of the totality of the universe. In short, rather than looking for the components of Knowledge, the point of education is to help us to find the source of Knowledge. We turn now to a discussion of how this search for Knowledge took place in traditional Hindu educational practice.

TRADITIONAL HINDU EDUCATIONAL PRACTICE

Given the very long history of Hinduism, it is hardly surprising that traditional Hindu educational thought has been manifested in practice in a variety of ways. Mookerji, for example, distinguished among the educational practices of the Rigvedic era, later Vedic educational practices, educational practices described in the Sutra literature, education in the time of Panini, and so on.[53] Although traditional Hindu education has, indeed, taken a variety of forms, there has also been an underlying unity that holds these different sets of practices together, and it is that underlying unity that is our focus here.

Hindu educational practice has focused on three distinct steps, discussed in detail in the *Upanishads*. Specifically, education is concerned with *shravana*, *manana*, and *nididhyasana*.[54] *Shravana* refers to the process of listening to one's teacher and learning the oral tradition on which the Hindu religious tradition is largely based. It is *shravana* that provides the content base necessary for a person to become educated. *Shravana* is followed by *manana*, which involves reflection on what is contained in the *shravana*. *Manana* is best understood as the process by which one begins to think about and reflect on the meaning of what one has learned and, is essentially, an intellectual rather than a spiritual process. *Manana* is followed by *nididhyasana*, or "meditation," in which the goal is the realization of truth and the "consciousness of the One." Each in its own way, all of the different traditional Hindu educational practices follow this same general process of increasing spirituality.

Formal education in traditional Indian society was almost exclusively the domain of males, and of Brahmin males at that.[55] To be sure, exceptions did exist, and one can make a case from the extensive Hindu literature that learning was intended, at least in principle, to be a far more general endeavor. Sures Banerji, for instance, argued that, "In matters of education, the narrow barriers of the caste-system appeared to have crumbled down."[56] In terms of typical practice, however, this does not, in fact, seem to have been the case for much of Hindu history, when non-Brahmins and girls were generally excluded from the educational sphere.[57]

Brahmin education began when the boy was about 5 years old, with a ritual called *vidyarambha* (which means "knowledge beginning"). This involved learning the Sanskrit alphabet in a ceremonial way, and generally lasted about an hour.[58] The boy would then commence studying at home, reading and writing, practicing on simple texts, as well as learning basic arithmetic. At around the age of 8, the boy would undergo what is called the "sacred thread ceremony" (*upanayana*), which involved his new teacher whispering his *gayatri mantra* to him and beginning the more formal part of his education.[59]

Formal education then commenced, with the boy living in the home of his teacher. A teacher, or *guru*, would accept only a small number of students, thus ensuring that education remained the highly individualized undertaking that Hinduism required. The student, in this system,

> lived with the [teacher] as a member of his family, ministered to his needs, obeyed his *guru*'s commands implicitly and treated him with divine reverence. He wore his hair long, dressed simply, practised penances, and studied under the direction of the *guru*. He had to collect fuel and tend the sacred fires, look after the cattle, help in agriculture and attend to the running of the household. If the need arose he had to go begging on behalf of his master.[60]

At the age of 10, the boy would begin his study of the *Vedas* themselves, memorizing many texts and learning to perform the *samdhya* ("daily devotions") appropriately.[61] His education was also characterized by a commitment to sexual chastity, an important aspect of the vow of *brahmacharya* that the student had to take.[62] Adolescence, marked by a special ceremony called *keshanta* ("the first shaving of the beard"), marked the end of formal education for many Brahmins.[63] For those who continued, study expanded and intensified and could last for as long as an additional 15 years.

Much traditional Hindu education took place as described previously, in *ashramas* run by individual teachers. As Mookerji noted, "The vital principle of ancient Indian education was that of individual and intimate relationship between pupils and their teachers, as members of the same family, living in a common home, the home of the teacher functioning as the school. . . ."[64] However, there were also notable educational institutions of a more formal, institution type in traditional Hindu society, often tied to temples and monasteries.[65] Still, even in these more institutional settings, the focus of traditional Hindu education was always on the individual and his personal spiritual growth.

CONCLUSION

The Hindu educational tradition is both one of the oldest and one of the richest in the world. It has functioned for millennia, in different forms, providing an education that emphasized the individual and his spiritual needs, even as it taught that only by renouncing the self could one achieve unity with the whole of the universe. Although sharing common roots with the West in the very distant past (as reflected in the ties of the Sanskrit language to other Indo-European languages), Hinduism presents us with a very different view of both the *educated person* and of the purposes of education than those with which most of us in the west are most familiar and comfortable.[66] Furthermore, as we see in the next chapter, Hinduism also provides the foundation on which Buddhism and, indeed, several other religious traditions, are based. In short, it is undoubtedly a good idea for us to reflect on the lessons that we can learn from the wisdom of Hinduism and its educational tradition.

QUESTIONS FOR REFLECTION AND DISCUSSION

1. Given your understanding of the difference between *schooling* and *education*, do you think that the traditional Hindu educational practice of placing students in the homes of their teachers, where they essentially became part of the teacher's household, is an example of *schooling* or *education*? Why?

2. To a very great extent, the whole point of Hindu education is spiritual. What are the advantages of such a focus in education? What are the disadvantages? How does this emphasis on spirituality differ from the approaches to education found in contemporary American society?
3. It was suggested in this chapter that oral tradition played an important role in traditional Hindu educational thought and practice and, yet, the Hindu tradition is very much text based. How can this seeming contradiction be reconciled?
4. The six "methods of knowing" that are discussed in this chapter provide us with an understanding of Hindu epistemology. In what ways, and to what extent, do these "methods of knowing" differ from the "scientific method"?
5. Traditional Hindu education is based on the student's progress through three stages, *shravana*, *manana*, and *nididhyasana*. Are these stages reflected at all in contemporary American public schooling? What lessons can be learned by considering these stages as we examine public schooling in our society?

RECOMMENDED FURTHER READINGS

In terms of general introductions to Hinduism, some of the better works currently available are Stephen Cross, *The Elements of Hinduism* (Shaftsbury, Dorset: Element, 1994), A. L. Herman, *A Brief Introduction to Hinduism: Religion, Philosophy, and Ways of Liberation* (Boulder, CO: Westview, 1991), and Ed Viswanathan, *Am I a Hindu? The Hinduism Primer* (San Francisco: Halo Books, 1992). Among the Hindu texts available in translation are Juan Mascaró (trans.), *The Upanishads* (Harmondsworth: Penguin, 1965), Wendy Doniger O'Flaherty (trans.), *The Rig Veda: An Anthology* (Harmondsworth: Penguin, 1981), and S. Radhkrishnan (ed.), *The Principal Upanishads* (New Delhi: Indus, 1994). In addition, the *Bhagavad Gita*, which is considered to be one of the more accessible and readable Hindu texts, is widely available in a number of translations. A very readable collection of short essays on contemporary Hinduism is provided in Eleanor Zelliot and Maxine Bernsten (eds.), *The Experience of Hinduism* (Albany: State University of New York Press, 1988).

NOTES

1. See S. Gopalan, *Outlines of Jainism* (New York: Halsted, 1973), 3. Although Jainism is not discussed in this book, it is a fascinating religious tradition well worth examination. In addition to Gopalan's book, see Paul

Dundas, *The Jains* (London: Routledge, 1992), and Caroline Humphrey and James Laidlaw, *The Archetypal Actions of Ritual: A Theory of Ritual Illustrated by the Jain Rite of Worshop* (Oxford, England: Clarendon Press, 1994).

2. Klaus Klostermaier, *A Survey of Hinduism* (Albany: State University of New York Press, 1989), 30–31.

3. Mary Pat Fisher, *Living Religions*, 2nd ed. (Englewood Cliffs, NJ: Prentice-Hall, 1994), 64–66.

4. Klostermaier noted that, "The very name *Hinduism* owes its origin to chance; foreigners . . . extended the name of the province of Sindh to the whole country lying across the Indus river and simply called all its inhabitants *Hindus* and their religion *Hinduism*." See Klostermaier, *A Survey of Hinduism*, 31.

5. Klostermaier, *A Survey of Hinduism*, 31; see also Arvind Sharma, "Hinduism," in Arvind Sharma (ed.), *Our Religions: The Seven World Religions Introduced By Preeminent Scholars From Each Tradition* (San Francisco: Harper, 1993), 36–38; R. C. Zaehner, *Hinduism* (London: Oxford University Press, 1962), 19–22; David Knipe, *Hinduism* (San Francisco: Harper, 1991), 17–25; K. M. Sen, *Hinduism* (Harmondsworth: Penguin, 1961), 17–21.

6. Klostermaier, *A Survey of Hinduism*, 45.

7. Fisher, *Living Religions*, 62; Zaehner, *Hinduism*, 2–4.

8. Klostermaier, *A Survey of Hinduism*, 31.

9. Fisher, *Living Religions*, 62.

10. Troy Organ, *The Hindu Quest for the Perfection of Man* (Athens: Ohio University Press, 1970), 4.

11. Stephen Cross, *The Elements of Hinduism* (Shaftesbury, Dorset: Element, 1994), 3. See also A. K. Banerjee, *Discourses on Hindu Spiritual Culture* (Delhi: S. Chand & Co., 1967), 3–4.

12. Klostermaier, *A Survey of Hinduism*, 40–41.

13. Sharma, "Hinduism," 6.

14. Sharma, "Hinduism," 7–11.

15. Sharma, "Hinduism," 11.

16. Cross, *The Elements of Hinduism*, 3–4; see also Sharma, "Hinduism," 26–27.

17. Klostermaier, *A Survey of Hinduism*, 61.

18. Zaehner, *Hinduism*, 11–13.

19. Fisher, *Living Religions*, 66.

20. Klostermaier, *A Survey of Hinduism*, 26; Cross, *The Elements of Hinduism*, 16–17.

21. Klostermaier, *A Survey of Hinduism*, 26; Cross, *The Elements of Hinduism*, 17.

22. Klostermaier, *A Survey of Hinduism*, 27; Sharma, "Hinduism," 26–27.

23. Sharma, "Hinduism," 27.

24. There is actually a third level of Hindu scripture as well, *Itihasas*, which is comprised essentially of histories of individuals who, by virtue of the sanctity of their lives, have come to be seen as incarnations of God. Two works in

particular are generally classified as *Itihasas*: the *Ramayana* ("The Deeds of Rama") and the *Mahabharata*, of which the *Bhagavadgita* is a part. See Sharma, "Hinduism," 29–30.

25. Sharma, "Hinduism," 27.

26. Sharma, "Hinduism," 27.

27. Klostermaier, *A Survey of Hinduism*, 67.

28. Gerald Larson, "Hinduism in India and in America," in Jacob Neusner (ed.), *World Religions in America* (Louisville, KY: Westminster/John Knox Press, 1994), 185–186.

29. Zaehner, *Hinduism*, 15–16.

30. Cross, *The Elements of Hinduism*, 12.

31. Victoria Fromkin and Robert Rodman, *An Introduction to Language*, 2nd ed. (New York: Holt, Rinehart, and Winston, 1978), 295–296. See also Leonard Bloomfield, "Language," in O. L. Chavarria-Aguilar (ed.), *Traditional India* (Englewood Cliffs, NJ: Prentice-Hall, 1964), 112–113.

32. Quoted in Larson, "Hinduism in India and in America," 197. For an extensive presentation of contemporary Hindu beliefs, see Satguru Sivaya Subramuniyaswami, *Dancing with Siva: Hinduism's Contemporary Catechism* (Concord, CA: Himalayan Academy, 1993); also of interest here is Bansi Pandit, *The Hindu Mind: Fundamentals of Hindu Religion and Philosophy for All Ages*, 2nd ed. (Glen Ellyn, IL: B & V Enterprises, 1993).

33. Fisher, *Living Religions*, 68; Cross, *The Elements of Hinduism*, 15–16; Madeleine Biardeau, *Hinduism: The Anthropology of a Civilization* (Delhi: Oxford University Press, 1994), 45.

34. Cross, *The Elements of Hinduism*, 16; see also Sen, *Hinduism*, 27–31.

35. Cross, *The Elements of Hinduism*, 16; see also Sen, *Hinduism*, 27–31.

36. Cross, *The Elements of Hinduism*, 16; see also Sen, *Hinduism*, 27–31.

37. Larson, "Hinduism in India and in America," 189; Sharma, "Hinduism," 24; Biardeau, *Hinduism*, 41–68.

38. Larson, "Hinduism in India and in America," 189; Sharma, "Hinduism," 24; Biardeau, *Hinduism*, 41–68.

39. Larson, "Hinduism in India and in America," 189. See also Patrick Olivelle, *The Ashrama System: The History and Hermaneutics of a Religious Institution* (New York: Oxford University Press, 1993).

40. See Organ, *The Hindu Quest for the Perfection of Man*.

41. Organ, *The Hindu Quest for the Perfection of Man*, 173.

42. Organ, *The Hindu Quest for the Perfection of Man*, 47.

43. Klostermaier, *A Survey of Hinduism*, 69–70.

44. Organ, *The Hindu Quest for the Perfection of Man*, 47.

45. Organ, *The Hindu Quest for the Perfection of Man*, 48.

46. Organ, *The Hindu Quest for the Perfection of Man*, 48–49.

47. Klostermaier, *A Survey of Hinduism*, 69–70.

48. Organ, *The Hindu Quest for the Perfection of Man*, 49.

49. Organ, *The Hindu Quest for the Perfection of Man*, 49.

50. Organ, *The Hindu Quest for the Perfection of Man*, 50.

51. Radha Mookerji, *Ancient Indian Education* (Delhi: Motilal Banarsidass, 1969), XXIII.

52. Mookerji, *Ancient Indian Education*, XXIII–XXIV.

53. Mookerji, *Ancient Indian Education*, XXIII–XXIV.

54. Mookerji, *Ancient Indian Education*, XXXI–XXXIII.

55. Benjamin Walker, *The Hindu World: An Encyclopedic Survey of Hinduism*, Vol. 1 (New York: Praeger, 1968), 320.

56. Sures Banerji, *Society in Ancient India: Evolution Since the Vedic Times Based on Sanskrit, Pali, Prakrit and Other Classical Sources* (New Delhi: D. K. Printworld, 1993), 228–229.

57. For discussions of the role and place of women in Hindu society, see Julia Leslie (ed.), *Roles and Rituals for Hindu Women* (Rutherford, NJ: Fairleigh Dickinson University Press, 1991). Also of interest here is C. J. Fuller's *The Camphor Flame: Popular Hinduism and Society in India* (Princeton, NJ: Princeton University Press, 1992), 182–203 and A. L. Basham's *The Origins and Development of Classical Hinduism* (Boston: Beacon Press, 1989), 104–106.

58. Walker, *The Hindu World*, 320; Mookerji, *Ancient Indian Education*, 173.

59. Mookerji, *Ancient Indian Education*, 174–175; see also David Miller and Dorothy Wertz, *Hindu Monastic Life and the Monks and Monasteries of Bhubaneswar* (Montreal: McGill-Queen's University Press, 1976), 3.

60. Walker, *The Hindu World*, 320–321.

61. Walker, *The Hindu World*, 321.

62. Walker, *The Hindu World*, 321.

63. Walker, *The Hindu World*, 321.

64. Mookerji, *Ancient Indian Education*, 366.

65. See Mookerji, *Ancient Indian Education*, 366–373; Walker, *The Hindu World*, 322.

66. See Sushila Raval, *Basic Education in Modern India: A Critique of Gandhian Educational Philosophy* (MA thesis, The American University, 1958), 2–8.

7

The Buddhist
Educational Tradition

Buddhism emerged in India during the period between the 7th and 5th centuries B.C., which was a time of intense intellectual ferment in the subcontinent.[1] Developing in the context of classical Hinduism, Buddhism shared many common ideas and themes with Hinduism, even as it seems to have diverged from the Hindu tradition in significant ways.[2] Nonetheless, the distinction between Hinduism and Buddhism is often a difficult one to articulate in practice. As Ananda Coomaraswamy wrote in his comparative study of the two religions:

> The more superficially one studies Buddhism, the more it seems to differ from the Brahmanism in which it originated; the more profound our study, the more difficult it becomes to distinguish Buddhism from Brahmanism, or to say in what respects, if any, Buddhism is really unorthodox. The outstanding distinction lies in the fact that Buddhist doctrine is propounded by an apparently historical founder. . . . Beyond this there are only broad distinctions of emphasis.[3]

As this passage suggests, the obvious starting point in trying to understand Buddhism is with its founder, the Buddha ("the Awakened One"). As Noble Ross Reat wrote in his book *Buddhism: A History*:

> Given his enormous historical significance, remarkably few Westerners are even vaguely acquainted with the Buddha or the religion he founded. . . . In terms of influence upon human history, the Buddha can be compared with only two historical individuals: Jesus and Muhammad, the founders of Christianity and Islam. As with Jesus and Muhammad, little is known of the early life of the Buddha, but in his later years as a teacher he stands out as one of the first figures ever to be recorded in history as a real, recognizable human personality rather than as a two-dimensional character in a mythologized narrative. In this sense, he is comparable to the Greek philosopher Socrates (5th century B.C.) and to some of the figures in the *Hebrew Bible* or *Old Testament.*[4]

The man who became the Buddha was born in the village of Lumbini, in what is today southern Nepal, and the most common dates for his life are 563 to 483 B.C. (although Chinese sources give the significantly later dates of roughly 445 to 365 B.C.).[5] His name was Siddhattha Gotama (also commonly written Gautama) and, as a prince, he was born into a life of privilege and comfort. However, he was a sensitive youth, concerned about human suffering around him, and so gave up his privileged life to become a wandering "seeker of truth." He studied meditation, and ultimately, at the age of 35, achieved what is known in Buddhism as the *Great Enlightenment* one night while sitting under the Bodhi tree (the "tree of enlightenment").[6] The "awakening" achieved by the Buddha, which can be achieved by others as well, is both difficult to attain and to describe. As Reat noted, "Buddhist doctrine emphasizes that the specific content of the Buddha's experience on the night of enlightenment—or the equivalent experience of an *arahat* [one who has achieved the awakening]—can never be conveyed by mere words."[7] In general terms, however, the Buddha is said to have experienced what are called the "three knowledges": "remembrance of his past rebirths in detail, ability to discern the past and future rebirths of other beings, and knowledge that he himself was free of all faults and illusions and would therefore never be reborn again. The "third knowledge" is synonymous with the realization of nirvana."[8]

Although originating in India, Buddhism spread through Asia and has come to be identified more with other countries than with India itself. Buddhism remains the dominant religious tradition in Tibet, Sri Lanka, and Thailand, and has had a powerful impact both culturally and religiously in a number of other societies, including those of China, Korea, and Japan (see Fig. 7.1).[9] There are, as a consequence, many varieties and forms of Buddhism that coexist, both with each other and with other religious traditions.[10] As Malcolm Eckel noted,

FIG. 7.1. The spread of Buddhism [From Mary Pat Fisher, *Living Religions*, 2nd ed. (Englewood Cliffs, NJ: Prentice-Hall, 1994), p. 122]. Reprinted with permission.

If you have never thought of religion without thinking of God, or if you think that a religion has to have clear boundaries that separate insiders from outsiders, you will be intrigued and challenged by your encounter with Buddhism. For over two thousand years in Asia, and more recently in Europe and North America, the Buddhist tradition has brought joy, consolation, and meaning to human life without affirming the existence of a personal God, and it has found ways to exist side by side with other religious traditions without many of the great conflicts that have plagued religious life in the West.[11]

We turn now to an exploration of this intriguing and challenging religious tradition, focusing on the two major streams of Buddhism—Theravada and Mahayana Buddhism—and then moving on to a discussion of traditional Buddhist educational thought and practice.

AN OVERVIEW OF BUDDHISM

The core of Buddhism is expressed in what is called the *Triple Refuge* (*trisharana*), which is the basic profession of faith for the Buddhist. Every Buddhist recites the Triple Refuge (which is also sometimes called the *Three Jewels* or the *Three Treasures*) daily, and one becomes a Buddhist by reciting it three times. The Triple Refuge is as follows: "I go to refuge to the Buddha; I go for refuge to the Doctrine (*Dharma*); I go for refuge to the community (*Sangha*)."[12] Included in the Triple Refuge, then, are the place of the Buddha himself, the place of his teachings, and the role of the Buddhist community. We have already briefly discussed the Buddha, and so we now turn to the teachings of Buddhism.

Buddhism is, at its core, arguably less concerned with metaphysical and theological matters than with psychological ones.[13] The teachings of the Buddha are all basically concerned with human suffering and achieving freedom from that suffering.[14] Summarized in the "Four Noble Truths," which are common to all of the different types of Buddhism, the teachings of the Buddha include the ideas that:

1. Human life inevitably involves suffering (*dukkha*),
2. Suffering arises from our desires (*samudaya*),
3. There is a state of being in which there is no suffering (*nirodha*),
4. There is a way to achieve this state of being (*marga*).[15]

The way to achieve this state of being free from suffering is a systematic approach taught by the Buddha called the *Eightfold Path of Liberation*. As Mary Pat Fisher explained, "The Eightfold Path offers ways to burn up all past demerits, avoid accumulating new demerits, and build up merit for a favorable rebirth. Perfection of the path means final escape from the cycle of death and rebirth, into the peace of Nirvana."[16] The eight factors that comprise the

"Eightfold Path" can be divided into three broad categories (known as *khandha*, or *pillars*), dealing respectively with wisdom (*panna*), ethics (*sila*), and meditation (*samadhi*).[17] The particular factors included in each of these three broad categories are discussed briefly next.

Wisdom

The factors included in this category include right understanding (*samma-ditthi*) and right intention (*samma-sankappa*). Right understanding refers to making sense of the world and questioning one's assumptions within the framework provided by the "Four Noble Truths." Right intention in essence involves the application of right understanding in one's life, and constitutes the core of Buddhist morality. Specifically, right intention includes renunciation (*nekkhama*), benevolence (*avyapada*), and nonviolence (*avihimsa*).[18]

Ethics

This category is concerned with conduct and the rules that underlie appropriate conduct. Taken as a whole, they seek to ensure that one's conduct is harmful neither to oneself nor to others. Specifically, the factors included here are right speech (*samma-vacha*), right action (*samma-kammanta*), and right livelihood (*samma-ajiva*). Right speech focuses on the need to avoid gossip, lying, slander, and other kinds of idle or hurtful language. Right action involves what are known as the "five precepts" (*sikkha-pada*) in Buddhism, which include the avoidance of violence toward any living thing, stealing, harmful speech, sexual misconduct, and abuse of drugs and alcohol.[19] Right livelihood refers to the need to ensure that one's way of earning a living in no way violates any of the "five precepts."[20]

Meditation

The final three factors in the "Eightfold Path" are right effort (*samma-yayama*), right self-possession or mindfulness (*samma-sati*), and right meditation (*samma-samadhi*). These three factors are all very closely related, and basically involve "the cultivation of the wholesome (*kusala*) and rejection of the unwholesome (*akusala*)." They involve continuous striving to reject unwholesome states of mind, and to develop the mental quietness that leads to liberation.[21]

The ultimate goal of the "Eightfold Path," as suggested here, is to avoid the ongoing cycle of death and rebirth, and to achieve Nirvana. This is done by leading a passion-free existence that has no karmic consequences, as is suggested by the term *Nirvana* itself, which actually refers to "the extinguishing of a flame from lack of fuel."[22]

For Westerners, one of the more puzzling aspects of Buddhism is its lack of concern for or interest in a personal God. Melford Spiro, for example, in his book *Buddhism and Society*, commented that:

> Buddhism is a religion without a God. Just as the body has no soul which guides and directs its action, so the universe has no Creator who brought it into being, who guides its course, or who presides over the destiny of man. More important, there is no Being—no savior God—to whom man can turn for salvation. Each man, as it were, must save himself.[23]

Having said this, it is important to note that the Buddha did not actually deny the existence of God. Rather, the Buddha argued that: "curiosity about such matters was like a man who, upon being wounded by a poisoned arrow, refused to have it pulled out until he was told the caste and origin of his assailant, his name, his height, the color of his skin, and all details about the bow and arrow. In the meantime, he died."[24]

In other words, for Buddhism "speculations concerning the origin of the Universe are held to be immaterial. . . . They are not merely a waste of time but they may also postpone deliverance from suffering by engendering ill-will in oneself and in others."[25] In short, Buddhism is best understood simply as a "nontheistic" religion that does not, like other religions, presuppose the existence of a personal God.[26] Furthermore, although the monotheistic religions with which most of us are most familiar identify God with supreme good, for Buddhism it is emptiness—that is, the absence of both good and evil—that is the ultimate goal.[27] As Masao Abe explained:

> [Buddhism] overcomes all duality completely and attains a nondualistic position. This means that both ends of duality, for instance good and evil, are equally overcome through the double negation of the two ends—i.e., good and evil. This double negation of both ends of duality does not entail the supreme good, but that which is neither good nor evil. This is the reason why in Buddhism ultimate reality is not God as the supreme good, but Emptiness, which is neither good nor evil. . . . Buddhism *completely* overcomes the duality of value judgment in the axiological dimension through the negation of negation, and thus reaches the religious dimension, which is entirely free from even the notion of absolute good.[28]

For the most part, the beliefs discussed thus far are common to all Buddhists. Within Buddhism, however, there coexist a number of different schools of thought. The two most important of these schools of thought are those of Theravada Buddhism and Mahayana Buddhism. The distinction between Theravada Buddhism and Mahayana Buddhism is one of both geography and emphasis. *Theravada Buddhism*, which emphasizes the original Buddhist scriptural tradition (hence its name, which means "Teaching of the Elders"), is sometimes called the Southern School because it is found primarily in the south Asian countries (Sri Lanka, Myanmar, Thailand, Kampuchea, and

Laos). *Mahayana Buddhism* is, on the other hand, known as the Northern School, and is the kind of Buddhism found in Nepal, Tibet, China, Korea, Mongolia and Japan. Theravada Buddhism is a somewhat more austere kind of Buddhism and involves an emphasis not only on the early Buddhist scriptures but also on the monastic life, whereas Mahayana Buddhism accepts a wider variety of scriptural traditions and gives greater freedom in terms of devotional and metaphysical beliefs and practices than does Theravada Buddhism, which tends to be more uniform.[29] At heart, however, there is an essential unity in Buddhism, as Edward Conze explained:

> Throughout its history, Buddhism has the unity of an *organism*, in that each new development takes place in continuity from the previous one. Nothing could look more different from a tadpole than a frog, and yet they are stages of the same animal, and evolve continuously from each other. The Buddhist capacity for metamorphosis must astound those who only see the end-products separated by long intervals of time, as different as chrysalis and butterfly. In fact they are connected by many gradations, which lead from one to the other, and which only close study can detect. There is in Buddhism really no innovation, but what seems so is in fact a subtle adaptation of pre-existing ideas.[30]

This essential unity includes not only Theravada Buddhism and Mahayana Buddhism, but also Tibetan Buddhism (which is actually a distinctive branch of Mahayana Buddhism) and Zen Buddhism, as well as the many different varieties of each that have developed in different social and cultural contexts.[31] With this brief introduction to Buddhism in mind, we turn now to a discussion of the educational thought and practice associated with Buddhism.

TRADITIONAL BUDDHIST EDUCATIONAL THOUGHT AND PRACTICE

Education in traditional Buddhism, at least in a formal sense, existed almost exclusively within the context of the monastery, both in terms of secular and religious education. As Radha Mookerji noted in his book *Ancient Indian Education:*

> The history of the Buddhist system of education is practically that of the Buddhist Order or *Sangha.* Buddhist education and learning centred round monasteries . . . The Buddhist world did not offer any educational opportunities apart from or independently of its monasteries. All education, sacred as well as secular, was in the hands of the monks. They had the monopoly of learning and the leisure to impart it.[32]

In other words, our discussion of traditional Buddhist educational thought and practice brings us back to the final element of the Triple Refuge: the religious (i.e., monastic) community. As Heinrich Dumoulin observed:

> Taking refuge in the *sangha* is an essential co-condition of the other two refuges. From its beginnings, the Buddhist religion confronts us as a communal, and specifically as a monastic formation. . . . Though Buddhism has not yet developed a theology of community, it is clear that Buddhist faith has an essential communal dimension.[33]

The fact that traditional education was controlled by the *sangha*, however, in no way means that it was jealously guarded or hidden; indeed, quite the reverse is true. Buddhist monasteries are not separate from the surrounding world. Rather, they are closely tied to the surrounding community in a sort of symbiotic relationship, and monasteries are commonly the center of village life.[34] Furthermore, at least in Theravadin societies, it is quite common for young men to take what are, essentially, temporary vows of monkhood (during, for instance, the rainy season when they are not required for agricultural work).[35]

A number of general themes characterized traditional Buddhist educational practice. Traditional Buddhist education was based on the close, intimate relationship that existed between the student and his teacher, whom he was to serve in much the same way as was expected in Vedic education. The relationship between student and teacher was a reciprocal one, however, and although the obligations of the student to the teacher were substantial, so too were the obligations of the teacher to the student.[36] All students observed the two fundamental principles that demarcate monastic life from that of the laity: celibacy and poverty.[37] Instruction was primarily oral, and was based on a knowledge of the Buddhist scriptural tradition, although an introduction to basic literacy was also provided.

The focus of education was on far more than mere memorization of texts, however. Debate played a central role in the educational process in traditional Buddhism. As Mookerji argued, "Buddhist education made dialectic skill and ability in argumentation a most important part of intellectual equipment essential to leadership."[38] The importance of such skill is made clear in a number of written texts in the Buddhist tradition, one of which, composed around the year 400 A.D., contains a detailed discussion of the subject of debate, the place in which debate should take place, the means by which a debate should be conducted, the qualifications of the debaters, the points of defeat in a debate, the fitness or appropriateness of a debate and, finally, the need for self-confidence in the debater.[39] It is interesting to note here that in a comparative study of traditional and contemporary education in Tibet, David Eckel observed that:

> In the traditional monastery, even with its emphasis on memorization and rote learning, students were required from an early age to defend what they had learned in formal debate. The debating hall was a lonely place, where rank and authority were no help. A student or teacher had to be able to defend his understanding before the whole assembly. It is hard to picture a 12-year-old monk standing up in a doctoral examination to question a scholar more than

twice his age and still think of the traditional system as fostering only the values of dependence and submission. The irony of the Tibetan transition to modern styles of education is that it endangers not only the sense of dependence and respect for tradition, but the formal means for developing a sense of self-reliance and autonomy.[40]

Traditional Buddhist education, in short, involved what would today be called basic schooling for young boys, as well as more advanced education for monks (including a noteworthy university level educational system).[41] For the most part, however, it did not concern itself with the educational needs of girls and women and, although there were notable exceptions (including female monasteries where women were indeed well educated), traditional Buddhism paid relatively little attention to females' education.[42]

CONCLUSION

Given the highly decentralized nature of Buddhist institutions, as well as the tolerance for diversity within the Buddhist tradition, it is hardly surprising that traditional Buddhist education took somewhat different forms in different Buddhist societies. What is remarkable is the degree of uniformity that, in fact, seems to have existed on a number of important points. Perhaps most interesting in this regard is the role of the monastery as the sole educational institution in Buddhist societies, and the reliance on the monasteries for both secular and religious education.[43] Furthemore, it is clear that traditional Buddhist educational thought and practice had a powerful impact on the societies in which they existed, in many instances providing a cultural and intellectual base for the society concerned. This was, for instance, the case in Japan, as B. H. Chamberlain noted: "All education was for centuries in Buddhist hands, Buddhism introduced art, introduced medicine, moulded the folklore of the country, created its dramatic poetry, deeply influenced politics and every sphere of social and intellectual activity. In a word, Buddhism was the teacher under whose instruction the nation grew up."[44]

In short, traditional Buddhist educational thought and practice successfully served a wide array of social, cultural, and spiritual, as well as educational, functions, and did so in ways generally accepted in various Buddhist societies for centuries. This alone would merit our attention.

QUESTIONS FOR REFLECTION AND DISCUSSION

1. The role of the *sangha* in traditional Buddhist education presents an interesting parallel to that of the monastery in medieval Europe. In what ways are the educational undertakings of these two kinds of religious

communities similar and in what ways do they differ? How can the similarities and the differences be explained?

2. Explain the educational significance of each of the three components of the Triple Refuge. How do these three components relate to one another and what are the social and educational implications of these relationships?

3. If the spiritual goal of Buddhism is emptiness, then what purpose does education serve? Why is education needed in the quest for nirvana?

4. Given your own understanding of *religion*, was traditional Buddhist education a religious education? Was it a spiritual education? What, in your view, is the difference between these two kinds of education?

5. What, in your view, were the strengths of traditional Buddhist education? What were its weaknesses? Can you identify any lessons from the study of traditional Buddhist education for contemporary schooling in our own society?

RECOMMENDED FURTHER READINGS

Among the better general introductions to Buddhism that are readily available are Heinrich Dumoulin's *Understanding Buddhism: Key Themes* (New York: Weatherhill, 1994), Nolan Pliny Jacobson's *Understanding Buddhism* (Carbondale: Southern Illinois University Press, 1986), and Nancy Wilson Ross' *Buddhism: A Way of Life and Thought* (New York: Vintage, 1980). An especially powerful contemporary work is Thich Nhat Hanh's *Old Path White Clouds: Walking in the Footsteps of the Buddah* (Berkeley, CA: Parallax, 1991). Also of considerable value is Eric Cheetham, *Fundamentals of Mainstream Buddhism* (Boston: Tuttle, 1994). For an interesting and insightful personal account, see Tenzin Gyatso, *Freedom in Exile: The Autobiography of the Dalai Lama* (New York: Harper Perennial, 1990). Finally, there is a plethora of works readily available that deal explicitly with Zen Buddhism. Good basic introductions to Zen Buddhism include Kazuaki Tanahashi and Tensho David Schneider, *Essential Zen* (San Francisco: HarperCollins, 1994) and David Scott and Tony Doubleday, *The Elements of Zen* (Shaftesbury, Dorset: Element, 1992).

NOTES

1. William T. de Bary (ed.), *The Buddhist Tradition in India, China and Japan* (New York: Modern Library, 1969), 3.

2. See, for example, Amamda Coomaraswamy, Hinduism and Buddhism (Westport, CT: Greenwood, 1971); Roderick Hindery, *Comparative Ethics in Hindu and Buddhist Traditions* (Delhi: Motilal Banarsidass, 1978); Bansi

Pandit, *The Hindu Mind: Fundamentals of Hindu Religion and Philosophy for All Ages*, 2nd ed. (Glen Ellyn, IL: B & V Enterprises, 1993), 85–86.

3. Coomaraswamy, *Hinduism and Buddhism*, 45.

4. Noble Ross Reat, *Buddhism: A History* (Berkeley, CA: Asian Humanities Press, 1994), 1.

5. Reat, *Buddhism*, 1–2; see also Mary Pat Fisher, *Living Religions*, 2nd ed. (Englewood Cliffs, NJ: Prentice-Hall, 1994), 113.

6. See David Kalupahana, *A History of Buddhist Philosophy: Continuities and Discontinuities* (Honolulu: University of Hawaii Press, 1992), 22–29; Fisher, *Living Religions*, 114.

7. Reat, *Buddhism*, 12.

8. Reat, *Buddhism*, 12.

9. Malcolm Eckel, "Buddhism in the World and in America," in Jacob Neusner (ed.), *World Religions in America: An Introduction* (Louisville, KY: Westminster/John Knox Press, 1994), 203.

10. See John Snelling, *The Buddhist Handbook: A Complete Guide to Buddhist Schools, Teaching, Practice, and History* (Rochester, VT: Inner Traditions, 1991), 103–189; Masao Abe, "Buddhism," in Arvind Sharma (ed.), *Our Religions* (San Francisco: Harper, 1993), 85–100.

11. Eckel, "Buddhism in the World and in America," 203.

12. Abe, "Buddhism," 73–74.

13. de Bary, *The Buddhist Tradition in India, China and Japan*, 9.

14. Melford Spiro, *Buddhism and Society* (New York: Harper & Row, 1970), 38–39; see also Hindery, *Comparative Ethics in Hindu and Buddhist Traditions*, 226–228.

15. Fisher, *Living Religions*, 116; Abe, "Buddhism," 86; Heinrich Dumoulin, *Understanding Buddhism: Key Themes* (New York: Weatherhill, 1994), 21–24; Snelling, *The Buddhist Handbook*, 43–46.

16. Fisher, *Living Religions*, 117.

17. Reat, *Buddhism*, 40; see also A. K. Warder, *Indian Buddhism* (Delhi: Motilal Banarsidass, 1970), 100–106.

18. Reat, *Buddhism*, 40–41; Fisher, *Living Religions*, 117–118.

19. See Edward Conze (trans.), *Buddhist Scriptures* (Harmondsworth: Penguin, 1959), 69–73.

20. Reat, *Buddhism*, 41–42; Fisher, *Living Religions*, 117.

21. Reat, *Buddhism*, 42; Fisher, *Living Religions*, 118–119.

22. Fisher, *Living Religions*, 120.

23. Spiro, *Buddhism and Society*, 7.

24. Fisher, *Living Religions*, 115.

25. Edward Conze, *Buddhism: Its Essence and Development* (New York: Harper & Row, 1975), 39.

26. Eckel, "Buddhism in the World and in America," 212.

27. The doctrine of emptiness (*sunyata*) is a very important one in Buddhist thought. In actuality, there are two distinct theories of emptiness in Buddhism,

a moderate view and a more extreme view. See Kalupahana, *A History of Buddhist Philosophy*, 130–131; Reat, *Buddhism*, 56–58; Conze, *Buddhism*, 130–135.

28. Abe, "Buddhism, " 119.

29. For discussions of the distinctions between Theravada Buddhism and Mahayana Buddhism, see de Bary, *The Buddhist Tradition in India, China and Japan*; Christmas Humphries, *Buddhism: An Introduction and Guide* (Harmondsworth: Penguin, 1951).

30. Edward Conze, *A Short History of Buddhism* (Bombay: Chetana, 1960), xi—xii.

31. For Tibetan Buddhism, see Emil Schlagintweit, *Buddhism in Tibet*, 2nd ed. (London: Susil Gupta, 1968). For works that deal with Zen Buddhism, see David Scott and Tony Doubleday, *The Elements of Zen* (Sahftsbury, Dorset: Element, 1992); Daisetz Teitaro Suzuki, *An Introduction to Zen Buddhism* (New York: Philosophical Library, 1949); Trevor Leggett (ed.), *Zen and the Ways* (London: Routledge & Kegan Paul, 1978); Kenneth Kraft (ed.), *Zen: Tradition and Transition* (New York: Grove, 1988); Christopher Ives, *Zen Awakening and Society* (Honolulu: University of Hawaii Press, 1992).

32. Radha Mookerji, *Ancient Indian Education* (Delhi: Motilal Banarsidass, 1969), 394.

33. Dumoulin, *Understanding Buddhism*, 56–57.

34. Abe, "Buddhism," 110.

35. Fisher, *Living Religions*, 123.

36. Mookerji, *Ancient Indian Education*, 403–405.

37. Mookerji, *Ancient Indian Education*, 409–412.

38. Mookerji, *Ancient Indian Education*, 454.

39. Mookerji, *Ancient Indian Education*, 454.

40. Quoted in Susan Pollak, *Ancient Buddhist Education (Papers from the Bernard Van Leer Foundation Project on Human Potential)* (Cambridge, MA: Harvard Graduate School of Education, 1983), 18. This publication, available through ERIC, is taken directly from Mookerji's earlier work.

41. Mookerji, *Ancient Indian Education*, 557–610.

42. Mookerji, *Ancient Indian Education*, 462–464. See also Diane Y. Paul, *Women in Buddhism: Images of the Feminine in the Mahayana Tradition* (Berkeley: University of California Press, 1985).

43. Pollak, *Ancient Buddhist Education*, 17.

44. Quoted in Pollak, *Ancient Buddhist Education*, 16–17; see also Alicia Matsunaga, *The Buddhist Philosophy of Assimilation: The Historical Development of the Honji-Suijaku Theory* (Tokyo: Sophia University, 1969).

8

The Islamic
Educational Enterprise

It is, in an important sense, inappropriate for a book concerned with non-Western educational traditions to include a chapter on Islam and the Islamic educational heritage. Islam is one of the world's three great monotheistic religions, along with Judaism and Christianity, and approximately one fifth of the world's population are Muslim. (see Fig. 8.1).[1] More important, Islam as a religion is not independent of the religions of the West in the way that Buddhism and Hinduism are. Rather, Islam is part of what can be termed the *Judeo-Christian-Islamic tradition*, sharing with Judaism and Christianity many core beliefs, ideas, and values.[2] To be sure, the idea that all three religions are part of a single, unified tradition is for some people a problematic one, because just as they share many elements, so too do they disagree about key issues.[3] Nevertheless, historically the three faiths are closely related in ways quite different from their relationships with most other religions. This suggests, of course, that Islam is not really "non-Western" in the way that the other societies and religions we have examined thus far in this book can be said to be. Indeed, much of what we consider to be the basis for the Western tradition from the period of classical antiquity was preserved for us not in the West, but rather by Islamic scholars in the Middle Ages.[4] Why, then, is Islam included in this book?

The answer is a pragmatic and straightforward one. Although Islam may well be closely connected with Judaism and Christianity, it has, throughout Western history, been perceived to be alien and different.[5] This view of Islam as "the other" in our own culture is, in many ways, as powerful today as ever before, encouraged by the resurgence of what has been called "militant Islam."[6] For many in the West, a lack of knowledge about and understanding of Islam is coupled quite closely with a fear and, in some cases, an active dislike for both the faith and its practitioners. In short, although Islam ought not be seen as non-Western, it nevertheless is seen in this light, and so should be treated here if for no other reason than to encourage a more accurate understanding of both Islam and the place of Islam in our own heritage. As John Esposito argued, "A basic knowledge of Islam is becoming essential for

FIG. 8.1. The Islamic World [From John Esposito, Islam: The Straight Path, exp.
and rev. ed. (New York: Oxford University Press, 1991), p. 2].
Reprinted with permission.

every American today. There are five million Muslims living in America. In
fact, Islam is the third largest U.S. religion, and by the year 2010 it is expected
to be second largest . . . Islam, like Judaism and Christianity, is an American
religion."[7]

Furthermore, given the historical relationship between the west and the
Islamic world, one can offer an even stronger case for including the study of
Islamic education in a book of this type. As Carolyn Fluehr-Lobban suggested
in *Islamic Society in Practice*:

> Perhaps if the recent history of the world were different and Western society
> did not have the imperial advantage that it has inherited from the legacy of
> colonialism and economic domination, we might have studies of our culture
> by non-western people. A chapter entitled "Western Values and Social
> Practice" in such a study might include sections on individualism, self-suffi-
> ciency, entrepreneurial spirit, male supremacy, or optimism. The treatise,
> written in Arabic, might be read in translation by some "natives" who think
> it is reductionist and a simplification of their complex, multifaceted social
> reality.[8]

Just as such a chapter might have been written had recent history been different, then, so must a chapter such as this one be included in a book on non-Western educational traditions.

In this chapter, we begin by exploring the basic tenets of Islam as a religion, and then discuss the implications of these tenets for an understanding of what can be called an "Islamic philosophy of education." Finally, we examine the ways in which this Islamic philosophy of education has been manifested in traditional Islamic education practice.

ISLAM: AN OVERVIEW

Discussions of Islam intended for non-Muslims often begin with Muhammad, but this is perhaps misleading. The word *Islam* actually means "submission," as in "submission to the will of God," and the real focus of Islam is not Muhammad, but rather, Allah (God).[9] Muhammad is important both in his role as God's Prophet (as God's messenger bringing the word of God to humanity), and as an example of how a Muslim should seek to lead his life. As Mary Pat Fisher explained, "Muhammad's life story is important to Muslims, for his example is considered a key that opens the door to the Divine Presence."[10] Nevertheless, Muhammad was a man, the last prophet (*nabi*) in a long series of prophets sent by God to reveal His will—a series of prophets that included Adam, Abraham, Noah, Moses, and Jesus, among others.[11] Islam, however, is far more than its messenger. With this in mind, we turn now to a brief account of the life of Muhammad.

The Life of Muhammad

Muhammad was born in 569 or 570 A.D. in the Arabian city of Mecca. His father had died before his birth and his mother died when he was still quite young. He was initially cared for by his impoverished grandfather, but his grandfather died when Muhammad was only 8 years old. The boy was then raised by an uncle, Abu Talib, working first as a shepherd and later accompanying his uncle on caravan trade missions. As a young adult, Muhammad was well known in Mecca for his spirituality and his honesty. He was hired by a wealthy widow, Khadijah, who eventually married him.[12]

From the age of 35 on, Muhammad often spent time alone in spiritual retreats in order to engage in prayer and meditation.[13] At the age of 40, during one of these retreats, the angel Gabriel appeared to him and told him that God had chosen him to be His messenger to all mankind. The angel insisted that Muhammad recite what he was told, and it was in this way that what we now know as the *Qur'an* was transmitted from Gabriel through Muhammad to humanity. Three years later, after a pause during which Muhammad continued to pray and meditate, Gabriel appeared again to Muhammad and commanded him to begin publicly proclaiming God's revelation. His message was simple and clear: "the belief in One Transcendent God, in Resurrection and the Last Judgment."[14] His message was a profoundly moral one, grounded in the revelations he was receiving from God—revelations that continued throughout his life and that his followers were expected to learn by heart. It was also a message that contained hope for the oppressed, which helps to explain both the historical and contemporary power of Islam in many parts of the world.

Muhammad and his followers were persecuted by the Meccan leaders who saw Muhammad as a social and political revolutionary, threatening the status quo, much as Jesus had been seen in his time. This led, in the year 622 A.D., to Muhammad's departure from Mecca to the more welcoming town of Yathrib (now Medina), where he established the first Muslim community.[15] This event, called the *hijrah* ("migration"), was a crucial one in the development of Islam, and it is from the date of the *hijrah*—not that of Muhammad's birth, or even of the first appearance of Gabriel to Muhammad—that the Muslim calendar begins. Ultimately, in 630 A.D., Muhammad and his followers returned triumphantly to Mecca and then onward to Northern Africa, the Persian states, and beyond.

The Central Beliefs of Islam

For Islam, there is a close interrelationship between belief and practice, and the distinction between being a believer (*mu'min*) and an unbeliever (*kafir*) is to a significant extent based on one's practice.[16] This is so because the basic beliefs of Islam in large part presume certain practices, as we see later in this chapter. Having said this, it is nonetheless possible for us to delineate the beliefs that are at the core of the Islamic worldview. These core beliefs of Islam are identified clearly in the *Qur'an* itself: "The Prophet believes in what has been revealed to him from his Lord, and so do the Believers. They all believe in God, His angels, His scriptures and His messengers, making no distinction among His prophets. And they say, 'We hear and we obey. Grant us Thy forgiveness, our Lord, and unto Thee is the journeying'" (Sura 2: 285).

As these core beliefs are discussed, it is important to keep in mind the following warning from Suzanne Haneef: "the principles on which the Islamic systems are based are constant, unalterable and universal ones originating in Divine revelation. However, the details of their application may certainly be adjusted as necessary within the Islamic framework to fit existing needs and circumstances."[17] In other words, although the core beliefs may be the same, the ways in which they will be manifested in practice may differ in various social and cultural contexts.[18]

The most fundamental belief of Islam is in the unity and Oneness of God. From a Muslim point of view, "the Oneness of God is the primordial religion taught by all prophets of all faiths. Muhammad merely served to remind people of it."[19] In Arabic, the concept of the unity of God is expressed in the term *tawhid*, which Khurshid Ahmad explains as follows: "*Tawhid* is a revolutionary concept and constitutes the essence of the teachings of Islam. It means that there is only One Supreme Lord of the universe. He is Omnipotent, Omnipresent and the Sustainer of the world and of mankind."[20]

Islam, as noted earlier, teaches that God has sent a series of prophets to mankind—in fact, according to a saying of Muhammad, there have been some 124,000 prophets, beginning with Adam.[21] Before Muhammad, each prophet was sent to renew the message of God's Oneness and unity to a particular people.[22] Only Muhammad, however, "was entrusted with the final and complete statement of God's guidance for the whole of humanity for all time to come."[23] Because of his special role, Muhammad is called the "Seal of the Prophets" in the *Qur'an*, and is believed by Muslims to be the last and final authority in the prophetic tradition.[24]

Two Islamic beliefs that are closely related to the role of the prophetic tradition are the belief in angels and the role of revealed Scriptures. It was the angel Gabriel who appeared to Muhammad, and this was necessary, as Haneef explained:

> Because the glory and majesty of the Creator is so awesome and overwhelming that a limited, flesh-and-blood human being is unable to bear direct contact with Him, God chose to convey His revelation to the prophets, including Muhammad . . . through the agency of an angel. . . . It is because of this vital role of angels as bringers of the Divine revelation to the prophets that belief in them is so important as to form a fundamental article of faith in Islam.[25]

Many of the prophets were also messengers (*rasul*), which is to say that the revelation they left was in written form. Thus, Islam accepts both the Hebrew Torah and the Christian Gospels as revealed scripture, and Jews and Christians are both recognized in Islam as "people of the Book" (*ahl al-kitab*).[26] The status of the *Qur'an*, however, is somewhat different than that of other scripture, as we see later in this chapter. For now, it is sufficient to note that for a Muslim, the "*Qur'an* is the only divinely-revealed scripture in the history of mankind which has been preserved to the present time in its exact original form."[27]

Finally, Muslims believe in both an afterlife and in a "Last Judgment" at which each person will have to answer for his or her sins. As stipulated in the *Qur'an*, "The works of each person We have bound about his neck. On the Day of Resurrection, We shall confront him with a book spread wide open, saying, 'Read your book. Enough for you this day that your own soul should call you to account'" (Sura 17: 13–14).

Islam teaches that there will be a physical, bodily resurrection, followed by either eternal paradise or eternal punishment, depending on God's judgment. Much has been made by writers about the descriptions of paradise found in the *Qur'an*, which emphasize physical and material pleasures. As John Esposito, using the *Qur'an* as his source, described it, the "Garden of Paradise is a heavenly mansion of perpetual peace and bliss with flowing rivers, beautiful gardens, and the enjoyment of one's spouses and beautiful, dark-eyed female companions."[28] Granting that such descriptions are indeed to be found in the Qur'an, Hamidullah compellingly pointed out that:

> All this is easily explained when one thinks of the vast majority of men, of the common masses, to whom the Divine message is addressed. It is necessary to speak to every one according to his capacity of understanding and of intelligence. . . . The Qur'an speaks of Paradise and Hell simply as a means of persuading the average man to lead a just life and to march in the path of truth; it attaches no importance to details whether they describe a place or a state of things. . . .[29]

We turn now to a discussion of how these different core beliefs of Islam are manifested in practice in the lives of Muslims.

The Five Pillars of Islam

Although there is a great deal of diversity in the Islamic world with respect to religious practice, there are a core of practices that are shared by all Muslims. Specifically, there are five essential practices, commonly called the *pillars of Islam*, that are universally accepted throughout the Islamic world.[30] These five pillars of Islam are:

1. The profession of faith,
2. Prayer,
3. Almsgiving,
4. Fasting,
5. The pilgrimage to Mecca.[31]

The *profession of faith* (or *shahadah*, literally "witness" or "testimony") refers to the obligation of the Muslim to declare his or her faith that "There is no god but Allah, and Muhammad is His Prophet" ("*La ilaha illa Allah, Muhammadu Rasul Allah*" in Arabic).[32] In other words, the believer accepts the absolute monotheism of Islam, the oneness and unity (*tawhid*) of God, and accepts Muhammad as God's final messenger to humanity. Furthermore, this implies that one accepts the obligation to inform others of the faith, although the Qur'an explicitly rejects the use of coercion in such efforts: "Let there be no compulsion in religion; truth stands out clear from error: whoever rejects evil and believes in God has grasped the most trustworthy handle, that never breaks" (Sura 2: 256).

The second pillar of Islam is prayer (*salah*); Muslims pray five times a day, at daybreak, noon, midafternoon, sunset, and evening.[33] Prayer is preceded by ritual ablutions (*wudu'*), normally done with water, which help to prepare the individual for worship. The Muslim then faces Mecca and recites a series of prayers and Qur'anic passages. On Fridays, the noon prayer is a congregational one, led by a religious leader (called an *imam*). Prayer is, thus, both an individual and a communal obligation for the Muslim.

Almsgiving (*zakah*) "is an act both of worship or thanksgiving to God and of service to the community."[34] Although the basic goal of almsgiving is to redress economic inequities and to support the poor, it is not charity in that it is obligatory rather than voluntary.[35] Muslims are required to donate at least 2½% of their income in this manner,[36] and the funds are used both for the poor (including widows and orphans) and for the spread of the faith (which includes support for religious and educational institutions). This emphasis on the obligation to help those in need is one that occurs repeatedly in the *Qur'an*: "Who denies religion? It is the person who repulses the orphan and does not promote feeding the poor. Woe to those who worship but are neglectful, those who want to be noticed but who withhold assistance from those in need" (Sura 107: 1–7).

Once each year, during the entire month of Ramadan, all adult Muslims who are able are required to fast (*sawm*) from sunrise to sunset.[37] During the fast, Muslims must abstain from food, drink, smoking, and sexual activity. This is a time for reflection and self-discipline, and "a time to thank God for His blessings, repent and atone for one's sins, discipline the body and strengthen moral character, remember one's ultimate dependence on God, and respond to the needs of the poor and hungry."[38] The fifth pillar of Islam is the pilgrimage (*hajj*) to Mecca.[39] All Muslims who can possibly do so are expected to make the pilgrimage at least once in their lifetime. The *hajj*:

> constitutes a form of worship with the totality of the Muslim's being: with his body, mind and soul, with his time, possessions and the temporary sacrifice of all ordinary comforts, conveniences and tokens of status and individuality which human beings normally enjoy, to assume for a few days the condition of a pilgrim totally at God's service and disposal, His slave who seeks only His pleasure.[40]

Underlying all five of the pillars of Islam is the unity of belief and practice, as well as the idea that Islam is not simply a body of religious beliefs but is, rather, a unified and consistent way of life for both the individual and the community.[41] *Shari'a*, or Islamic religious law, provides the framework within which Islamic communities should exist, thus ensuring consistency with the mandates of the *Qur'an*.[42] As Ghulam Sarwar explained:

> Islam is a complete way of life. It is the guidance provided by Allah, the Creator of the Universe, for all mankind. It covers all the things people do in their lifetime. Islam tells us the purpose of our creation, our final destiny and our place among other creatures. It shows us the best way to conduct our private, social, political, economic, moral and spiritual affairs.[43]

One of the more controversial aspects of Islam has been the role and place of women in society, and this is an area about which there is considerable debate in the West and in many contemporary Islamic societies.[44] There can be little doubt that in the time of the Prophet the status of women was improved markedly by Islam, and women are indeed accorded important rights and privileges by *shari'a*.[45] Islamic law grants women the right to enter into contracts, to earn money, and to possess goods in their own right, as well as ensuring their right to inherit.[46] Even more important for our concerns here, women are: "equal to [men] in the pursuit of education and knowledge. When Islam enjoins the seeking of knowledge upon Muslims, it makes no distinction between man and woman. Almost fourteen centuries ago, Muhammad declared that the pursuit of knowledge is incumbent on every Muslim male and female."[47]

There are, however, significant distinctions in the rights, duties, and responsibilities of men and women. The distinctions in treatment between them are argued to be manifestations of the different natures of the two genders, and it is commonly asserted that men and women are indeed equal in Islam, but they are not the same, and that Islam therefore accords them appropriately different social positions and responsibilities.[48] As David Waines explained the "Islamic feminist" view:

> Women have the right to education, to religious instruction, to honor and respect, to the vote, and to employment. There are, however, restrictions sanctioned by the religious law for the welfare and stability of society as a whole. A woman can be neither a political leader nor a judge; she must only appear in public modestly dressed, and her natural and sacred task is to keep the household smoothly functioning and to raise and instruct her children to be good Muslims. Men, for their part, must shoulder the burden of providing for the family in material ways. Liberation for a woman does not mean being like a male, or taking up male tasks, but rather being herself and fulfilling the destiny Allah created for her.[49]

In short, both with respect to the role of women and in terms of other aspects of social organization, Islam provides far more than a framework for social organization; it is a total, comprehensive way of life[50] in which religion is integral to economics,[51] politics,[52] law, and society.[53]

The Role of the Qur'an

An understanding of Islam is possible only with an understanding of the *Qur'an*, which holds a unique place in Islam. Although both Judaism and Christianity have scriptural traditions that include sacred texts, these texts are viewed by most believers in a way quite different from the view of the *Qur'an* in Islamic thought. The *Qur'an* is not the "inspired" Word of God, nor is it a record of what was reported to have been told to Muhammad. Rather, for the Muslim, the *Qur'an* is the exact, literal transcription of the words of God Himself, precisely as they were given to Muhammad. In other words, the *Qur'an* is "the unadulterated word of God, which has become audible through Muhammad."[54] As Suzanne Haneef, writing as a Muslim herself, commented, "The Holy *Qur'an* is the only divinely-revealed scripture in the history of mankind which has been preserved to the present time in its exact original form."[55] This means, of course, that because the Qur'an was revealed in Arabic, it was spoken by God in Arabic, and should, therefore, only be read and recited in that language: "To recite the Qur'an is the most sublime and edifying occupation for the Muslim, even when he or she does not intellectually understand its words, as is the case with most non-Arab believers. Since the Qur'an is the Divine Word *par excellence*, Muslims consider it inconceivable to "translate" it into any language."[56]

Nor is the Qur'an merely written in Arabic; the Arabic in which it is composed is believed by Muslims to be "inimitable and of superhuman beauty and power."[57] Not only do Muslims believe that it is impossible to match the beauty of the style of the Qur'an, but they use this style as compelling evidence for its divine origin.[58] Because Muhammad was illiterate, and because the records we have in the *Hadith* ("Traditions of the Prophet") of his speech makes clear that he spoke in a language quite different than that of the Qur'an, it follows that he was, as he claimed, only the means of transmission for the Qur'an.[59] Therefore, it makes no sense to talk meaningfully about an English language Qur'an, nor can one really talk about a translation into English of the Qur'an. Instead, for Muslims, English language translations are best discussed as "interpretations" of the Qur'an. As Haneef explained:

> Because of its extremely distinctive style and language, it is impossible for a translation to do more than convey its bare meaning. The great nobility of its form of expression, the earnest, moving, eloquent style which is its outstanding characteristic, cannot be translated, and hence any translation must be regarded (as all translators themselves confirm) as a mere approximation to the sense of the words.[60]

Finally, unlike both Jewish and Christian scriptures, which were in the most part created as written texts, the Qur'an is, in essence, an oral text preserved in written form—in fact, the word itself is often translated, "the Recitation." The oral nature of the Qur'an is reinforced by the inclusion of Qur'anic passages in daily prayers and by the emphasis placed on its recitation by Muslims.[61]

This understanding of the nature of the Qur'an, of course, has important educational implications for the Muslim.[62] First, literacy becomes an important religious obligation. Indeed, the name of the Qur'an itself—which can also be translated as "that which is to be read"—entails a challenge to become literate. Muslims the world over not only read the Qur'an, but, regardless of their native language, memorize the Qur'an in Arabic. Thus, the role of Arabic, as the language not only of the Qur'an, but also of Islamic prayer, takes on a great significance for the believer as well. With this background in mind, we turn now to a discussion of what might be termed an *Islamic philosophy of education*.

ISLAMIC PHILOSOPHY OF EDUCATION

Education has, since the time of the Prophet, played a key role in Islam. As A. L. Tibawi commented, "The mosques, became the first schools in Islam [and] it would be equally true to say that the Qur'an was the first textbook."[63] In fact, education from an Islamic point of view makes little sense if one removes it from a religious context, and it is in the Qur'an that educational thought should be grounded.[64] As Abdul-Rahman Salih Abdullah explained:

> Since the Qur'an provides the Muslim with an outlook towards life, its principles must guide Islamic education. One cannot talk about Islamic education without taking the Qur'an as one's starting point . . . the Qur'an lays down the foundation for education aims and methods. Moreover, the Muslim educator will find in the Qur'an the guiding principles which help in selecting the content of the curriculum.[65]

Given the view of the nature of the Qur'an discussed earlier in this chapter, such a view of its centrality for educational thought is hardly surprising. Islamic educational thought, although based on the Qur'an and the Hadith, has, nevertheless, been further developed and articulated by Muslim scholars and educators. Among the best examples of such educational philosophers in the Islamic tradition is the theologian, mystic, and teacher al-Ghazali, about whom Tibawi wrote, "Classical Arabic literature contains no theory of education more authoritative, systematic and comprehensive than had been bequeathed by al-Ghazali."[66] al-Ghazali's philosophy of education provided the bedrock for Islamic educational thought for generations and "practically all educational literature down to the beginning of modernization in the nineteenth century is either inspired by his writings or directly derived from them."[67]

al-Ghazali's view of education was characterized by a deep spirituality coupled with both a good deal of common sense and an obvious concern and affection for children. In essence, al-Ghazali believed that there were two ways in which knowledge might be acquired: through human reason and from "light from God." In a good educational setting, a balance will be achieved between these two, albeit one in which the latter is viewed as of greater significance than the former—a resolution of the faith-reason problem reminiscent of that of Aquinas. Furthermore, al-Ghazali believed that all children have the capacity to learn: "Knowledge exists potentially in the human soul like a seed in the soil; by learning the potential becomes actual."[68] The focus of education for al-Ghazali was largely on what might today be called *moral education* rather than on academic learning alone. As Tibawi explained:

> "The child," [al-Ghazali] wrote, "is a trust [placed by God] in the hands of his parents, and his innocent heart is a precious element capable of taking impressions." If the parents, and later on the teachers, brought him up in righteousness he would live happily in this world and the next and they would be rewarded by God for their good deed. If they neglected the child's upbringing and

education he would lead a life of unhappiness in both worlds and they would bear the burden of the sin of neglect.[69]

It is worth noting here that within an Islamic framework, unlike in Christianity with its doctrine of "original sin," children are believed to have a basically good nature (*fitrah*),[70] and thus the purpose of education is not viewed as one of "correcting" a sinful nature but rather one of guidance—precisely the same goal as of the *Qur'an* itself.[71]

Another Islamic scholar who contributed important insights to the development of an Islamic philosophy of education was the historian Ibn Khaldun. Ibn Khaldun believed that education could only take place in a civilized social order and, like the American philosopher of education John Dewey centuries later, he focused on the social nature of education: "Ibn Khaldun starts from first principles: education is a social phenomenon and teaching is one of the social crafts; man is a social animal and his prosecution of learning is conditioned by the nature of the material, intellectual and spiritual forces of the civilization in which he lives."[72]

Ibn Khaldun, like al-Ghazali before him, also addressed the role of reason in the learning process. It is reason that provides the base for education, on Ibn Khaldun's account. As he himself wrote, "Man is distinguished from animals by a capacity to reason. His reason guides him to make a living, to cooperate with other members of his society and to accept what God has revealed through His prophets for man's welfare in this world and the next. Man is therefore a reasoning animal, and reasoning is the foundation of all learning."[73] The ability to reason is not, however, given equally to all people, and there are innate intellectual differences among people. Furthermore, all learning ultimately rests on divine guidance—Ibn Khaldun recommended that learners "seek God's guidance which had illuminated the way of learners before you and taught them that which they knew not."[74]

It is possible for us to identify some of the broad outlines of an Islamic philosophy of education. Abdul-Rahman Salih Abdullah articulated some of the key elements in such a philosophy of education (although he prefers the term *hikmah*) as follows:

> The Islamic theory of education is fundamentally based upon the *Qur'anic* concepts. In this theory the door is left open for concepts which come from different fields of knowledge provided that they fit the *Qur'anic* perspective. All elements which cannot be reconciled with Islamic principles should be excluded. It has been pointed out that traditional philosophy which gives excessive weight to reason cannot offer any help to our theory.[75]

Islamic philosophy of education recognizes three distinct kinds of educational aims. Specifically, there are physical aims (*ahdaf jismiyyah*), spiritual aims (*ahdaf ruhiyyah*), and mental aims (*ahdaf 'aqliyyah*).[76] In essence, these aims taken together are concerned with ensuring that education results not merely in the Platonic goal of "a sound mind in a sound body," but rather in a thoroughly integrated personality grounded in the *Qur'an* and in *Qur'anic* morality, because "a person who truly accepts the message of Islam should accept all the ideals embodied in the *Qur'an*."[77] Underlying these different kinds of educational aims in Islamic philosophy of education are a number of common, unifying characteristics, including:

1. Islamic education should be concerned with developing the unique characteristics of the individual human being in such a way as to allow him/her to adapt to the standards of his/her society (which should share the ideals of Islam).
2. Islamic educational aims should be both realistic and idealistic. In other words, Islamic education must take into account biological needs, while at the same time not accepting an individual's yielding to temptation.
3. Since the *Qur'an* and its ideals are timeless and unchangeable, so to must educational ideals grounded in the *Qur'an* be seen as timeless and unchanging. The aims of Islamic philosophy of education are thus universal in nature.
4. Islamic education should be concerned both with preparation for this life and with preparation for the Hereafter.
5. Islamic educational aims and objectives should be translated into observable behavior.[78]

Having briefly discussed Islamic educational thought, we now turn to an examination of the ways in which this Islamic philosophy of education has been manifested in practice in traditional Islamic schools.

TRADITIONAL ISLAMIC EDUCATIONAL PRACTICE

The traditional Islamic educational system has varied from time to time and from place to place in a number of ways, but underlying the diversity in terms of curricula, teaching methods, and so on there has been a common core that allows us to talk about a general approach to *Qur'anic* education in the Islamic world.[79] It is important to keep in mind, however, that what is being discussed here is the Islamic educational tradition, rather than the Western-inspired, formal educational systems that are found today in most Islamic countries. Although such modern systems may include religious instruction, they are not "Islamic" in the same sense as traditional *Qur'anic* schools, and often coexist with such *Qur'anic* schools even today.

The basis of traditional Islamic education is the *kuttab*, or *Qur'anic* school. This institution bears the responsibility for providing all children with the foundations necessary for the practice of their faith. The curriculum focuses on the memorization of the *Qur'an* and the ability to read Arabic, although in some societies this basic curriculum was expanded to include the study of

Arabic grammar and poetry, writing, and often penmanship.[80] However, it is important to note here that by "reading Arabic" what is often meant for non-Arabic-speaking children is simply an ability to decode written Arabic for purposes of pronunciation, rather than fluent reading for meaning in what is for them a second language. Nonetheless, such skills are both valuable and necessary in the context of an Islamic society and, in comparing such traditional schooling with that of other societies, it is clear that although such *Qur'anic* schooling:

> did not take [children] very far . . . it fulfilled the requirements of the great mass of Muslims in the Middle Ages, indeed up to quite recent times, in that it gave them basic literacy. It is worth observing . . . that the level of literacy among the masses of the people in the Islamic world during the Middle Ages, and perhaps even up to the establishment of state primary education in European countries, was probably higher than in Christendom.[81]

Beyond the level of the *kuttab* are other Islamic educational institutions that are responsible for the preparation of Islamic professionals—the scribes, theologians, magistrates, and so on, on whom an Islamic society relies. These advanced institutions are called the *madaris*, and provide curricula that include the study of *tafsir* (*Qur'anic* exegesis), the *Hadith, shari'a, fiqh* (Islamic jurisprudence), and a variety of other appropriate subjects, often at very sophisticated levels of scholarship.[82]

CONCLUSION

Traditional Islamic educational thought and practice are, in short, inseparable from the fabric of Islamic religious thought and practice. As Carolyn Fluehr-Lobban commented about Islam in general, "Islam has been a power unifier because . . . its teachings blend religious, moral, and social practice into an indivisible whole for the believer-practitioner."[83] This unity of Islam is the context in which its educational thought and practice must be understood. To a very considerable extent, an understanding of the *Qur'an* is a necessary condition for a real understanding of traditional Islamic educational thought and practice. Indeed, the Islamic view of the importance of education is nowhere articulated more clearly than in the *Qur'an* itself, where we read, "And say, O Muhammad, 'My Lord, increase me in knowledge'" (Sura 20: 114). Finally, as we come to the end of this chapter, two beautiful passages from the *Hadith* provide as good a conclusion as one might wish:

> The Prophet prayed, "O my Lord, do not let the sun set on any day during which I did not increase in knowledge."
>
> No gift among all the gifts of a father to his child is better than education.[84]

QUESTIONS FOR REFLECTION AND DISCUSSION

1.   Memorization constitutes a central feature of traditional *Qur'anic* educational practice. What are the advantages of learning selected texts (e.g., in the case of Islamic education the *Qur'an*) by heart? Are there comparable advantages, in our own society, for memorizing other kinds of literature? What, in your view, are the problems associated with the use of extensive memorization in education?

2.   In earlier chapters, we have discussed the distinction between "education" and "schooling." How does this distinction apply to the case of traditional Islamic thought and practice?

3.   In this chapter, it is suggested that Muslims, when discussing the issue of gender and gender relations in Islam, commonly argue that men and women are indeed equal in Islam, but they are not the same, and that Islam therefore accords them appropriately different social positions and responsibilities. What are the educational implications for this argument? How does this view differ from those generally advocated by Western educators?

4.   For the Muslim educator, what is the role of moral development in the educational process? Does moral education "come with the territory," or is there an even stronger relationship between the two than this suggests?

5.   In contemporary American society, are there other religious groups whose view of the role and purpose of education would parallel that found in Islam? What other commonalities are there between the groups you identify and Muslims? How might one explain these similarities?

RECOMMENDED FURTHER READINGS

There are a number of excellent introductions to Islam. David Waines' *An Introduction to Islam* (Cambridge, England: Cambridge University Press, 1995) is a recent work of this sort; John Esposito's *Islam: The Straight Path*, expanded edition (New York: Oxford University Press, 1991) is widely used and available. A very thorough guide to Islam is provided in Caesar Farah's *Islam: Beliefs and Observations*, 5th ed. (Hauppage, NY: Barron's Educational Series, 1994). Other good general works include Thomas Lippman, *Understanding Islam: An Introduction to the Muslim World*, 2nd rev. ed. (New York: Meridan, 1995), Kenneth Cragg, *The Event of the Qur'an: Islam and Its Scripture* (Oxford, England: Oneworld, 1994), Akbar S. Ahmed's *Discovering Islam: Making Sense of Muslim History and Society* (London: Routledge, 1988), and Frederick Denny's *Islam* (San Francisco: Harper, 1987). Suzanne Haneef provided an outstanding introduction to Islam from the perspective of an American convert to the faith in her book, *What Everyone Should Know About Islam and Muslims* (Des Plaines, IL: Library of Islam, 1985), and Ruqaiyyah Maqsood's *Islam* (London: NTC, 1994) provides a useful "hands on" introduction to Islam. Finally, a fascinating and sophisticated treatment of contemporary Islam is found in Akbar S. Ahmed's *Postmodernism and Islam: Predicament and Promise* (London: Routledge, 1992).

NOTES

1. See Mary Pat Fisher, *Living Religions*, 2nd ed. (Englewood Cliffs, NJ: Prentice-Hall, 1994), 297.
2. Fisher, *Living Religions*, 297.
3. See, for example, the fascinating discussion of the way in which the three religions view Abraham in Hans Küng, *Judaism: Between Yesterday and Tomorrow* (New York: Crossroad, 1992), 11–18.
4. See George Holmes (ed.), *The Oxford Illustrated History of Medieval Europe* (Oxford, England: Oxford University Press, 1988), 50–51; see also Majid Fakhry, *A History of Islamic Philosophy*, 2nd ed. (New York: Columbia University Press, 1983).
5. See Edward Said, *Orientalism* (New York: Vintage, 1978).
6. G. H. Jansen, *Militant Islam* (New York: Harper & Row, 1979).
7. John Esposito, "Islam in the World and in America," in Jacob Neusner (ed.), *World Religions in America: An Introduction* (Louisville, KY: Westminster/John Knox, 1994), 243.
8. Carolyn Fluehr-Lobban, *Islamic Society in Practice* (Gainesville: University of Florida Press, 1994), 44.
9. See Hammudah Abdalati, *Islam in Focus* (Indianapolis, IN: American Trust Publications, 1975), 1. This is a very important point, and helps to explain why the term *Mohammedan*, which implies (falsely) that Muslims worship Muhammad, is deeply offensive to Muslims. See Maryam Jameelah, *Islam in Theory and Practice* (Lahore: Mohammad Yusuf Khan & Sons, 1986), 20–21; Fluehr-Lobban, *Islamic Society in Practice*, 6–7.
10. Fisher, *Living Religions*, 298; see also Esposito, "Islam in the World and in America," 244–245.
11. Esposito, "Islam in the World and in America," 244; M. Hamidullah, *Introduction to Islam* (Chicago: Kazi, 1981), 58–61.
12. A very thorough description of Muhammad's early life is provided in Muhammad Husayn Haykal, *The Life of Muhammad* (Indianapolis, IN: American Trust Publications, 1976). See also Karen Armstrong, *Muhammad: A Biography of the Prophet* (San Francisco: Harper, 1992); Ibn Ishaq, *The Life of Muhammad* (London: Oxford University Press, 1967); Martin Lings, *Muhammad: His Life Based on the Earliest Sources* (Rochester, VT: Inner Traditions, 1983); Abdul Hameed Siddiqui, *Life of Muhammad* (Des Plaines, IL: Library of Islam, 1991); Syed Ameer Ali, *The Spirit of Islam: A History of the Evolution and Ideals of Islam with a Life of the Prophet* (Delhi: Low Price Publications, 1990); Maxime Rodinson, *Mohammed* (New York: Vintage, 1974).

13. Hamidullah, *Introduction to Islam*, 6–7; see also Fazlur Rahman, *Islam*, 2nd ed. (Chicago: University of Chicago Press, 1979), 11–29.

14. Hamidullah, *Introduction to Islam*, 8

15. Esposito, "Islam in the World and in America," 245.

16. John Esposito, *Islam: The Straight Path* (New York: Oxford University Press, 1988), 68–69.

17. Suzanne Haneef, *What Everyone Should Know About Islam and Muslims* (Des Plaines, IL: Library of Islam, 1985), 93.

18. See Alfred Willms, "Nordafrika," in Michael Ursinus (ed.), *Der Islam in der Gegenwart* (München: Verlag C. H. Beck, 1984), 561–569; Lode Frank Brakel, "Indonesien," in Michael Ursinus (ed.), *Der Islam in der Gegenwart* (München: Verlag C. H. Beck, 1984), 570–581; Merwyn Hiskett, *The Development of Islam in West Africa* (London: Longman, 1984).

19. Fisher, *Living Religions*, 308.

20. Khurshid Ahmad, "Islam: Basic Principles and Characteristics," in Khurshid Ahmad (ed.), *Islam: Its Meaning and Message* (London: The Islamic Foundation, 1980), 29; see also Ghulam Sarwar, *Islam: Beliefs and Teaching* (London: Muslim Educational Trust, 1989), 19.

21. Sarwar, *Islam*, 27.

22. Haneef, *What Everyone Should Know About Islam and Muslims*, 20–21.

23. Haneef, *What Everyone Should Know About Islam and Muslims*, 20.

24. Fisher, *Living Religions*, 309.

25. Haneef, *What Everyone Should Know About Islam and Muslims*, 16–17; see also Fisher, *Living Religions*, 310–311; Sarwar, *Islam*, 27–28.

26. Annemarie Schimmel, *Islam: An Introduction* (Albany: State University of New York Press, 1992), 70; Hamidullah, *Introduction to Islam*, 57–58.

27. Haneef, *What Everyone Should Know About Islam and Muslims*, 18.

28. Esposito, *Islam*, 35.

29. Hamidullah, *Introduction to Islam*, 61.

30. Esposito, "Islam in the World and in America," 247; Fisher, *Living Religions*, 319; Fluehr-Lobban, *Islamic Society in Practice*, 23–37.

31. See Fisher, *Living Religions*, 320–323; Sarwar, *Islam*, 40–83; Shaykh Fadhlalla Haeri, *The Elements of Islam* (Shaftesbury, Dorset: Element, 1993), 37–42.

32. See Haneef, *What Everyone Should Know About Islam and Muslims*, 11–15, 42–43; Hamidullah, *Introduction to Islam*, 51–53; Fluehr-Lobban, *Islamic Society in Practice*, 23–24.

33. See Abdalati, *Islam in Focus*, 55–86; Haneef, *What Everyone Should Know About Islam and Muslims*, 43–46; Fluehr-Lobban, *Islamic Society in Practice*, 25–28.

34. Esposito, *Islam*, 92.

35. Esposito, *Islam*, 92.

36. Fisher, *Living Religions*, 321.

37. Sarwar, *Islam*, 76–78; Haneef, *What Everyone Should Know About Islam and Muslims*, 46–48.

38. Esposito, "Islam in the World and in America," 249.

39. For a fascinating history of the *hajj*, see F. E. Peters, *The Hajj: The Muslim Pilgrimage to Mecca and the Holy Places* (Princeton, NJ: Princeton University Press, 1994).

40. Haneef, *What Everyone Should Know About Islam and Muslims*, 51.

41. Ahmad, "Islam," 35–37; Jansen, *Militant Islam*, pp. 17–18. Also of interest here is C. van Nieuwenhuijze, *The Lifestyles of Islam: Recourse to Classicism, Need of Realism* (Leiden: Brill, 1985), 93–132.

42. See Joseph Schacht, *An Introduction to Islamic Law* (Oxford, England: Clarendon Press, 1964); Bassam Tibi, *Islam and the Cultural Accomodation of Social Change* (Boulder, CO: Westview, 1990), 59–75; Ahmad Ibrahim, "Islam and the Law," in *Toward Islamization of Disciplines* (Herndon, VA: International Institute of Islamic Thought, 1989), 381–391; Hamidullah, *Introduction to Islam*, 122–138; Fluehr-Lobban, *Islamic Society in Practice*, 115–141; Ignaz Goldziher, *Introduction to Islamic Theology and Law* (Princeton, NJ: Princeton University Press, 1981).

43. Sarwar, *Islam*, 13.

44. See Sarwar, *Islam*, 166–170; Haneef, *What Everyone Should Know About Islam and Muslims*, 142–148; Abdalati, *Islam in Focus*, 184–191; John Esposito, *Women in Muslim Family Law* (Syracuse, NY: Syracuse University Press, 1982); Fatima Mernissi, *The Veil and the Male Elite: A Feminist Interpretation of Women's Rights in Islam* (Reading, MA: Addison-Wesley, 1987); Fatima Mernissi, *Beyond the Veil: Male-Female Dynamics in Modern Muslim Society* (Bloomington: Indiana University Press, 1987).

45. Sarwar, *Islam*, 166–167; Abdalati, *Islam in Focus*, 184–185.

46. Abdalati, *Islam in Focus*, 187.

47. Abdalati, *Islam in Focus*, 186.

48. Haneef, *What Everyone Should Know About Islam and Muslims*, 145–146; Abdalati, *Islam in Focus*, 187–191.

49. David Waines, *An Introduction to Islam* (Cambridge, England: Cambridge University Press, 1995), 255.

50. See Ahmad, "Islam," 37–38; Maxime Rodinson, *Islam et capitalisme* (Paris: Éditions du Seuil, 1966).

51. For detailed discussions about the nature of Islamic economics, see Hamidullah, *Introduction to Islam*, 139–154; Muhammad Najatullah Siddiqi, "Islamizing Economics," in *Toward Islamization of Disciplines* (Herndon, VA: International Institute of Islamic Thought, 1989), 253–261; Mahmoud Abu Saud, "Toward Islamic Economics," in *Toward Islamization of Disciplines* (Herndon, VA: International Institute of Islamic Thought, 1989), 265–270; Muhammad Abdul Mannan, "The Frontiers of Islamic Economics: Some Philosophical Underpinnings," in *Toward Islamization of Disciplines* (Herndon, VA: International Institute of Islamic Thought, 1989), 295–311.

52. See Johannes Reissner, "Die innerislanische Diskussion zur modernen Wirtschafts- und Sozialordnung," in Michael Ursinus (ed.), *Der Islam in der Gegenwart* (München: Verlag C. H. Beck, 1984), 155–169; Hamidullah,

Introduction to Islam, 107–121; Aziz Al-Azmeh, *Islams and Modernities* (London: Verso, 1993), 89–103.

53. See Schacht, *An Introduction to Islamic Law*; Tibi, *Islam and the Cultural Accomodation of Social Change*, 59–75; Ahmad Ibrahim, "Islam and the Law"; Hamidullah, *Introduction to Islam*, 122–138; Fluehr-Lobban, *Islamic Society in Practice*, 115–141.

54. Schimmel, *Islam*, 29; see also Alfred Guillaume, *Islam* (Harmondsworth: Penguin, 1956), 55; Mohammed Arkoun, *Rethinking Islam: Common Questions, Uncommon Answers* (Boulder, CO: Westview, 1994), 35–39.

55. Haneef, *What Everyone Should Know About Islam and Muslims*, 18; see also Sarwar, *Islam*, 32–33.

56. Haneef, *What Everyone Should Know About Islam and Muslims*, 18.

57. Schimmel, *Islam*, 30; see also W. Montgomery Watt and Richard Bell, *Introduction to the Qur'an* (Edinburgh: Edinburgh University Press, 1970).

58. See Abdalati, *Islam in Focus*, 193; Esposito, *Islam*, 22–23.

59. Haneef, *What Everyone Should Know About Islam and Muslims*, 19.

60. Haneef, *What Everyone Should Know About Islam and Muslims*, 19.

61. See Waines, *An Introduction to Islam*, 23–24.

62. Allahbukhsh Brohi, "The *Qur'an* and Its Impact on Human History," in Khurshid Ahmad (ed.), *Islam: Its Meaning and Message* (London: The Islamic Foundation, 1980), 89–91.

63. A. L. Tibawi, *Islamic Education: Its Traditions and Modernization into the Arab National Systems* (London: Luzac & Co., 1972), 24.

64. Seyyed Hossein Nasr, "Islamic Education and Science: A Summary Appraisal," in Yvonne Haddad, Byron Haines, and Ellison Findly (eds.), *The Islamic Impact* (Syracuse: Syracuse University Press, 1984), 48; see also Seyyed Hossein Nasr, *Traditional Islam in the Modern World* (London: Routledge & Kegan Paul, 1987), 147–163.

65. Abdul-Rahman Salih Abdullah, *Educational Theory: A Qur'anic Outlook* (Makkah, Saudi Arabia: Umm Al-Qura University, 1982), 25.

66. Tibawi, *Islamic Education*, 39.

67. Tibawi, *Islamic Education*, 41.

68. Quoted in Tibawi, *Islamic Education*, 40.

69. Tibawi, *Islamic Education*, 40.

70. Abdullah, *Educational Theory*, 31.

71. See Nasr, "Islamic Education and Science," 48.

72. Tibawi, *Islamic Education*, 42.

73. Quoted in Tibawi, *Islamic Education*, 42.

74. Quoted in Tibawi, *Islamic Education*, 43.

75. Abdullah, *Educational Theory*, 43.

76. Abdullah, *Educational Theory*, 119.

77. Abdullah, *Educational Theory*, 121.

78. Abdullah, *Educational Theory*, 129–133.

79. Seydon Cissé, *L'enseignement islamique en Afrique noire* (Paris: L'Harmattan, 1992); Hiskett, *The Development of Islam in West Africa*, 55; Dale

Eickelman, *Knowledge and Power in Morocco: The Education of a Twentieth-Century Notable* (Princeton, NJ: Princeton University Press, 1985), 59–65.

80. See Tibawi, *Islamic Education*, 43.

81. Hiskett, *The Development of Islam in West Africa*, 55.

82. Hiskett, *The Development of Islam in West Africa*, 55; see Arkoun, *Rethinking Islam*, 35–48.

83. Fluehr-Lobban, *Islamic Society in Practice*, 2.

84. Quoted in Haneef, *What Everyone Should Know About Islam and Muslims*, 162.

9

Themes and Lessons
in the Study of Non-Western
Educational Traditions:
Concluding Thoughts

In the first chapter of this book, it was suggested that "it is neither idealistic nor unrealistic to suggest that we can learn much from non-Western educational traditions." We have explored and examined a number of non-Western educational traditions in *Non-Western Educational Traditions: Alternative Approaches to Educational Thought and Practice*, and are now in a better position to evaluate this claim. In each of the traditions that we have studied, there have been similarities to both other non-Western educational traditions and our own western tradition, just as each of the traditions has offered unusual and even unique features. In this final chapter, we look at some of the themes that appear to be fairly common across the different traditions we have examined, and try to determine what lessons might be learned from these common themes. We also briefly discuss some of the many non-Western educational traditions that have not been addressed in this book, but that might merit the attention of scholars and educators in the future.

SOME COMMON THEMES IN NON-WESTERN
EDUCATIONAL TRADITIONS

Underlying the common themes that seem to be reflected in the various non-Western educational traditions that we have studied is a powerful answer to the question, "Have we lost something important and valuable in Western education?" Until recently, Western scholars tended to view non-Western educational traditions as largely irrelevant and unrelated to their concerns, and, when they dealt with such areas at all, they all too often did so through a very potent and distorting lens. That lens was the assumption that non-Western educational traditions were in some significant way "primitive." Thus, when

George Pettitt wrote in the mid-1940s what remains the single most comprehensive study of Native American educational thought and practice, he and others saw nothing odd about naming his monograph *Primitive Education in North America.*[1] And yet, if there is any single conclusion that can reasonably be reached from the cases that we have examined in this book, it is that there is much that those of us in the West can and should learn from the traditions of the non-Western world. In short, we have indeed lost something important and valuable, and that "something" can be found in the very traditions that were wrongly labeled "primitive." As Adam Kuper forcefully argued, the very idea of a "primitive society" is a concept developed by Western scholars to delegitimize the societies and social systems of others.[2] Given the evidence now available, it is simply not credible to believe that non-Western approaches to childrearing and education are in any way inferior to those with which we are more familiar. They are different, to be sure, and they functioned to prepare children and young people for very different kinds of societies—but they did so, for the most part, effectively and humanely.

Moving beyond the rejection of the view of non-Western educational traditions as primitive, we find that there are at least seven broad themes that seem to be fairly (although not universally) common among the different traditions that we have studied in this book. Each of these themes are now briefly discussed.

A fundamental distinction between contemporary Western conceptions of education and many of the non-Western systems that we have examined is that between formal schooling and education. Formal schooling played important roles in many non-Western traditions (consider, e.g., its potency in traditional Chinese education), and it was to some extent present in most of the traditions that we studied (e.g., in initiation schools in Africa). However, it is also clear that the common tendency in our own society to conflate and confuse "formal schooling" with "education"—a tendency reflected in our concern with formal certification and degrees rather than with competence per se—has been far less common in non-Western traditions. To be sure, this may well be explained in large part by the nature and needs of different kinds of social organization. Our concerns with formal schooling no doubt reflect the nature of modern society, and in earlier times our tradition was far less concerned with formal schooling. The difference between formal schooling and education is, nonetheless, an important one for us to keep in mind, and the study of non-Western educational traditions certainly functions effectively to bring it to the forefront of our attention.

A second common theme in the non-Western educational traditions that we have studied is that education, to a great extent, has tended to be community based and communal in nature. Not only have adults and older children in the community tended to play important educational roles in the society but, with relatively few exceptions, there has been relatively little focus on identifying educational specialists in non-Western societies. Education and childrearing have commonly been seen as a social responsibility shared by all

of the members of the community. Although individuals may play greater or
lessor roles in this undertaking, it is significantly seen as the province of
everyone. Thus, the concept of some adults being *teachers* and others (pre-
sumably) being *non-teachers* is a somewhat alien one to many traditions.
Furthermore, it is interesting to note that in none of the cases examined
here—even those with the most fully articulated formal educational systems—was there any explicit, formal training for those who would play
teaching roles. The idea of teachers engaging in a profession, with specialized
knowledge and expertise not held by others, appears to be a Western, and
indeed relatively recent, innovation.

Related to the community-based focus of many non-Western educational
traditions is the broadly shared concern with what might be called *civic
education.* In every case we have studied, there is a concern with helping the
child grow into the kind of adult who will function effectively and appropriately in his or her society. In many of the non-Western traditions that we have
examined, this focus has clear political overtones, whereas in others a more
spiritual concern is at issue. Furthermore, although there is a common concern
with preparing the child for life in his or her society, this is not to say that there
is a blind acceptance of the status quo. Indeed, just the opposite seems to be
true—even in the more conservative instances, there is always room for the
individual to challenge his or her society, albeit often at considerable personal
cost. Thus, for instance, in the African tradition we find the role of the *imbongi*;
whereas in the Chinese case we learn that all relationships the rights and
privileges of the educated person are seen in reciprocal terms; and in Aztec
society, the higher one's rank, the greater the punishment for violating social
norms.

Not only do non-Western educational traditions stress what can be called
civic education, but they also emphasize the need for every child to be
prepared to function economically in his or her society. Thus, what would
today be called *vocational education* can be found in every case that we have
studied. In some cases occupations can be chosen by the child or the child's
family, whereas in others special skills and aptitudes are required. Still other
occupations are open only to selected individuals, often on the basis of birth.
Finally, it is in the area of preparation to function economically that one finds
the greatest degree of gender stratification. In most non-Western societies, the
roles of men and women are different, and the differences are clearly demar-
cated. Thus, girls learn the skills they will need from the mothers (and, often,
from other female relatives), whereas boys learn the skills that they will need
from their fathers, uncles, and other adult male role models. It is also
important in this context to note that although all of the traditions examined
in this book pay attention to the vocational needs of the individual, this focus
is different from that found in contemporary American society in a significant
way. In modern capitalist societies in general, and in American society in
particular, educational institutions are often expected to serve the needs of
the economy (or, more accurately, of employers) rather than the needs of

individual workers. To be sure, one could suggest that these two sets of needs ought to be, at least in the ideal, very similar, but they are by no means the same. In the cases examined in this book, the emphasis placed on vocational preparation is largely an empowering one, with the greater emphasis normally placed on the needs and aptitudes of the individual rather than on the needs of the employer.

The role of the family is, in every case we have examined, the central facet of education. Other social institutions may well play important and valuable roles, and nonfamily members may also perform important educational roles, but it is the family that is the key to the child's education. To be sure, different societies define the family in different ways, but what is common is the idea that it is the family as a unit that bears the ultimate responsibility for the child and for his or her education and upbringing. At the same time, in the cases examined here (and, in fact, in non-Western traditions generally), it is clear that the final say in decisions about childrearing and education almost always rests with the family rather than with the society at large.

The role of language plays a surprisingly important part in almost all non-Western educational traditions. Although many non-Western traditions do indeed have rich written traditions, others have been entirely oral. This has meant that the way in which language skills are taught and used may vary among different non-Western societies, but the concern with the *proper* use of language, knowledge of the spoken traditions of the community, and the ability to use language creatively to reason and to argue are all powerful components of language use, and they are virtually universal in the cases we have examined.

Last, we come to the issue of values, morality, and spirituality in education. In every educational tradition that we have studied in *Non-Western Educational Traditions: Alternative Approaches to Educational Thought and Practice*, the principal goal of education seems to be the development of a *good person*. Although there may be differences of opinion about selective aspects of the nature of this good person there are also a number of core features (such as honesty) that are agreed on in every case we have studied. As Jack Forbes, writing about Native American education, argued:

> The main thing I want to emphasize is that there can be no education that is multicultural involving the Native American tradition unless it gets into this area of the meaning of life, unless it gets into the area of values. . . . I don't have the answer as to how you bring a spiritual path into schools in a society which is going in the opposite direction. I don't have the answer as to how you do that, except that we must try.[3]

Each of these common themes that have been identified and briefly discussed here has much to teach us about not only what others have done and believed about education, but also what we ourselves seem to assume and believe about education. There are many valuable lessons that could be learned from the wisdom of others, and such insights should not be lightly put aside.

We turn now to a discussion of some of the non-Western educational traditions that we have not examined in this book.

AREAS FOR FUTURE RESEARCH

In *Non-Western Educational Traditions: Alternative Approaches to Educational Thought and Practice*, we have examined seven different non-Western educational traditions, but there are, of course, far more non-Western educational traditions that have not even been mentioned thus far. It is certainly not the point of this chapter to cover all of the ground that remains; indeed, even if we wished to do so, it would not be possible. What we can do, however, is to simply identify other non-Western educational traditions that merit further, careful study. Among those traditions that have much to teach us, and that provide both interesting counterpoints to some of the cases discussed in this book and often strong support for the common themes that we have identified, are:

1. The traditional educational thought and practice of the different peoples in Oceania, including certainly the fascinating case of the Maori civilization.
2. The traditional educational thought and practice of different groups of the Australian Aborigines (the indigenous peoples of Australia).
3. A detailed study of both childrearing and formal education in the Inca empire before the Conquest.
4. Detailed, focused examinations of particular groups in Africa, the Americas, and so on.
5. The traditional educational thought and practice of various societies in Asia (and, in particular, those of Japan and Korea), especially with respect to how indigenous practices have interacting with those imported from China.

Needless to say, this list is far from exhaustive. This book is intended to be, at most, a first step in our study of non-Western educational traditions, and it is a first step on a very long road. Having said this, it should also be kept in mind that every trip, no matter how long, must begin with a first step.

CONCLUSION

The first chapter of this book ended with an intriguing quote from Ali Mazrui. Mazrui, a noted African scholar, argued that: "I cannot help feeling that it is about time Africa sent missionaries to Europe and America, as well as teachers, engineers, doctors, and ordinary workers. . . . It is indeed time that Africa counter-penetrated the western world.[4]

If Mazrui is correct, then perhaps not only Africa but the rest of the non-Western world as well needs to send us missionaries, because they do indeed have much to teach us. At the same time, we need not reject everything in our own tradition. In *The Mikado*, Gilbert and Sullivan wrote disparagingly about "the man who loves every century but this and every country but his own." Other societies and traditions have many strengths, as does our own, just as they have many weaknesses, as does our own. The fundamental point of this book has been that there is much in every society that is worthwhile and valuable, and that we need to learn to do a better job of learning from one another.

QUESTIONS FOR REFLECTION AND DISCUSSION

1. What are some examples of educational activities in our own society that take place apart from formal schooling, and are not connected with it? What role, if any, do professional educators play in these activities?

2. It is pointed out in this chapter that "the idea of teachers engaging in a profession, with specialized knowledge and expertise not held by others, appears to be a Western, and indeed relatively recent, innovation." What are the benefits of viewing teachers as a specialized profession? What problems do you see with this development in our society?

3. One of the common themes identified in this chapter is the role of spirituality in education. In your view, should spirituality play a significant role in a secular, public education? What limits, if any, need to be observed in "spiritual education?"

4. How are the common themes found in the non-Western educational traditions discussed in this chapter reflected or manifested in contemporary American education? What lessons can we learn from these themes?

5. In your view, what is the single most important idea that has emerged in our study of non-Western educational traditions and practices? How do you see that idea affecting your practice as an educator?

RECOMMENDED FURTHER READINGS

There are no other works currently available that deal with non-Western educational traditions in a broad, general way. Works dealing with specific non-Western traditions are cited in the bibliography.

NOTES

1. George Pettitt, *Primitive Education in North America* (Berkeley: University of California Press, 1946).

2. See Adam Kuper, *The Invention of Primitive Society: Transformations of an Illusion* (London: Routledge, 1988).

3. Jack Forbes, "Traditional Native American Philosophy and Multicultural Education," in *Multicultural Education and the American Indian* (Los Angeles: American Indian Studies Center, University of California, 1979), 11.

4. Ali Mazrui, *The African Condition: The Reith Lectures* (London: Heinemann, 1980), 16.

Bibliography

Abdalati, H. (1975). *Islam in focus*. Indianapolis, IN: American Trust Publications.

Abdullah, R.S. (1982). *Educational theory: A Qur'anic outlook*. Makkah, Saudi Arabia: Umm Al-Qura University.

Abe, M. (1993). Buddhism. In Arvind Sharma (ed.), *Our religions* (San Francisco: Harper), 69–137.

Achebe, C. (1958). *Things fall apart*. London: Heinemann.

Achebe, C. (1960). *No longer at ease*. London: Heinemann.

Achebe, C. (1966). *A man of the people*. London: Heinemann.

Achebe, C. (1974). *Arrow of god* (2nd ed.). London: Heinemann.

Adams, D. (1970). *Education and modernization in Asia*. Reading, MA: Addison-Wesley.

Adegbola, E. (Ed.), (1983). *Traditional religion in West Africa*. Nairobi: Uzima.

Ahmad, K. (1980a). Islam: Basic principles and characteristics. In Khurshid Ahmad (Ed.), *Islam: Its meaning and message* (pp. 27–44). London: Islamic foundation.

Ahmad, K. (Ed.), (1980b). *Islam: Its meaning and message*. London: Islamic Foundation.

Ahmed, A. S. (1988). *Discovering Islam: Making sense of Muslim history and society*. London: Routledge.

Ahmed, A. S. (1992). *Postmodernism and Islam: Predicament and promise*. London: Routledge.

Aizpuro, P. (1990). *Historia de la educación en la época colonial: El mundo indígena* [History of education in the colonial period: the indiginous world]. México: El Colegio de México.

Al-Azmeh, A. (1993). *Islams and modernities*. London: Verso.

Ali, S. A. (1990). *The spirit of Islam: A history of the evolution and ideals of Islam with a life of the prophet.* Delhi: Low Price Publications.

Amdouni, H. (1992). *La famille musulmane: Relations familiales et éducations* [The Muslim family: Familial and educative relations]. Paris: Al Qalam.

Andrews, J. (1975). *An introduction to classical Nahuatl.* Austin: University of Texas Press.

Appiah, K. (1992). *In my father's house: Africa in the politics of culture.* Oxford, England: Oxford University Press.

Arkoun, M. (1994). *Rethinking Islam: Common questions, uncommon answers.* Boulder, CO: Westview.

Armstrong, K. (1992). *Muhammad: A biography of the Prophet.* San Francisco: Harper.

Asante, M., & Asante, K. (Eds.). (1990). *African culture: Rhythms of unity.* Trenton, NJ: Africa World Press.

Atwood, M. (1991). *Spirit healing: Native American magic and medicine.* New York: Sterling.

Austin, A. (1976). El fundamento mágico-religioso del poder [The magical-religious foundation of power]. *Estudios de Cultura Náhuatl, 12,* 197–240.

Aveni, A. (Ed.). (1992). *The sky in Mayan literature.* Oxford, England: Oxford University Press.

Ayers, W. (1971). *Chang Chih-tung and educational reform in China.* Cambridge, MA: Harvard University Press.

Ayisi, E. (1979). *An introduction to the study of African culture.* London: Currey.

Ball, J. (1925). *Things Chinese, or, notes connected with China* (5th ed., rev. by E. C. Werner). Shanghai: Kelly and Walsh.

Ball, S. (Ed.). (1990) *Foucault and education: Disciplines and knowledge.* London: Routledge.

Banerjee, A. K. (1967). *Discourses on Hindu spiritual culture.* Delhi: S. Chand & Co.

Banerji, S. (1993). *Society in ancient India: Evolution since the Vedic times based on Sanskrit, Pali, Prakrit and other classical sources.* New Delhi: D. K. Printworld.

Barman, J. Hébert, Y., & McCaskill, D. (1987). The challenge of Indian education: An Overview. In J. Barman, Y. Hébert, & D. McCaskill (eds.), *Indian Education in Canada, Volume 2: The Challenge* (pp. 1–21). Vancouver: University of British Columbia Press.

Barman, J., Hébert, Y., & McCaskill, D. (Eds.). (1987). *Indian education in Canada, volume 2: The challenge.* Vancouver: University of British Columbia Press.

Barrett, T. H. (1990). Religious traditions in Chinese civilization: Buddhism and Taoism. In P. Ropp (Ed.), *Heritage of China: Contemporary perspectives on Chinese civilization* (pp. 138–163) Berkeley: University of California Press.

Bascom, W. (1975). *African dilemma tales.* The Hague: Mouton.

Basham, A. L. (1989). *The origins and development of classical Hinduism.* Boston: Beacon.

Bastid, M. (1987). Servitude or liberation? The introduction of foreign educational practices and systems to China. In R. Hayhoe & M. Bastid (Eds.), *China's education and the industrialized world* (pp. 3–20). London: M. E. Sharpe.

Bauer, W. (1976). *China and the search for happiness: Recurring themes in four thousand years of Chinese cultural history.* New York: Seabury.

Belenky, M. F., Clinchy, B. M., Goldberger, N. R., & Tarule, J. M. (1986). *Women's ways of knowing: The development of self, voice, and mind.* New York: Basic.

Bell, B. (ed.) (1967). *Indian Mexico: Past and present.* Los Angeles: University of California at Los Angeles, Latin American Center.

Berdan, F. (1976). La organización del tributo en el imperio azteca [The organization of tribute in the Aztec Empire]. *Estudios de Cultura Náhuatl* 12: 185–195.

Bernal, M. (1987). *Black Athena: The Afroasiatic roots of classical civilization, volume 1: The fabrication of ancient Greece, 1785–1985.* New Brunswick, NJ: Rutgers University Press.

Bernal, M. (1991). *Black Athena: The Afroasiatic roots of classical civilization, volume 2: The archeological and documentary evidence.* New Brunswick, NJ: Rutgers University Press.

Berrelleza, J. (1987). Offering 48 of the Templo Mayor: A case of child sacrifice. In E. Boone (Ed.), *The Aztec templo mayor: A symposium at Dumbarton Oaks, 8th and 9th October 1983* (pp. 131–143). Washington, DC: Dumbarton Oaks Research Library and Collection.

Besmer, F. (1983). *Horses, musicians, and gods: The Hausa cult of possession-trance.* Zaria, Nigeria: Ahmadu Bello University Press.

Biardeau, M. (1994). *Hinduism: The anthropology of a civilization.* Delhi: Oxford University Press.

Bill, M. C. (1991). Rhythmical patterning of Tsonga children's traditional oral poetry. *South African Journal of African Languages 11,* (4), 133–143.

Biot, É. (1847). *Essai sur l'histoire de l'instruction publique en Chine* [An essay on the history of public education in China]. Paris: Benjamin Duprat.

Birge, B. (1989). Chu Hsi and women's education. In W. de Bary and J. Chaffee (Eds.), *Neo-Confucian education: The formative stage* (pp. 325–367). Berkeley: University of California Press.

Bloom, I. 1987. *Knowledge painfully acquired: The K'un-chih chi by Lo Ch'in-shun*. New York: Columbia University Press.

Bloomfield, L. (1964). Language. In O. L. Chavarria-Aguilar (Ed.), *Traditional India* (pp. 112–113). Englewood Cliffs, NJ: Prentice-Hall.

Boateng, F. (1990). African traditional education: A tool for intergenerational communication. In M. Asante & K. Asante (Eds.), *African culture: Rhythms of unity* (pp. 109–122) Trenton, NJ: Africa World Press.

Bodde, D. (1967). *China's first unifier: A study of the Ch'in Dynasty as seen in the life of Li Ssu*. Hong Kong: Hong Kong University Press. (Original work published 1938)

Bodde, D. (1981). *Essays on Chinese civilization*. Princeton, NJ: Princeton University Press.

Boe, P. (1983). Circumcision: The rites of manhood in the Bille tribe. In E. Adegbola (Ed.), *Traditional religion in West Africa* (pp. 73–89) Nairobi: Uzima Press.

Bol, P. (1989). Chu Hsi's redefinition of literati learning. In W. de Bary & J. Chaffee (Eds.), *Neo-Confucian education: The formative stage* (pp. 151–185) Berkeley: University of California Press.

Bond, M. (Ed.) (1986). *The psychology of the Chinese people*. Hong Kong: Oxford University Press.

Bond, M. & Kwang-kuo, H. (1986). The social psychology of the Chinese people. In M. Bond (Ed.), *The psychology of the Chinese people* (pp. 213–266). Hong Kong: Oxford University Press.

Boone, E. (Ed.). (1987). *The Aztec templo mayor: A symposium at Dumbarton Oaks, 8th and 9th October 1983*. Washington, DC: Dumbarton Oaks Research Library and Collection.

Boone, E. & Walter, M. (Eds.). (1994). *Writing without words: Alternative literacies in Mesoamerica and the Andes*. Durham, NC: Duke University Press.

Borland, C. H. (1969). The oral and written culture of the Shona. *LIMI: Bulletin of the Department of Bantu Languages, University of South Africa, 8*, 1–27.

Boyer, R. M. & Gayton, N. (1992). *Apache mothers and daughters: Four generations of a family*. Norman: University of Oklahoma Press.

Brakel, L. F. (1984). Indonesien. In M. Ursinus (Ed.), *Der Islam in der Gegenwart* [Islam in the present] (pp. 570–581). München: Verlag C. H. Beck.

Bray, W. (1968). *The everyday life of the Aztecs.* New York: Dorset.

Brohi, A. (1980). The *Qur'an* and its impact on human history. In K. Ahmad (Ed.), *Islam: Its Meaning and Message* (pp. 81–97). London: Islamic Foundation.

Brown, D. (1971). *Bury my heart at Wounded Knee: An Indian history of the American West.* New York: Bantam.

Brundage, B. (1972). *A rain of darts: The Mexica Aztecs.* Austin: University of Texas Press.

Brundage, B. (1975). *Two heavens, two earths: An essay contrasting the Aztecs and the Incas.* Albuquerque: University of New Mexico Press.

Brundage, B. (1979). *The fifth sun: Aztec gods, Aztec world.* Austin: University of Texas Press.

Calnek, E. (1988). The *calmécac* and *telpochcalli* in pre-Conquest Tenochtitlán. In J. J. Klor de Alva, H. Nicholson, & E. Keber (Eds.), *The work of Bernardino de Sahagun: Pioneer ethnographer of sixteenth-century Aztec Mexico* (pp. 169–177) Albany: Institute for Mesoamerican Studies, State University of New York.

Calvert, L.-J. (1984). *La tradition orale* [The oral tradition]. Paris: Presses Universitaires de France.

Campos, R. (1936). *La producción literaria de los Aztecas* [The literary production of the Aztecs]. México: Talleres Gráficos del Museo Nacional de Arqueología, Historia y Etnografía.

Carrasco, D. (1982). *Quetzalcoatl and the irony of empire: Myths and prophecies in the Aztec tradition.* Chicago: University of Chicago Press.

Carrasco, D. (1990). *Religions of Mesoamerica.* San Francisco: Harper.

Carroll, D. (1980). *Chinua Achebe.* London: Macmillan.

Chaffee, J. (1979). *Education and examinations in Sung society.* Unpublished doctoral dissertation, University of Chicago.

Chaffee, J. (1989). Chu Hsi in Nan-k'ang: *Tao-hsüeh* and the politics of education. In W. De Bary & J. Chaffee (Eds.), *Neo-Confucian education: The formative stage* (pp. 414–431). Berkeley: University of California Press.

Chase, D., & Chase, A. (Eds.). (1992). *Mesoamerican elites: Anarcheological assessment.* Norman: University of Oklahoma Press.

Chavarria-Aguilar, O. L. (Ed.). (1964). *Traditional India.* Englewood Cliffs, NJ: Prentice-Hall.

Cheetham, E. (1994). *Fundamentals of mainstream Buddhism.* Boston: Tuttle.

Chen L.-F. (1976). *Why Confucius has been reverenced as the model teacher of all ages.* New York: Center of Asian Studies, St. John's University, and the Institute of Chinese Culture.

Cheng, H. (1991). Confucian ethics and moral education of contemporary students. In S. Krieger & R. Trauzettel (Eds.), *Confucianism and the modernization of China* (pp. 193–202). Mainz: v. Hase & Koehler.

Cheng, T.-H. (1947). *China moulded by Confucius: The Chinese way in Western light.* London: Stevens & Sons.

Chew, P. G. L. (1991). The great Tao. *The Journal of Bahá'í Studies, 4,* (2), 11–39.

Chisholm, J. (1983). *Navajo infancy: An ethological study of child development.* Hawthorne, NY: Aldine.

Chu, R. (1989). Chu Hsi and public instruction. In W. De Bary & J. Chaffee (Eds.), *Neo-Confucian education: The formative stage* (pp. 252–273). Berkeley: University of California Press.

Chün-fang, Y. (1989). Ch'an education in the Sung: Ideals and procedures. In W. De Bary & J. Chaffee (Eds.), *Neo-Confucian education: The formative stage* (pp. 57–104). Berkeley: University of California Press.

Cissé, S. (1992). *L'enseignement islamique en Afrique noire* [Islamic education in black Africa]. Paris: L'Harmattan.

Clendinnen, I. (1991). *Aztecs: An interpretation.* Cambridge, England: Cambridge University Press.

Cleverley, J. (1985). *The schooling of China: Tradition and modernity in Chinese education.* Sydney: Allen & Unwin.

Coe, M. (1987). *The Maya* (4th rev. ed.). London: Thames and Hudson.

Coe, M. (1992). *Breaking the Maya code.* London: Thames and Hudson.

Cohen, P., & Goldman, M. (Eds.). (1990). *Ideas across cultures: Essays on Chinese thought in honor of Benjamin I. Schwartz.* Cambridge, MA: Harvard University Press.

Coleman, M. (1993). *American Indian children at school, 1850–1930.* Jackson: University Press of Mississippi.

Commeaux, C. (1970). *La vie quotidienne en Chine sous les Mandchous* [Daily life in China under the Manchus]. Paris: Librairie Hachette.

Conrad, G., & Demarest, A. (1984). *Religion and empire: The dynamics of Aztec and Inca expansionism.* Cambridge, England: Cambridge University Press.

Conze, E. (trans.). (1959). *Buddhist scriptures.* Harmondsworth: Penguin.

Conze, E. (1960). *A short history of Buddhism.* Bombay: Chetana.

Conze, E. (1975). *Buddhism: Its essence and development.* New York: Harper & Row.

Coomaraswamy, A. (1971). *Hinduism and Buddhism.* Westport, CT: Greenwood.

Cope, T. (Ed.). (1968). *Izibongo: Zulu praise poems.* Oxford, England: Oxford University Press.

Cordier, H. (1921). *Histoire générale de la Chine* [General history of China] (4 Vols.). Paris: Geuthner.

Cornyn, J. (1930). *The song of Quetzalcoatl.* Yellow Springs, OH: Antioch.

Coulehan, J. (1980). Navajo Indian medicine: Implications for healing. *Journal of Family Practice, 10*: 55–61.

Cowan, J. (1992). *The elements of the Aborigine tradition.* Shaftesbury, Dorset: Element.

Cragg, K. (1994). *The event of the Qur'an: Islam and its scripture.* Oxford, England: Oneworld.

Creel, H. (1949). *Confucius and the Chinese way.* New York: Harper & Row.

Cross, S. (1994). *The elements of Hinduism.* Shaftsbury, Dorset: Element.

Crystal, D. (1991). *A dictionary of linguistics and phonetics* (3rd ed.). Oxford, England: Blackwell.

Culin, S. (1975). *Games of the North American Indians.* New York: Dover.

Curtin, P., Feierman, S., Thompson, L., & Vansina, J. (1995). *African history: From earliest times to independence* (2nd ed.). London: Longman.

Curtis, S., & Boultwood, M. (1953). *A short history of educational ideas.* London: University Tutorial Press.

Davidson, B. (1991a). *Africa in history* (rev. ed.). New York: Macmillan.

Davidson, B. (Ed.). (1991b). *African civilization revisited: From antiquity to modern time.* Trenton, NJ: African World Press.

Davies, C. (1973). *Los mexicas: Primeros pasos hacia el imperio* [The Mexicas: First steps to empire]. México: Universidad Nacional Autónoma de México, Instituto de Investigaciones Históricas.

Davies, N. (1982). *The ancient kingdoms of Mexico.* New York: Penguin.

Davies, N. (1987). *The Aztec empire: The Toltec resurgence.* Norman: University of Oklahoma Press.

Dawson, R. (1978). *The Chinese experience.* London: Weidenfeld and Nicholson.

Day, J. (1992). *Aztec: The world of Moctezuma.* Niwot, CO: Denver Museum of Natural History and Roberts Rinehart.

de Bary, W. (Ed.). (1969). *The Buddhist tradition in India, China and Japan.* New York: Modern Library.

de Bary, W. (1981). *Neo-Confucian orthodoxy and the learning of the mind-and-heart.* New York: Columbia University Press.

de Bary, W. (1983). *The liberal tradition in China.* Hong Kong: Chinese University Press.

de Bary, W. (1989). Chu Hsi's aims as educator. In W. de Bary & J. Chaffee (Eds.), *Neo-Confucian education: The formative stage* (pp. 186–218). Berkeley: University of California Press.

de Bary, W., & Chaffee, J. (Eds.). (1989). *Neo-Confucian education: The formative stage.* Berkeley: University of California Press.

Denny, F. M. (1987). *Islam.* San Francisco: Harper.

de Villiers, S., & Hartshorne, S. H. (1981). Education. In A. Myburgh (Ed.), *Anthropology for Southern Africa* (pp. 145–150). Pretoria: van Schaik.

Diop, C. A. (1962). *The cultural unity of Negro Africa.* Paris: Presence Africaine.

Diop, C. A. (1989). *The cultural unity of Black Africa.* London: Karnak House.

Diop, C. A. (1991). *Civilization or barbarism: An authentic anthropology.* Chicago: Hill.

Doolittle, J. (orig. published 1865; 1966). *Social life of the Chinese: With some account of their religious, governmental, educational, & business customs and opinions* (2 Vols.). Taipe: Ch'eng-Wen.

Duminy, P. (Ed.) (1967). *Trends and challenges in the education of the South African Bantu.* Pretoria: van Schaik.

Duminy, P. (1973). *African pupils and teaching them.* Pretoria: van Schaik.

Dumoulin, H. (1994). *Understanding Buddhism: Key themes.* New York: Weatherhill.

Dundas, P. (1992). *The Jains.* London: Routledge.

Durán, D. (1964). *The Aztecs: The history of the Indies of New Spain.* New York: Orion.

Durant, W. (1963). *The story of civilization: Our Oriental heritage.* New York: Simon and Schuster.

Eberhard, W. (1977). *A history of China.* Berkeley: University of California Press.

Ebrey, P. (1989). Education through ritual: Efforts to formulate family rituals during the Sung period. In W. de Bary & J. Chaffee (Eds.), *Neo-Confucian education: The formative stage* (pp. 277–306). Berkeley: University of California Press.

Ebrey, P. (1990). Women, Marriage, and the Family in Chinese history. In P. Ropp (Ed.), *Heritage of China: Contemporary perspectives on Chinese civilization.* Berkeley: University of California Press.

Ebrey, P. (1991). *Confucianism and family rituals in imperial China: A social history of writing about rites.* Princeton, NJ: Princeton University Press.

Ebrey, P. (Ed.). (1993). *Chinese civilization: A sourcebook* (2nd ed.). New York: Free Press.

Eckel, M. (1994). Buddhism in the World and in America. In J. J. Neusner (Ed.), *World religions in America: An introduction* (pp. 203–218). Louisville, KY: Westminster/John Knox Press.

Edmonson, M. (1988). *The book of the year: Middle American calendrical systems.* Salt Lake City: University of Utah Press.

Eichhorn, W. (1969). *Chinese civilization: An introduction.* New York: Praeger.

Eickelman, D. (1985). *Knowledge and power in Morocco: The education of a twentieth-century notable.* Princeton, NJ: Princeton University Press.

Elvin, M. (1973). *The pattern of the Chinese past.* Stanford, CA: Stanford University Press.

Elzey, W. (1976). Some remarks on the space and time of the "center" in Aztec religion. *Estudios de Cultura Náhuatl, 12,* 315–334.

Esposito, J. (1982). *Women in Muslim family law.* Syracuse, NY: Syracuse University Press.

Esposito, J. (1988). *Islam: The straight path.* New York: Oxford University Press.

Esposito, J. (1991). *Islam: The straight path* (expanded ed.). New York: Oxford University Press.

Esposito, J. (1994). Islam in the World and in America. In J. Neusner (Ed.), *World religions in America: An introduction* (pp. 243–258). Louisville, KY: Westminster/John Knox.

Fadipe, N. (1970). *The sociology of the Yoruba.* Ibadan: Ibadan University Press.

Fafunwa, A. B. (1974). *A history of education in Nigeria.* London: Allen & Unwin.

Fagan, B. (1984). *The Aztecs.* New York: Freeman.

Fairbank, J. (1992). *China: A new history.* Cambridge, MA: Harvard University Press.

Fairbank, J., & Kwang-Ching L. (Eds.). (1980). *The Cambridge history of China, Volume 11: Late Ch'ing, 1800–1911, Part 2.* Cambridge, England: Cambridge University Press.

Fajana, A. (1986). Traditional methods of education in Africa: The Yoruba example. In J. Okpaku, A. Opubor, & B. Oloruntimehin (Eds.), *The arts and civilization of Black and African peoples: Volume 6, Black civilization and pedagogy* (pp. 42–59). Lagos: Center for Black and African Arts and Civilization.

Fakhry, M. (1983). *A history of Islamic philosophy* (2nd ed.). New York: Columbia University Press.

Farah, C. (1994). *Islam: beliefs and observances* (5th ed.). Hauppage, NY: Barron's Educational Series.

Finlayson, R. (1982). *Hlonipha*: The women's language of avoidance among the Xhosa. *South African Journal of African Languages* (Sup. 1), 35–59.

Finlayson, R. (1986). Linguistic terms of respect among the Xhosa. In P. Raper (Ed.), *Names 1983: Proceedings of the Second South African Names Congress* (pp. 128–138). Pretoria: Human Sciences Research Council.

Finnegan, R. (1970). *Oral literature in Africa*. Nairobi: Oxford University Press.

Finnegan, R. (1992). Reflecting back on *Oral literature in Africa*: Some reconsiderations after 21 years. *South African Journal of African Languages* 12 (2), 39–47.

Fisher, M. P. (1994). *Living religions* (2nd ed.) Englewood Cliffs, NJ: Prentice-Hall.

Fluehr-Lobban, C. (1994). *Islamic society in practice*. Gainesville: University of Florida Press.

Forbes, J. (1979). Traditional Native American philosophy and multicultural education. In *Multicultural Education and the American Indian* (pp. 3–13) Los Angeles: American Indian Studies Center, University of California.

Fortes, M. (1979). Foreward. In E. Ayisi (Ed.), *An introduction to the study of African culture* (2nd ed.). (pp. vii–ix). London: Currey.

Freidel, D., Schele, L., & Parker, J. (1993). *Maya cosmos: Three thousand years on the shaman's path*. New York: Morrow.

Fromkin, V., & Rodman, R. (1978). *An introduction to language* (2nd ed.). New York: Holt, Rinehart and Winston.

Fu, S. (1991). A brief account of the positive factors in Confucius' thinking. In S. Krieger & R. Trauzettel (Eds.), *Confucianism and the Modernization of China* (pp. 175–192). Mainz: v. Hase & Koehler.

Fuller, C. J. (1992). *The camphor flame: Popular Hinduism and society in India*. Princeton, NJ: Princeton University Press.

Furniss, G., & Gunner, L. (Eds.). (1995). *Power, marginality and African oral literature*. Cambridge, England: Cambridge University Press.

Gallenkamp, C. (1985). *Maya: The riddle and rediscovery of a lost civilization* (3rd rev. ed.). New York: Penguin .

Galt, H. (1951). *A history of Chinese educational institutions* (Vol. 1). London: Probsthain.

Gendrop, P. (1992). *Les mayas* [The Mayas] (5th ed.). Paris: Presses Universitaires de France.

Gernet, J. (1982). *A history of Chinese civilization.* Cambridge, England: Cambridge University Press.

Gilligan, C. (1982). *In a different voice: Psychological theory and women's development.* Cambridge, MA: Harvard University Press.

Goetz, D., & Morley, S. (trans.). (1950). *Popol Vuh: The sacred book of the ancient Quiché Maya.* Norman: University of Oklahoma Press.

Goldziher, I. (1981). *Introduction to Islamic theology and law.* Princeton, NJ: Princeton University Press.

Gopalan, S. (1973). *Outlines of Jainism.* New York: Halsted.

Granet, M. (1968). *La civilisation chinoise: La vie publique et la vie privée* [Chinese civilization: public life and private life]. Paris: Éditions Albin Michel.

Guillaume, A. (1956). *Islam.* Harmondsworth: Penguin.

Guma, S. (1977). *The form, content and technique of traditional literature in Southern Sotho* (2nd ed.). Pretoria: van Schaik.

Gutek, G. (1972). *A history of the Western educational experience.* Prospect Heights, IL: Waveland.

Gutek, G. (1991). *Cultural foundations of education: A biographical introduction.* New York: Macmillan.

Gutek, G. (1993). *American education in a global society: Internationalizing teacher education.* New York: Longman.

Gyatso, T. (1990). *Freedom in exile: The autobiography of the Dalai Lama.* New York: Harper Perennial.

Haddad, Y., Haines, B., & Findly, E. (Eds.). (1984). *The Islamic impact.* Syracuse, NY: Syracuse University Press.

Haeri, S. F. (1993). *The elements of Islam.* Shaftesbury, Dorset: Element.

Hamidullah, M. (1981). *Introduction to Islam.* Chicago: Kazi.

Hammond, N. (1988). *Ancient Maya civilization.* New Brunswick, NJ: Rutgers University Press.

Hammond-Tooke, W. (Ed.). (1974). *The Bantu-speaking peoples of Southern Africa.* London: Routledge & Kegan Paul.

Handlin, J. (1983). *Action in late Ming thought: The reorientation of Lü K'un and other scholar-officials.* Berkeley: University of California Press.

Haneef, S. (1985). *What everyone should know about Islam and Muslims.* Des Plaines, IL: Library of Islam.

Hanh, T. N. (1991). *Old path white clouds: Walking in the footsteps of the Buddah.* Berkeley, CA: Parallax.

Hansen, C. (1992). *A Daoist theory of Chinese thought: A philosophical interpretation*. New York: Oxford University Press.

Hassig, R. (1985). *Trade, tribute, and transportation: The sixteenth century political economy of the valley of Mexico*. Norman: University of Oklahoma Press.

Hassig, R. (1988). *Aztec warfare: Imperial expansion and political control*. Norman: University of Oklahoma Press.

Hassig, R. (1992). *War and society in ancient Mesoamerica*. Berkeley: University of California Press.

Hayhoe, R., & Bastid, M. (Eds.). (1987). *China's education and the industrialized world: Studies in cultural transfer*. London: M. E. Sharpe.

Haykal, M. H. (1976). *The Life of Muhammad*. Indianapolis, IN: American Trust Publications.

Headland, I. (1914). *Home life in China*. London: Methuen & Co..

Hellbrom, A. (1967). *La participación cultural de las mujeres: Indias y mestizas en el México precortesiano y postrevolucionario* [The cultural participation of women: Indians and Mesticas in pre-Cortesian and post revolutionary Mexico]. (Monograph Series, Publication 10). Stockholm: The Ethnographic Museum

Heren, L., Fitzgerald, C. P., Freeberne, M., Hook, B., & Bonavia, D. (1973). *China's three thousand years: The story of a great civilisation*. New York: Collier.

Herman, A. L. (1991). *A brief introduction to Hinduism: Religion, philosophy, and ways of liberation*. Boulder, CO: Westview.

Hindery, R. (1978). *Comparative ethics in Hindu and Buddhist traditions*. Delhi: Motilal Banarsidass.

Hiskett, M. (1984). *The development of Islam in West Africa*. London: Longman.

Holmes, G. (Ed.). (1988). *The Oxford illustrated history of medieval Europe*. Oxford, England: Oxford University Press.

Hsiung-huei, L. (1995). *Education in Taiwan during the Ch'ing dynasty, 1683–1895*. Unpublished doctoral dissertation, University of Connecticut, Storrs.

Hsü, I. C. Y. (1990). *The rise of modern China*. New York: Oxford University Press.

Huang, R. (1988). *China: A macro history*. London: Sharpe.

Hucker, C. (1975). *China's imperial past: An introduction to Chinese history and culture*. Stanford, CA: Stanford University Press.

Hulbert, J. (1935). *Bright's Anglo-Saxon reader*. New York: Henry Holt.

Humphrey, C., & Laidlaw, J. (1994). *The archetypal actions of ritual: A theory of ritual illustrated by the Jain rite of worshop*. Oxford, England: Clarendon Press.

Humphries, C. (1951). *Buddhism: An introduction and guide*. Harmondsworth: Penguin.

Hurtado, A., & Iverson, P. (Eds.). (1994). *Major problems in American Indian history: Documents and essays*. Lexington, MA: Heath.

Hymes, R. (1989). Lu Chiu-yüan, academies, and the problem of the local community. In W. de Bary & J. Chaffee (Eds.), *Neo-Confucian education: The formative stage* (pp. 432–456) Berkeley: University of California Press.

Ibrahim, A. (1989). Islam and the law. In *Toward Islamization of disciplines* (pp. 381–391). Herndon, VA: International Institute of Islamic Thought.

Infante, F. (1983). *La educación de los Aztecas* [The education of the Aztecs]. México: Panorama Editorial.

Irele, A. (Ed.) (1992). *African education and identity*. Ibadan: Spectrum.

Ishaq, I. (1967). *The life of Muhammad*. London: Oxford University Press.

Ishumi, A. (1986). Black civilization and pedagogy: A search for modern methods. In J. Okpaku, A. Opubor, & B. Oloruntimehin (Eds.), *The arts and civilization of Black and African peoples: Volume 6, Black civilization and pedagogy* (pp. 60–79). Lagos: Center for Black and African Arts and Civilization.

Ives, C. (1992). *Zen awakening and society*. Honolulu: University of Hawaii Press.

Izquierdo, A. (1983). *La educación Maya en los tiempos prehispánicos* [Mayan education in prehispanic times]. México: Universidad Nacional Autónoma de México.

Jacobson, N. P. (1986). *Understanding Buddhism*. Carbondale: Southern Illinois University Press.

Jameelah, M. (1986). *Islam in theory and practice*. Lahore: Mohammad Yusuf Khan & Sons.

Jansen, G. H. (1979). *Militant Islam*. New York: Harper & Row.

Jolly, J. (1989). *Histoire de continent Africain* (2 Vols.). Paris: Editions l'Harmattan.

Josephy, A., Jr. (Ed.). (1991a). *America in 1492: The world of the Indian peoples before the arrival of Columbus*. New York: Vintage.

Josephy, A., Jr. (1991b). *The Indian heritage of America*. Boston: Houghton Mifflin.

Josephy, A., Jr. (1994). *500 nations: An illustrated history of North American Indians*. New York: Knopf.

Josserand, J. K., & Dakin, K. (Eds.). (1988). *Smoke and mist: Mesoamerican studies in memory of Thelma D.Sullivan, Part II.* Oxford, England: B.A.R.

Kahn, M. (Ed.). (1981). *Education and society in the Muslim world.* Jeddah: King Abdulaziz University.

Kalupahana, D. (1992). *A history of Buddhist philosophy: Continuities and discontinuities.* Honolulu: University of Hawaii Press.

Karttunen, F., & Lockhard, J. (Eds.). (1987). *The art of Nahuatl speech: The Bancroft dialogues.* Los Angeles: UCLA Latin American Center Publications.

Kaschula, R. (1991). The role of Xhosa oral poetry in contemporary South African society. *South African Journal of African Languages 11,* (2), 47–54.

Kaschula, R. (Ed.). (1993). *Foundations in Southern African oral literature.* Johannesburg: Witwatersrand University Press.

Katengo, M., & Mwale, G. (1986). Can traditional education be integrated with the modern educational system? In S. Moyo, T. Sumaili, & J. Moody (Eds.), *Oral traditions in Southern Africa* (Vol. 6., pp. 456–481). Lusaka: Division for Cultural Research, Institute for African Studies, University of Zambia.

Katz, F. (1966). *Situación social y económica de los Aztecas durante los siglos XV y XVI* [The social and economic situation of the Aztecs during the 15th and 16th centuries]. México: Universidad Nacional Autónoma de México, Instituto de Investigaciones Históricas.

Keen, B. (1971). *The Aztec image in Western thought.* New Brunswick, NJ: Rutgers University Press.

Kelleher, M. T. (1989). Back to basics: Chu Hsi's *Elementary learning (Hsiao-hsüeh).* In W. de Bary & J. Chaffee (Eds.), *Neo-Confucian education: The formative stage* (pp. 219–251). Berkeley: University of California Press.

Kellogg, S. (1988). Cognatic kinship and religion: Women in Aztec society. In J. K. Josserand & K. Dakin (Eds.), *Smoke and mist: Mesoamerican studies in memory of Thelma D. Sullivan, Part II* (pp. 665–681). Oxford, England: B.A.R.

Kiang K.-H. (1934). *On Chinese studies.* Shanghai: Commercial.

Kincheloe, T. S. (1984). The wisdom of the elders: Cross-cultural perspectives. *Journal of Thought 19,* (3), 121–127.

Klein, C. (1987). The ideology of autosacrifice at the Templo Mayor. In E. Boone (Ed.), *The Aztec templo mayor: A symposium at Dumbarton Oaks, 8th and 9th October 1983* (pp. 293–370). Washington, DC: Dumbarton Oaks Research Library and Collection.

Klor de Alva, Jorge J., Nicholas, H., & Keber, E. (Eds.). (1988). *The work of Bernardino de Sahagun: Pioneer ethnographer of sixteenth century Aztec*

Mexico. Albany: Institute for Mesoamerican Studies, The University of Albany, State University of New York.

Klostermaier, K. (1989). *A survey of Hinduism*. Albany: State University of New York Press.

Kluckhohn, C., & Leighton, D. (1962). *The Navajo* (rev. ed.). Garden City, NY: Doubleday.

Knipe, D. (1991). *Hinduism*. San Francisco: Harper.

Kraft, K. (Ed.). (1988). *Zen: Tradition and transition*. New York: Grove.

Krieger, S., & Trauzettel, R. (Eds.). (1991). *Confucianism and the modernization of China*. Mainz: V. Hase & Koehler Verlang.

Kroeber, K. (1981). The art of traditional American Indian narration. In K. Kroeber (Ed.), *Traditional literatures of the American Indian: Texts and interpretations* (pp. 1–24). Lincoln: University of Nebraska Press.

Kroeber, K. (Ed.). (1981). *Traditional literatures of the American Indian: Texts and interpretations*. Lincoln: University of Nebraska Press.

Kuang Y. (1991). Modern values of the positive elements in Confucius' ideas concerning the study of man. In S. Krieger & R. Trauzettel (Eds.), *Confucianism and the modernization of China* (pp. 7–17). Mainz: v. Hase & Koehler.

Kubik, G. (1990). *Visimu vya mukatikati*: Dilemma tales and "arithmetical puzzles" collected among the Valuchazi. *South African Journal of African Languages 10*, (2), 59–68.

Kubik, G. (1992). A Luchazi riddle session: Analysis of recorded texts in a South-Central African Bantu language. *South African Journal of African Languages 12*, (2), 51–82.

Kuhn, T. (1970). *The structure of scientific revolutions* (2nd ed.). Chicago: University of Chicago Press.

Kuhn, T. (1977). *The essential tension: Selected studies in scientific tradition and change*. Chicago: University of Chicago Press.

Kunene, D. (1971). *Heroic poetry of the Basotho*. Oxford, England: Oxford University Press.

Küng, H. (1992). *Judaism: Between yesterday and tomorrow*. New York: Crossroad.

Kuper, A. (1988). *The invention of primitive society: Transformations of an illusion*. London: Routledge.

Lanczkowski, G. (1970). *Aztekische Sprach und Überlieferung [Aztc language and traditions]*. Berlin: Springer-Verlag.

Larson, G. (1994). Hinduism in India and in America. In J. Neusner (Ed.), *World religions in America* (pp. 185–186). Louisville, KY: Westminster/John Knox Press.

Lau, D. C. (trans). (1970). *Mencius.* Harmondsworth: Penguin.

Lau, D. C. (trans.). (1979). *The Analects.* Harmondsworth: Penguin.

Lee, G. (1967). *Crusade against ignorance: Thomas Jefferson on education.* New York: Teachers College Press.

Lee, T. H. C. (1985). *Government education and examinations in Sung China.* Hong Kong: Chinese University Press.

Lee, T. (1989). Sung schools and education before Chu Hsi. In W. de Bary and J. Chaffee (Eds.), *Neo-Confucian education: The formative stage* (pp. 105–136). Berkeley: University of California Press.

Leggett, T. (Ed.). (1978). *Zen and the ways.* London: Routledge & Kegan Paul.

León-Portilla, M. (Ed.). (1958). *Ritos, sacerdotes y atavíos de los dioses: Textos de los informantes de Sahagun, 1* [Rites, priests, and vestments of the gods: texts from Sahagun's informants]. México: Universidad Nacional Autónoma de México, Instituto de Historia.

León-Portilla, M. (1963). *Aztec thought and culture.* Norman: University of Oklahoma Press.

León-Portilla, M. (1966). *La filosofía Nahuatl: Estudio en sus fuentes* [Nahuatl philosphy: a study of its origins]. México: Universidad Nacional Autónoma de México.

León-Portilla, M. (1967). *Trece poetas del mundo azteca* [Thirteen poets of the Aztec world]. México: Universidad Nacional Autónoma de México, Instituto de Investigaciones Históricas.

León-Portilla, M. (1968). *Tiempo y realidad en el pensamiento maya* [Time and reality in Mayan thought]. México: Universidad Nactional Autónoma de México.

León-Portilla, M. (Ed.). (1971). *De Teotihuacán a los Aztecas: Antología de fuentes e interpretaciones históricas* [From Teotihuacán to the Aztecs: Anthology of historical sources and interpretations]. México: Universidad Nacional Autónoma de México, Instituto de Investigaciones Históricas.

León-Portilla, M. (1988). *Time and reality in the thought of the Maya.* Norman: University of Oklahoma Press.

León-Portilla, M. (1992a). *The Aztec image of self and society: An introduction to Nahua culture.* Salt Lake City, UT: University of Utah Press.

León-Portilla, M. (1992b). *Fifteen poets of the Aztec world.* Norman: University of Oklahoma Press.

Leslie, J. (Ed.). (1991). *Roles and rituals for Hindu women.* Rutherford, NJ: Fairleigh Dickinson University Press.

Lhuillier, A. (1963). El pensamiento náhuatl respecto de la muerte [Náhuatl thought concerning death]. *Estudios de Cultura Náhuatl, 4:* 251–261.

Liebenow, J. (1986). *African politics: Crises and challenges.* Bloomington: Indiana University Press.

Lincoln, Y., & Guba, E. (1985). *Naturalistic inquiry.* Newbury Park, CA: Sage.

Lings, M. (1983). *Muhammad: His life based on the earliest sources.* Rochester, VT: Inner Traditions.

Lippman, T. (1995). *Understanding Islam: An introduction to the Muslim world* (2nd rev. ed.). New York: Meridan.

Liu, J. (Ed.). (1974). *Political institutions in traditional China: Major issues.* New York: Wiley.

Liu, T.-Y. (1970). Taoist self-cultivation in Ming thought. In W. de Bary (Ed.), *Self and society in Ming thought* (pp. 291–330). New York: Columbia University Press.

Llasera, I. (1987). Confucian education through European eyes. In R. Hayhoe & M. Bastid (Eds.), *China's education and the industrialized world* (pp. 21–32). London:. Sharpe.

Locust, C. (1988). Wounding the spirit: Discrimination and traditional American Indian belief systems. *Harvard Educational Review, 58,* (3), 315–330.

Loewe, M. (1965). *Imperial China: The historical background to the modern age.* New York: Praeger.

Loewe, M. (1990). *The pride that was China.* New York: St. Martin's Press.

lo Liyong, T. (1969). *The last word.* Nairobi: East Africa Publishing House.

Lomawaima, K. T. (1994). *They called it prairie light: The story of Chilocco Indian school.* Lincoln: University of Nebraska Press.

Luis de Rojas, J. (1988). *México Tenochtitlan: Economía y sociedad en el siglo XVI.* México: El Colegio de Michoacán, Fondo de Cultura Económica.

Mahlangu, D. (1988). *Imiraro:* Ndebele riddles. *South African Journal of African Languages, 8* (Supplement 1), 147–172.

Malo, D. (1951). *Hawaiian antiquities* (2nd ed.). Bernice P. Bishop Museum, Special Publication 2. Honolulu: Bishop Museum Press.

Mannan, M. A. (1989). The frontiers of Islamic economics: Some philosophical underpinnings. In *Toward Islamization of disciplines* (pp. 295–311), Herndon, VA: International Institute of Islamic Thought.

Maqsood, R. (1994). *Islam.* London: NTC.

Marcus, J. (1992). *Mesoamerican writing systems: Propaganda, myth, and history in four ancient civilizations.* Princeton, NJ: Princeton University Press.

Markus, M. (1963). Estudio comparativo entre la educación nahuatl y la griega [Comparative study of Nahuatl and Greek education]. *Estudios de Cultura Náhuatl, 4*: 281–292.

Marrou, H. (1956). *A history of education in antiquity* (G. Lamb, Trans.). New York: Sheed & Ward.

Martin, C. (1994). Ethnohistory: A better way to write Indian history. In A. Hurtado & P. Iverson (Eds.), *Major problems in American Indian history: Documents and essays* (pp. 23–33), Lexington, MA: Heath.

Martin, J. R. (1982). The ideal of the educated person. In D. DeNicola (Ed.), *Philosophy of education: 1981* (pp. 3–20), Normal, IL: Philosophy of Education Society.

Martin, J. R. (1985). *Reclaiming a conversation: The ideal of the educated woman.* New Haven, CT: Yale University Press.

Martin, P., & O'Meara, P. (Eds.). (1995). *Africa* (3rd ed.). Bloomington: Indiana University Press.

Mascaró, J. (trans.). (1965). *The Upanishads.* Harmondsworth: Penguin.

Maspero, H., & Escarra, J. (1952). *Les institutions de la Chine: Essai historique* [The institutions of China: An historical essay]. Paris: Presses Universitaires de France.

Matsunaga, A. (1969). *The Buddhist philosophy of assimilation: The historical development of the Honji-Suijaku theory.* Tokyo: Sophia University.

Mazrui, A. (1980). *The African condition: The Reith lectures.* London: Heinemann.

Mazrui, A., & Wagaw, T. (1985). Towards decolonizing modernity: Education and culture conflict in Eastern Africa. In *The educational process and historiography in Africa* (pp. 35–62), Paris: UNESCO.

Mbiti, J. (1989). *African religions and philosophy* (2nd ed.). Oxford, England: Heinemann.

McKay, A. & McKay, B. (1987). Education as a total way of life: The Nisga'a experience. In J. Barman, Y. Hébert, & D. McCaskill (Eds.), *Indian education in Canada, Volume 2: The challenge* (pp. 64–85). Vancouver: University of British Columbia Press.

McKnight, B. (1989). Mandarins as legal experts: Professional learning in Sung China. In W. de Bary & J. Chaffee (Eds.), *Neo-Confucian education: The formative stage* (pp. 493–516). Berkeley: University of California Press.

McMullen, D. (1988). *State and scholars in T'ang China.* Cambridge, England: Cambridge University Press.

Medicine, B. (1987). My elders tell me. In J. Barman, Y. Hébert, & D. McCaskill (Eds.), *Indian education in Canada, Volume 2: The challenge* (pp. 142–152). Vancouver: University of British Columbia Press.

Mernissi, F. (1987). *Beyond the veil: Male-female dynamics in modern Muslim society.* Bloomington: Indiana University Press.

Mernissi, F. (1987). *The veil and the male elite: A feminist interpretation of women's rights in Islam.* Reading, MA: Addison-Wesley.

Meskill, J., & Gentzler, J. (Eds.). (1973). *An introduction to Chinese civilization.* New York: Columbia University Press.

Miller, D., & Wertz, D. (1976). *Hindu monastic life and the monks and monasteries of Bhubaneswar.* Montreal: McGill-Queen's University Press.

Miller, D. (1988). Hopi education: Before schools and teachers. *Tennessee Education 18,* (2), 28–32.

Miller, M. E. (1986). *The art of Mesoamerica from Olmec to Aztec.* London: Thames and Hudson.

Moctezuma, E. (1987). Symbolism of the Templo Mayor. In E. Boone (Ed.), *The Aztec Templo Mayor: A Symposium at Dumbarton Oaks, 8th and 9th October 1983* (pp. 185–209). Washington, DC: Dumbarton Oaks Research Library and Collection.

Mookerji, R. (1969). *Ancient Indian education.* Delhi: Motilal Banarsidass.

Morton, W. S. (1995). *China: Its history and culture.* New York: McGraw-Hill.

Mote, F., & Twitchett, D. (Eds.). (1988). *The Cambridge history of China, Volume 7: The Ming dynasty, 1368–1644, Part I.* Cambridge, England: Cambridge University Press.

Moumouni, A. (1968). *Education in Africa.* New York: Praeger.

Moyo, S., Sumaili, T., & Moody, J. (Eds.). (1986). *Oral traditions in Southern Africa* (Vol. 6). Lusaka: Division for Cultural Research, Institute for African Studies, University of Zambia.

Mudimbe, V. (1988). *The invention of Africa: Gnosis, philosophy, and the order of knowledge.* London: Currey.

Myburgh, A. (Ed.). (1981). *Anthropology for Southern Africa.* Pretoria: van Schaik.

Mzolo, D. (1988). Social function of clan praises. In A. Nkabinde (Eds.), *African linguistics and literature* (pp. 132–138). Johannesburg: Lexicon.

Nadel, S. (1942). *Black Byzantium: The kingdom of the Nupe in Nigeria.* London: International African Institute.

Nasr, S. H. (1984). Islamic education and science: A summary appraisal. In Y. Haddad, B. Haines, & E. Findly (Eds.), *The Islamic Impact* (pp. 47–68). Syracuse, NY: Syracuse University Press.

Nasr, S. H. (1987). *Traditional Islam in the modern world.* London: Routledge & Kegan Paul.

Needham, J. (1954). *Science and civilisation in China* (Vol. 1). Cambridge, England: Cambridge University Press.

Neusner, J. (Ed.). (1994). *World religions in America*. Louisville, KY: Westminster/John Knox Press.

Nicholson, H. (1967). The efflorescence of Mesoamerican civilization: A resume. In B. Bell (Ed.), *Indian Mexico: Past and present* (pp. 46–71). Los Angeles: University of California at Los Angeles, Latin American Center.

Nkabinde, A. (Ed.). (1988). *African linguistics and literature*. Johannesburg: Lexicon.

Nkara, J. (1992). *Bisisimi* or the language of the wise. *South African Journal of African Languages 12*, (4), 144–149.

Norman, J. (1988). *Chinese*. Cambridge, England: Cambridge University Press.

Nwosu, S. (1986). Pedagogic problems in Africa today. In J. Okpaku, A. Opubor, & B. Oloruntimehin (Eds.), *The arts and civilization of Black and African peoples: Volume 6, Black civilization and pedagogy* (pp. 102–118). Lagos: Center for Black and African Arts and Civilization.

Nyembezi, C. (1974). *Zulu proverbs*. Johannesburg: University of the Witwatersrand Press.

Obanewa, O. (1973). *Education of the children and youth in Ile-Ife: A comparison of formal and non-formal systems of education*. Unpublished master's thesis, University of Ife, Nigeria.

O'Flahery, W. D. (trans.). (1981). *The Rig Veda: An anthology*. Harmondsworth: Penguin.

Ogbalu, F., & Emenanjo, E. (Eds.). (1982). *Igbo language and culture* (Vol. 2). Ibadan: University Press.

Ogundijo, M. (1970). *Indigenous education in the Ejigbo district of Oshun division in the pre-colonial days and the coming of the missionaries*. Unpublished bachelor's thesis, Faculty of Education, University of Ife.

Okeke, A. (1982). Traditional education in Igboland. In F. Ogbalu & E. Emenanjo (Eds.), *Igbo language and culture* (Vol. 2, pp. 15–21). Ibadan: University Press.

Okpaku, J., Opubor, A., & Oloruntimehin, B. (Eds.). (1986). *The arts and civilization of Black and African peoples: Volume 6, Black civilization and pedagogy*. Lagos: Center for Black and African Arts and Civilization.

Olaniyan, R. (Ed.). (1982a). *African history and culture*. Lagos: Longman.

Olaniyan, R. (1982b). African history and culture: An overview. In R. Olaniyan *African history and culture* (pp. 1–13). Lagos: Longman.

Olivelle, P. (1993). *The Ashrama system: The history and heurmeneutics of a religious institution*. New York: Oxford University Press.

Opland, J. (1983). *Xhosa oral poetry: Aspects of a Black South African tradition*. Cambridge, England: Cambridge University Press.

Opland, J. (1990). Xhosa *izibongo*: Improvised line. *South African Journal of African Languages 10*, (4), 239–251.

Organ, T. (1970). *The Hindu quest for the perfection of man*. Athens: Ohio University Press.

Ortiz de Montellano, B. (1990). *Aztec medicine, health, and nutrition*. New Brunswick, NJ: Rutgers University Press.

Othón de Mendizábal, M. (1971). La cultura azteca y los sacrificios humanos [Aztec culture and human sacrifice]. In M. León-Portilla *De Teotihuacán a los Aztecas: Antología de fuentes e interpretaciones históricas* (pp. 208–214). México: Universidad Nacional Autónoma de México, Instituto de Investigaciones Históricas.

Oxendine, J. (1988). *American Indian sports heritage*. Champaign, IL: Human Kinetics.

Ozmon, H. & Craver, S. (1995). *Philosophical foundations of education* (5th Ed.). Englewood Cliffs, NJ: Prentice-Hall.

Pandit, B. (1993). *The Hindu mind: Fundamentals of Hindu religion and philosophy for all ages* (2nd Ed.). Glen Ellyn, IL: B & V.

Parrinder, G. (1969). *Religion in Africa*. Harmondsworth: Penguin.

Patton, M. (1978). *Utilization-focused evaluations*. Beverly Hills, CA: Sage.

Patton, M. (1990). Qualitative evaluation and research methods (2nd Ed.). Newbury Park, CA: Sage.

Paul, D. Y. (1985). *Women in Buddhism: Images of the feminine in the Mahayana tradition*. Berkeley, CA: University of California Press.

p'Bitek, O. (1967). *Song of Lawino and song of Ocol*. Ibadan: Heinemann.

p'Bitek, O. (1971). *African religions in Western scholarship*. Nairobi: East African Literature Bureau.

Pei-yi, W. (1989). Education of children in the Sung. In W. de Bary & J. Chaffee (Eds.), *Neo-Confucian education: The formative stage* (pp. 307–324). Berkeley: University of California Press.

Perkinson, H. (1980). *Since Socrates: Studies in the history of Western educational thought*. New York: Longman.

Peters, F. E. (1994). *The Hajj: The Muslim pilgrimage to Mecca and the holy places*. Princeton, NJ: Princeton University Press.

Pettitt, G. (1946). *Primitive education in North America*. Berkeley: University of California Press.

Phillips, H. (1975). *Basic education: A world challenge*. New York: Wiley.

Ping-Ti, H. (1962). *The ladder of success in Imperial China*. New York: Columbia University Press.

Pollak, S. (1983). *Ancient Buddhist education (Papers from the Bernard Van Leer Foundation Project on Human Potential)*. Cambridge, MA: Harvard Graduate School of Education.

Pretorius, W. J. (1990). A comparative look at the development of heroic poetry in Northern Sotho. *South African Journal of African Languages 10*, (3), 125–131.

Radhkrishnan, S. (Ed.). (1994). *The principal Upanishads*. New Delhi: Indus.

Rahman, F. (1979). *Islam* (2nd ed.) Chicago: University of Chicago Press.

Raper, P. (Ed.). (1986). *Names 1983: Proceedings of the second Southern African Names Congress*. Pretoria: Human Sciences Research Council.

Raum, O. (1967). An evaluation of indigenous education. In P. Duminy (Ed.), *Trends and Challenges in the Education of the South African Bantu* (pp. 89–105). Pretoria: J. L. van Schaik.

Raval, S. (1958). *Basic education in modern India: A critique of Gandhian educational philosophy*. Unpublished master's thesis, The American University, Washington DC.

Rawski, E. (1979). *Education and popular literacy in Ch'ing China*. Ann Arbor: University of Michigan Press.

Ray, B. (1976). *African religions: Symbol, ritual, and community*. Englewood Cliffs, NJ: Prentice-Hall.

Reat, N. R. (1994). *Buddhism: A history*. Berkeley, CA: Asian Humanities Press.

Reissner, J. (1984). Die innerislanische Diskussion zur modernen Wirtschafts- und Sozialordnung. In M. Ursinus (Ed.), *Der Islam in der Gegenwart* (pp. 155–169). München: Verlag C. H. Beck.

Ricoeur, P. (1965). *History and truth*. Evanston, IL: Northwestern University Press.

Rodinson, M. (1966). *Islam et capitalisme* [Islam and capitalism]. Paris: Éditions du Seuil.

Rodinson, M. (1974). *Mohammed*. New York: Vintage.

Rogers, J., & Wilson, S. (Eds.). (1993). *Ethnohistory and archaeology: Approaches to postcontact change in the Americas*. New York: Plenum.

Ron-guey, C. (1989). Chu Hsi and public instruction. In W. de Bary & J. Chaffee (Eds.), *Neo-Confucian education: The formative stage* (pp. 252–273). Berkeley: University of California Press).

Ropp, P. (Ed.). (1990). *Heritage of China*. Berkeley: University of California Press.

Ross, K. (Ed.). (1978). *Codex Mendoza*. Fribourg: Miller Graphics.

Ross, N. W. (1980). *Buddhism: A way of life and thought*. New York: Vintage.

Rubin, V. (1976). *Individual and state in ancient China: Essays on four Chinese philosophers*. New York: Columbia University Press.

Rycroft, D., & Ngcobo, A. (1981). *Say it in Zulu*. Pietermaritzburg: Language and Reading Laboratories, University of Natal.

Sáenz, J. (1988). Reto y educación en el México prehispánico. In J. K. Josserand & K. Dakin (Eds.), *Smoke and mist: Mesoamerican studies in memory of Thelma D. Sullivan, Part II* (pp. 681–695). Oxford, England: B.A.R.

Sahagun, B. (1981). *El Mexico antiguo: Selección y reordenación de la historia general de las cosas de Nueva España* [Ancient Mexico: Selection and reordering of the genral history of matters of New Spain]. Caracas: Biblioteca Ayachucho.

Said, E. (1978). *Orientalism*. New York: Vintage.

Said, E. (1993). *Culture and imperialism*. New York: Vintage.

Sakai, T. (1970). Confucianism and popular educational works. In W. de Bary (Ed.), *Self and society in Ming thought* (pp. 331–366). New York: Columbia University Press.

Sarwar, G. (1989). *Islam: Beliefs and teaching*. London: Muslim Educational Trust.

Saud, M. A. (1989). Toward Islamic economics. In *Toward Islamization of disciplines* (pp. 265–270). Herndon, VA: International Institute of Islamic Thought.

Schacht, J. (1964). *An introduction to Islamic law*. Oxford, England: Clarendon.

Schapera, I. (1965). *Praise-poems of Tswana chiefs*. Oxford, England: Oxford University Press.

Schele, L., & Freidel, D. (1990). *A forest of kings: The untold story of the ancient Maya*. New York: Morrow.

Schimmel, A. (1992). *Islam: An introduction*. Albany: State University of New York Press.

Schlagintweit, E. (1968). *Buddhism in Tibet* (2nd ed.). London: Susil Gupta.

Schwartz, B. (1985). *The world of thought in ancient China*. Cambridge, MA: Harvard University Press.

Scott, D., & Doubleday, T. (1992). *The elements of Zen*. Shaftsbury, Dorset: Element.

Sen, K. M. (1961). *Hinduism*. Harmondsworth: Penguin.

Senese, G. (1991). *Self-determination and the social education of Native Americans*. New York: Praeger.

Sharer, R. (1994). *The ancient Maya* (5th ed.). Stanford, CA: Stanford University Press.

Sharma, A. (1993a). Hinduism. In A. Sharma (Ed.), *Our religions: The seven world religions introduced by preeminent scholars from each tradition* (pp. 36–38). San Francisco: Harper.

Sharma, A. (Ed.). (1993b). *Our religions: The seven world religions introduced by preeminent scholars from each tradition*. San Francisco: Harper.

Sherzer, J. (1991). A richness of voices. In A. Josephy, Jr. (Ed.), *America in 1492: The world of the Indian peoples before the arrival of Columbus* (pp. 251–275). New York: Vintage.

Siddiqui, A. H. (1991). *Life of Muhammad*. Des Plaines, IL: Library of Islam.

Siddiqi, M. N. (1989). Islamizing economics. In (Ed.), *Toward Islamization of disciplines* (pp. 253–261). Herndon, VA: International Institute of Islamic Thought.

Siméon, R. (Ed.). (1889). *Annales de Domingo Francisco de San Anton Muñon Chimalpahim Quauhtlehuanitzin sixième et septième relations* [The Annas of Domingo]. Paris: Maisonneuve et Ch. LeClerc.

Siméon, R. (1963). *Dictionnaire de la langue Nahuatl ou Mexicaine* [Dictionary of the Nahuatl or Mexican language]. Graz: Akademische Druck U. Verlagsanstalt.

Smith, R. (1983). *China's Cultural heritage: The Ch'ing dynasty, 1644–1912*. Boulder, CO: Westview.

Snelling, J. (1991). *The Buddhist handbook: A complete guide to Buddhist schools, teaching, practice, and history*. Rochester, VT: Inner Traditions.

Snively, G. (1990). Traditional Native Indian beliefs, cultural values, and science instruction. *Canadian Journal of Native Education 17*(1), 44–59.

Soustelle, J. (1961). *Daily life of the Aztecs on the eve of the Spanish conquest*. Stanford, CA: Stanford University Press.

Soustelle, J. (1979). *The Olmecs: The oldest civilization in Mexico*. Norman: University of Oklahoma Press.

Soustelle, J. (1991). *Les aztèques* (6th ed.). Paris: Presses Universitaires de France.

Spiro, M. (1970). *Buddhism and society*. New York: Harper & Row.

Spores, R. (1984). *The Mixtecs in ancient and colonial times*. Norman: University of Oklahoma Press.

Sprenger, A. (1991). Confucius and modernization in China: An educational perspective. In S. Krieger & R. Trouzettel (Eds.), *Confucianism and the modernization of China* (pp. 454–472). Mainz: v. Hase & Koehler.

Staiger, B. (1991). The image of Confucius in China. In S. Krieger & R. Trauzettel (Eds.), *Confucianism and the modernization of China* (pp. 116–125). Mainz: v. Hase & Koehler.

Stover, L. (1974). *The cultural ecology of Chinese civilization: Peasants and elites in the last of the agrarian societies.* New York: Pica.

Stuart, G. (1981). *The mighty Aztecs.* Washington, DC: National Geographic Society.

Stumpfeldt, H. (1991). Confucius and Confucianism: On their history and status and on their present theoretical and practical potential. In S. Krieger & R. Trauzettel (Eds.), *Confucianism and the modernization of China* (pp. 18–28) Mainz: v. Hase & Koehler.

Suárez, J. (1983). *The Mesoamerican Indian languages.* Cambridge, England: Cambridge University Press.

Subramuniyaswami, S. S. (1993). *Dancing with Siva: Hinduism's contemporary catechism.* Concord, CA: Himalayan Academy.

Sudarkasa, N. (1982). Sex roles, education and development in Africa. *Anthropology and education 13*(3), 279–288.

Sullivan, T. (1963). Nahuatl proverbs, conundrums and metaphors collected by Sahagun. *Estudios de Cultura Náhuatl, 4*, 93–178.

Suzuki, D. T. (1949). *An introduction to Zen Buddhism.* New York: Philosophical Library.

Szasz, M. (1974). *Education and the American Indian: The road to self-determination, 1928–1973.* Albuquerque: University of New Mexico Press.

Tanahashi, K. & Schneider, T. D. (1994). *Essential Zen.* San Francisco: HarperCollins.

T'ang L.. (1928). *The foundations of modern China.* London: Noel Douglas.

Tannahill, R. (1992). *Sex in history* (rev. ed.). Lanham, MD: Scarborough House.

Telushkin, J. (1992). *Jewish humor.* New York: Morrow.

Thomas, N. W. (1969). *Proverbs, narratives, vocabularies and grammar: Anthropological report on the Ibo-speaking peoples of Nigeria, Part III.* New York: Negro Universities Press. (Original work published 1913)

Thompson, J. (1933). *Mexico before Cortez: An account of the daily life, religion, and ritual of the Aztecs and kindred peoples.* New York: Scribner's.

Thompson, J. E. (1962). *A catalog of Maya hieroglyphs.* Norman: Univeristy of Oklahoma Press.

Thompson, T. (1978). *The schooling of Native America*. Washington, DC: American Association of Colleges for Teacher Education, in collaboration with The Teacher Corps, U.S. Office of Education.

Tibawi, A. L. (1972). *Islamic education: Its traditions and modernization into the Arab national systems*. London: Luzac & Co.

Tibi, B. (1990). *Islam and the cultural accomodation of social change*. Boulder, CO: Westview.

Townsend, R. (1992). *The Aztecs*. London: Thames and Hudson.

Tozer, S., Violas, P., & Senese, G. (1993). *School and society: Educational practice as social expression*. New York: McGraw-Hill.

Turner, N. (1988). Comparison of the izibongo of the Zulu royal women, Mnkabayi and Nandi. *South African Journal of African Languages 8*(1), 28–33.

Tu, W. (1989). The Sung Confucian idea of education: A background understanding. In W. de Bary & J. Chaffee (Eds.), *Neo-Confucian education: The formative stage* (pp. 139–150). Berkeley: University of California Press.

Tu, W. (1990). The Confucian tradition in Chinese history. In P. Ropp (Ed.), *Heritage of China: Contemporary perspectives on Chinese civilization* (pp. 112–136). Berkeley: University of California Press.

Twitchett, D. (Ed.). (1979). *The Cambridge history of China, Volume 3: Sui and T'ang China, 589–906, Part I*. Cambridge, England: Cambridge University Press.

Twitchett, D. & Loewe, M. (Eds.). (1986). *The Cambridge history of China, volume 1: The Ch'in and Han empires, 221 B.C–A.D. 220*. Cambridge, England: Cambridge University Press.

Übelhör, M. (1989). The community compact (Hsiang-yüeh) of the Sung and its educational significance. In W. de Bary & J. Chaffee (Eds.), *Neo-Confucian education: The formative stage* (pp. 371–388). Berkeley: University of California Press.

Uka, N. (1986). Continuity and change: A challenge to African educators. In J. Okpaku, A. Opubor, & B. Oloruntimehin (Eds.), *The arts and civilization of Black and African peoples: Volume 6, Black civilization and pedagogy* (pp. 129–144). Lagos: Center for Black and African Arts and Civilization.

UNESCO. (1985). *The educational process and historiography in Africa*. Paris: UNESCO.

Ungar, S. (1986). *Africa: The people and politics of an emerging continent* (Rev. Ed.). New York: Simon & Schuster.

Ursinus, M. (Ed.). (1984). *Der Islam in der Gegenwart*. München: Verlag C. H. Beck.

van der Vliet, V. (1974). Growing up in a traditional society. In W. Hammond-Tooke (Ed.), *The Bantu-speaking peoples of Southern Africa* (pp. 211–245). London: Routledge & Kegan Paul.

van Nieuwenhuijze, C. (1985). *The lifestyles of Islam: Recourse to classicism, need of realism.* Leiden: Brill.

Vansina, J. (1985). *Oral tradition as history.* (rev. ed.). Madison: University of Wisconsin Press.

van Zantwijk, R. (1985). *The Aztec arrangement: The social history of pre-spanish Mexico.* Norman: University of Oklahoma Press.

Veytia, M. (1944). *Historia antigua de Mexico* (2 Vols.). México: Editorial Leyenda.

Viswanathan, E. (1992). *Am I a Hindu? The Hinduism primer.* San Francisco: Halo Books.

Waines, D. (1995). *An introduction to Islam.* Cambridge, England: Cambridge University Press.

Waley, A. (trans.). (1938). *The Analects of Confucius.* New York: Vintage.

Walker, B. (1968). *The Hindu world: An encyclopedic survey of Hinduism* (Vol. 1). New York: Praeger.

Wall, S. (1994) *Shadowcatchers: A journey in search of the teachings of Native American healers.* New York: HarperColins.

Walton, L. (1989). The institutional context of neo-Confucianism: Scholars, schools, and *Shu-yüan* in Sung-Yüan China. In W. de Bary & J. Chaffee (Eds.), *Neo-Confucian education: The formative stage* (pp. 457–492). Berkeley: University of California Press.

Wang, G. (1991). *The Chineseness of China.* Hong Kong: Oxford University Press.

Warder, A. K. (1970). *Indian Buddhism.* Delhi: Motilal Banarsidass.

Watson, B. (1961). *Records of the grand historian of China* (2 Vols.). New York: Coumbia University Press.

Watt, W. M., & Bell, R. (1970). *Introduction to the Qur'an.* Edinburgh: Edinburgh University Press.

Weaver, M. (1981). *The Aztecs, Maya, and their predecessors: archeology of Mesoamerica* (2nd ed.) New York: Academic Press.

Weibust, P. (1989). Tradition as process: Creating contemporary tradition in a rural Norwegian school and community. *Qualitative Studies in Education* 2(2), 107–122.

White, J. (1971). *Cortés and the downfall of the Aztec empire: A study in a conflict of cultures.* New York: St. Martin's Press.

Wilkinson, E. (1973). *The history of Imperial China: A research guide.* Cambridge, MA: Harvard University Press.

Williams, S. W. (1907). *The middle kingdom: A survey of the geography, government, literature, social life, arts, and history of the Chinese empire and its inhabitants* (2 Vols.). New York: Scribner's.

Willms, A. (1984). Nordafrika. In M. Ursinus (Ed.), *Der Islam in der Gegenwart* (pp. 561–569). München: Verlag C. H. Beck.

Wilson, J. (1963). *Education and changing West African culture.* New York: Teachers College, Bureau of Publications.

Wing-tsit, C. (1989). Chu Hsi and the academies. In W. de Bary & J. Chaffee (Ed.), *Neo-Confucian education: The formative stage* (pp. 389–413) Berkeley: University of California Press.

Witherspoon, G. (1977). *Language and art in the Navajo universe.* Ann Arbor: The Univeristy of Michigan Press.

Wong, E. (trans.). (1990). *Seven Taoist masters: A folk novel of China.* Boston: Shambhala.

Wright, R. (1992). *Stolen continents: The "new world" through Indian eyes.* Boston: Houghton Mifflin.

Wyatt, D. (1990). A language of continuity in Confucian thought. In P. Cohen & M. Goldman (Eds.), *Ideas Across cultures: Essays on Chinese thought in honor of Benjamin I. Schwartz* (pp. 33–61). Cambridge, MA: Harvard University Press.

Yellow Bird, R. (1990). Position paper on native education. *Humanity & Society 14*(3), 297–301.

Yu D. (1991). The concept of "great harmony" in the Book of Changes (Zhou Yi). In S. Krieger & R. Trauzettel (Eds.), *Confucianism and the modernization of China* (pp. 51–62). Mainz: v. Hase & Koehler.

Zaehner, R. C. (1962). *Hinduism.* London: Oxford University Press.

Zelliot, E., & Bernsten, M. (Eds.). (1988). *The experience of Hinduism.* Albany: State University of New York Press.

Zürcher, E. (1989). Buddhism and education in T'ang times. In W. de Bary & J. Chaffee (Eds.), *Neo-Confucian education: The formative stage* (pp. 19–56). Berkeley: University of California Press.

Index